TAUNTON'S

SMALL HOUSES

Editors of Fine Homebuilding

The Taunton Press

The Taunton Press, Inc., 63 South Main Street, PO Box 5506, Newtown, CT 06470-5506
e-mail: tp@taunton.com

Editors: Joeseph R. Provey, Kathleen D. Williams
Copy editor: Candace B. Levy
Indexer: Barbara Mortenson
Interior design: Carol Singer
Layout: Rita Sowins/Sowins Design

LIBRARY OF CONGRESS CATALOGING-IN-PUBLICATION DATA

Taunton's small houses / editors of Fine homebuilding.
pages cm
Includes index.
ISBN 978-1-60085-765-2
1. Architecture, Domestic--Designs and plans. 2. Dwellings--Designs and plans. 3. Architecture, Modern--21st century--Designs and plans. I. Fine homebuilding. II. Title: Small houses.
NA7110.T345 2012
728'.370222--dc23
2012028017

PRINTED IN THE UNITED STATES OF AMERICA
10 9 8 7 6 5 4

This book is compiled from articles that originally appeared in *Fine Homebuilding* magazine. Unless otherwise noted, construction costs listed were current at the time the articles first appeared.

Homebuilding is inherently dangerous. From accidents with power tools to falls from ladders, scaffolds, and roofs, builders risk serious injury and even death. We try to promote safe work habits throughout this book, but what is safe for one person under certain circumstances may not be safe for you under different circumstances. So don't try anything you learn about here (or elsewhere) unless you're certain that it is safe for you. If something about an operation doesn't feel right, don't do it. Look for another way. Please keep safety foremost in your mind whenever you're working.

ACKNOWLEDGMENTS

Special thanks to the authors, editors, art directors, copy editors, and other staff members of *Fine Homebuilding* who contributed to the development of the articles in this book.

Contents

PART 2

INTRODUCTION

Smaller Is Smarter

Building smaller is no longer the charming, quirky idea it was when architect Sarah Susanka wrote *The Not So Big House* (The Taunton Press) in 1998. Today, however, the idea of compact-but-quality house design has arrived. It's not just for retirement or vacation homes, or for co-op and condo dwellers: It's the way we'll build in the future.

For decades, house design was largely market driven. You needed that underutilized dining room, fourth bedroom, and enormous center hall for resale even if it didn't suit your lifestyle. All of those extra square feet (that you couldn't really afford) were a good investment because the equity of houses kept rising, and the more space the bigger return upon resale—or so our realtors told us. That's all in the past. Today, house designers can turn to the real issues of how we live, what we actually need, and what we don't.

The green building revolution has also contributed to the momentum for compact building. Turns out that we had somehow forgotten that a smaller footprint is a lighter footprint. Smaller houses use less of just about everything, including energy for heat and cooling, and dollars for building. The average size of newly constructed houses has already begun to trend downward in recent years from about 2,700 sq. ft. in 2009 to 2,300 sq. ft. in the latest survey by the National Association of Homebuilders. How much smaller houses will become is difficult to say, but with decreasing household size and tight budgets, it's a good bet newly built houses will continue to shrink in the coming years.

With this in mind, *Small Houses* serves up dozens of examples of carefully thought out small homes. Part 1, "Small from the Start," kicks off with 10 basic principles of small space design, ideas that can be incorporated into any remodeling or building project. The remainder of the section examines nearly 30 architect-designed homes—none over 2,300 sq. ft. You'll find floor plans for young families as well as retirees and everyone in between. There are vacation homes for beach lovers, modern-day farmhouses, and infill duplexes for young urbanites hailing from virtually every corner of the U.S. Each example is filled with ideas for living big in smaller spaces, including congestion-alleviating porches, decks and courtyards, space-saving storage solutions, double-duty rooms, and multipurpose outbuildings.

Part 2, "Adding On But Staying Small," shows how small-scale remodeling can transform older homes without destroying their charm or breaking the bank. There's one story of how an architect turned a living room from thoroughfare to sanctuary by changing the front door location and adding a mere 50 sq. ft. There are several others about how adding dormers or entire

second floors turned pumpkins into palaces—albeit modest ones. Still others show how old buildings can have new lives as contemporary and efficient homes.

In addition, *Small Houses* introduces readers to many homebuilding technologies and products that anyone contemplating a new house or addition should know about. They include super insulation details, structural insulated panels, insulating concrete forms, modular construction, solar thermal and electric systems, passive cooling, radiant heat, fiber-cement board and steel panel siding, rainwater and grey water collection systems, daylighting, and much more.

Begin planning your new *small* dream home right here!

—Joseph R. Provey, editor

SMALL HOME DESIGN can incorporate many fine details that you would expect to find in far bigger and more lavish homes.

PART 1

Small from the Start

Big Ideas for Small Houses

BY RUSSELL HAMLET

The greenhouse effect is everywhere these days. You just can't escape the news about how important it is to save energy with efficient appliances and ample insulation—and that's a good thing. But the simplest, most effective way to reduce a home's energy usage in the long run is to reduce its size from the outset. A shrinking energy bill is just for starters: The need for fewer building materials, less land, and less maintenance is a significant by-product of building smaller houses.

More and more of my clients ask whether a small house can work for them. They're concerned that it won't have enough room for family and friends on holiday visits or that it will just seem cramped. The reality is that a small house doesn't have to appear or feel small. With thoughtful design techniques, a small house can be made to seem larger and more gracious than its actual dimensions.

This chapter presents 10 guidelines that can be used to expand the perceived size of a small house. They make up an overall approach that will yield a house that is both practical and excellent. To be successful, a small house also should be straightforward, composed of simple architectural forms and construction techniques, quality materials, and careful detailing. Quality feels better than quantity, while spirit and personality bring a house to life.

1 OUTDOOR ROOMS

2
TRANSITIONAL SPACES

3
LIGHT AND COLOR CONTRAST

4
VARYING SCALE

5
DISTINCT ZONES

6
MULTIPLE VIEWS

7
ACCENTUATED DIMENSIONS

8
ILLUSION

9
THICK EDGES

10
MULTIPURPOSE ROOMS

1. Include an outdoor room

What you build outside the house can have a major impact on the way your home feels inside, especially if you make a roomlike space and connect it properly to the house. This outdoor space should have a definite boundary such as a stone wall, a fence, shrubs, a deck railing, or adjacent structures. It needs to be easily accessible from inside the house and to be linked to the interior by consistent materials, floor patterns, overhangs, plantings, and large doors and/or windows. An element such as an outdoor fireplace or an arrangement of table and chairs also can give this space an interior connection.

The outdoor room should be a bit bigger than the largest room in the house. I typically like to use spaces that are about 1¼ to 1½ times as big as the largest room. Ideally, the outdoor room should have an area that is hidden from view, creating a bit of mystery and tempting a visitor to explore, leaving guests with a sense that there is something to discover.

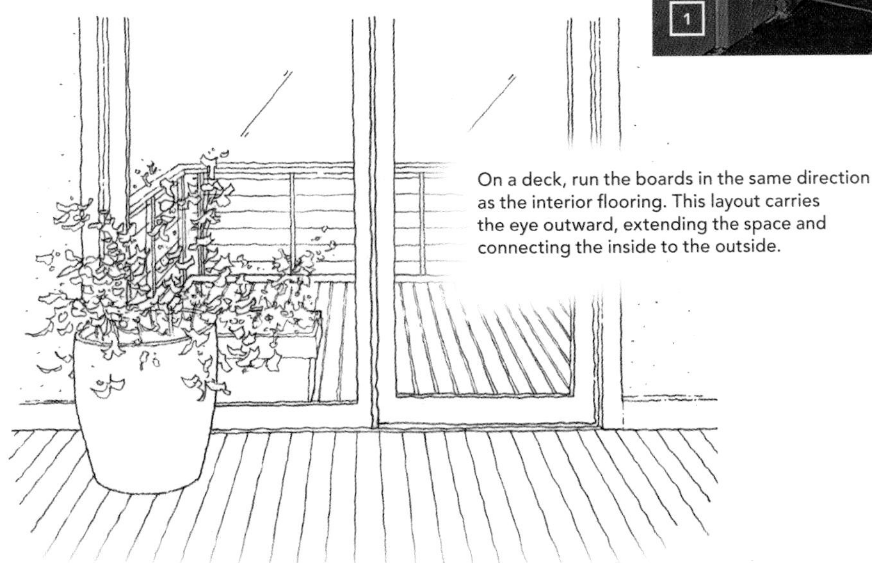

On a deck, run the boards in the same direction as the interior flooring. This layout carries the eye outward, extending the space and connecting the inside to the outside.

2. Invest space in transitions

By using transitions, you can emphasize distinct realms within a house. Transitions range from portions of the floor plan such as stairs, hallways, and balconies to details such as thick thresholds, substantial columns, overhead beams, and lowered ceilings. You can use these architectural elements to create a sense of mystery and a process of controlled discovery, heightening the impression that there is more to the house than immediately meets the eye.

Although it might be tempting to remove square footage from entry and circulation spaces, it is more important to be generous with these areas. Doing so will create the sense that you are living in a bigger house.

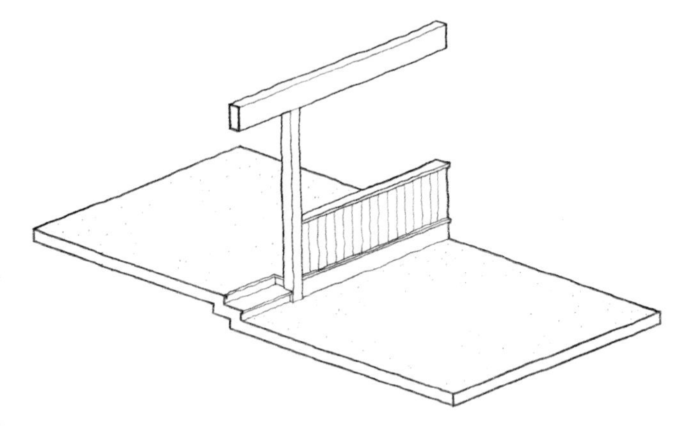

Define the divisions between rooms with elements such as beams, changes in floor or ceiling heights, or low walls.

3. Use contrasts in light and color

Light and color can be used to expand the perceived size of a house. Bright light in the foreground with slightly darker areas in the background creates a perspective that increases the perceived depth of a space. Light brought into the ends of a room draws the viewer's eye, increasing the perceived distance; so too does a window at the end of a hall or a skylight at the top of a staircase.

Natural light is a wonderful way to warm up and subjectively enlarge a space. Bring light into the house by using large windows, skylights, and clerestories. Interior spaces that are isolated from the exterior can use elements such as roof monitors and light tunnels or can borrow light from other areas via transoms and interior windows.

Artificial lighting also can be used to brighten a room and to illuminate features and tasks. Well-placed lighting provides contrast and shadow, gives definition and clarity to elements and edges, and creates a sense that the space is larger than it actually is.

Although a color scheme should be kept simple, contrasting colors can help expand a space. Light colors on ceilings and walls dissolve boundaries, making a room seem larger; darker colors enclose the volume of a room, making it feel smaller and more intimate. Warm colors seem to advance toward us, whereas cool colors tend to recede. Using color in creative ways really can open up small spaces.

Use layers of light and dark to exaggerate a sense of distance. A light source as a focal point intensifies the effect.

4. Create contrast with scale

Avoid downsizing everything in a small house; doing so just makes it seem even smaller. Instead, vary the scale of objects and elements from larger than normal to smaller than normal to evoke a sense of grandeur. For example, a tiny window placed next to a big piece of furniture makes the area seem larger.

Using elements that are monumental can achieve the same effect. A huge fireplace, a grand chimney, an oversize window, a massive door, giant columns, an overstuffed chair, and a formal garden all appear as if they belong to a "greater" house. Combining large pieces of comfortable furniture with large area rugs is another good idea; you just need to use fewer pieces. Raising the ceiling height from the standard 8 ft. to 9 ft. in the main living areas can also make a big impact.

A big window and chimney provide maximum contrast to a small house.

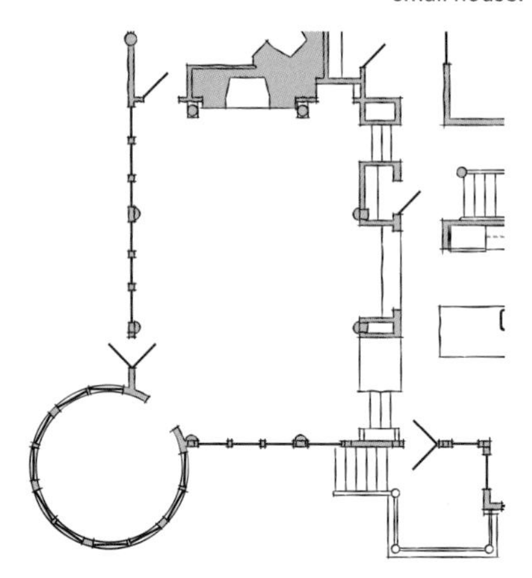

Varying the shape and size of neighboring spaces adds character and complexity to a small house.

5. Organize the house into distinct zones

If you clearly distinguish different areas within a small house, you can make it seem larger by creating the impression that it contains multiple rooms and spatial domains. Establish at least two realms; avoid making a one-room house, unless that is your intention. Creating public and private zones, separating competing functions, and making distinctions between quiet and noisy areas all are good ways to enlarge the perceived size of a small house. Use well-articulated transitions such as floor-level changes and varied ceiling heights (see guideline no. 2 on p. 10) to define and separate different areas.

Contrast spaces by making some of them intimate and snug and others open and airy. A sheltered inglenook off an open living area is a good example of this tactic.

A getaway space somewhere in the house also is important. A small house feels larger and more balanced if you know that it contains a secluded place for quiet and inward-focused activities.

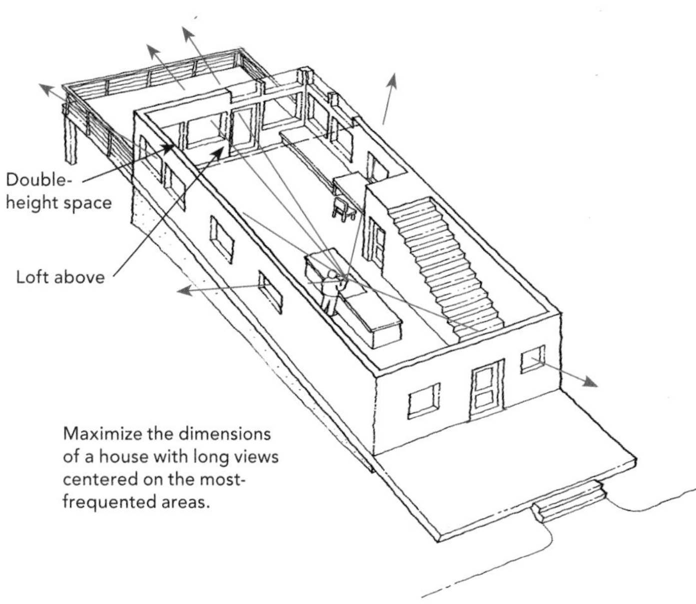

6. Develop multiple views

Use windows to vary the focus from nearby features to distant horizons. Try also to give each space natural light from at least two sides.

In the house pictured at right, for example, high and low windows frame both garden and hilltop views, open-riser stairs allow glimpses from one room to another, and a frosted-glass stair landing adds a surprising layer of light in the center of the house.

Avoid using large areas of glass in small rooms and large windows on only one wall. Doing so can create an uneasy imbalance that sucks the sense of enclosure from the room.

7. Accentuate the dimensions

Start by using sightlines to their full potential. Long hallways strategically placed, one-and-a-half- or two-story spaces, and diagonal views all are ways to gain a sense of spaciousness. Instead of a solid wall that limits a potential long view, use interior windows, transoms, and clerestories to maximize sightlines and to extend space beyond its perceived boundaries.

Keeping sightlines clear is important. Limit the number of furniture pieces and eliminate clutter to allow the eye to travel farther, extending perceived spatial dimensions.

8. Put illusion to work

You can combine tapered walls and ceilings and manipulate the scale of objects such as fireplaces, sculptures, and landscaping to create the illusion of expanded space. For example, an outdoor room with walls that taper toward one another creates a forced perspective that funnels the eye toward a focal point that seems more distant. Placed at that focal point, an object such as a small sculpture helps enhance this perception of expanded space (see the drawing below).

Another technique is to create a seductive curve by designing a space that beckons visitors into an area partly hidden from view. A curved or angled wall, a loft, or stairs going up or down can help create a sense of mystery.

Large mirrors set on closet or bathroom doors and in small rooms can enlarge perceived space. Be careful to avoid placing mirrors facing each other, however. This arrangement can create a disorienting fun-house effect of endlessly duplicated images. When deciding how big a mirror should be and where it should go, think of it like a window, a piece

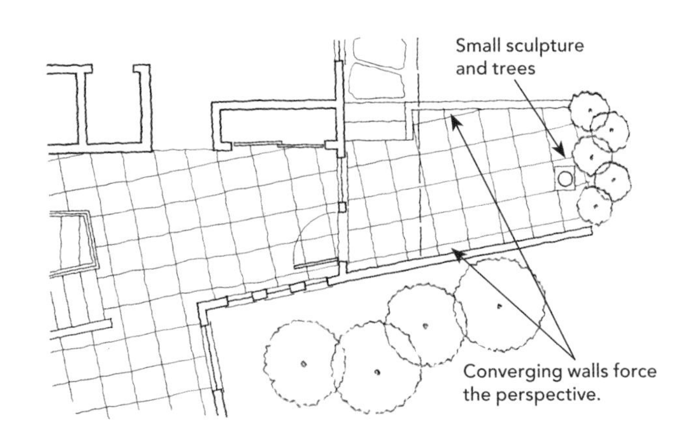

of artwork, or a framed picture. Paintings and photographs also can create the illusion of more space when they're placed strategically in a room or at the end of a hallway or staircase.

9. Use thick edges and built-ins

Thick countertops, deep window jambs, and wide door thresholds all are examples of thick edges. They give the impression of strength and longevity, and express a sense of grandeur.

Extending a window beyond the exterior plane of a wall creates thickness around the interior of the window. Inside, the wide jambs reflect light, brightening the room. Outside, shadows cast by the window bay add interest to the facade of the house. Likewise, recessing an entry door also creates the illusion of a thick wall.

By incorporating thick edges and built-in furniture around the perimeter of a room, the center of the space becomes liberated for living. Built-in furniture such as window seats, wall beds, Pullman bunks, booth seating, and fold-up tables can be used to keep spaces clear.

Nothing creates a sense of claustrophobia in a small house faster than clutter. Use bookshelves, cupboards, cabinets, drawers, and storage chests to keep clutter out of sight. Often, nooks and

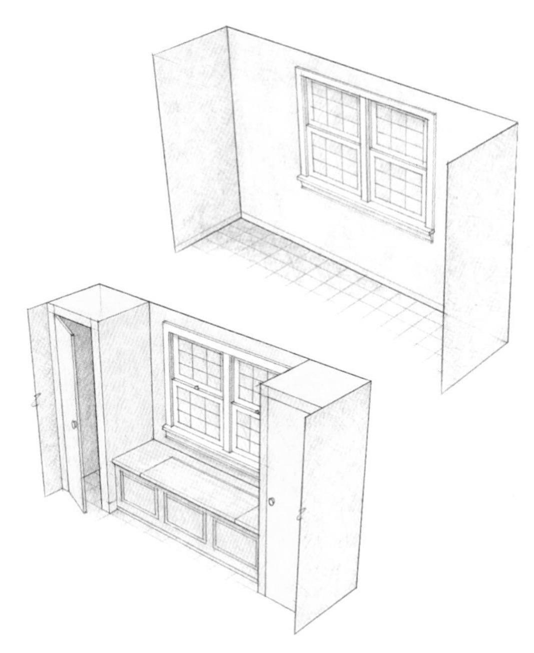

Add interest and utility to a wall by flanking a window with a pair of closets or built-in cabinets. Put a window seat in the middle, and within this 2-ft.-deep space, you've gained storage, a sunny reading nook, and reflective surfaces that bounce daylight into the room.

crannies present themselves during remodeling or construction. Think like a boat designer and look for these opportunities to provide places for stowing away items.

10. Include multipurpose rooms

Houses integrate numerous functions, but each one doesn't need its own space all the time. If you can combine different activities that occur at different times in the same space, you can eliminate the need for more rooms, but don't force it. Work through the functional requirements of different activities before combining them. Here are some typical combinations:

- Hall with laundry and storage
- Bathroom/laundry room
- Entry with bench, storage, and powder room
- Mudroom with workbench, sink, and clothes-drying racks
- Bedroom with a comfortable area for reading or meditation
- Stair landing expanded to include a desk
- Dining area that serves both formal and informal dining

The Big Little Backyard House

BY JOHN HOPKINS

Shortly after Suzie McKig moved her family from Los Angeles and bought a house in Berkeley, Calif., her mother, Billie, decided to follow suit. Billie's requirements were simple: She wanted a home of her own, and she wanted to live close to her daughter and grandchildren. However, Billie's limited budget put finding a house on a full-size lot in Berkeley out of the question. Suzie contacted me to explore building a new home for her mother in her own backyard.

The idea our firm proposed was to locate the new house at the rear of the property to maximize space for a garden between the two houses. A protected California live oak tree would have to be accommodated, and setback and height limits respected; most critical, zoning requirements would restrict living space to a mere 540 sq. ft. Our challenge was to create a home for Billie that would be compact and comfortable.

THE OUT-BACK RETIREMENT HOUSE. Billie McKig's cottage sits at the far end of her daughter's backyard, leaving plenty of space between the two houses for daylight and a future garden. Photo taken at B on floor plan.

Fitting full-size function in a compact package

Our first task was simply to make the tiny house work. After all, this was going to be Billie's permanent home, and it would have to accommodate all the typical functions of her previous house in one-third of the floor area. As a result, we had to omit wasted space, to consolidate activities, and to think small—very small.

Even in larger homes, we try to reduce wasted space by minimizing unnecessary circulation areas such as halls, stairs, and a dedicated entry. Why

PART ENTRYWAY, PART FOCAL POINT, the deck is an outdoor room that nearly doubles the living space. The live oak's canopy shades the cottage in the afternoon. Photo taken at A on floor plan.

spend money on space whose only purpose is to lead to other rooms? In Billie's house, we reduced such waste to zero: All circulation occurs within the main rooms themselves (see the floor plan on p. 20).

Next, we consolidated as many functions into as few rooms as possible, thus allowing different activities to share space. The living room, the kitchen, and the dining area are combined, and all enjoy a view of the fireplace and the garden. A desk tucked in to a corner of the same room fills the role of home office. The bedroom occupies a separate space. Combining these uses in only two main rooms helps make the house seem bigger. Each discrete space is similar to its counterpart in a house twice the size.

Given our mild climate, we also were able to eliminate space for mechanical equipment. A gas fireplace on a thermostat heats the house, and a direct-vent tankless water heater mounted outside on the back wall satisfies domestic hot-water needs. Even using these strategies, though, we were hard-pressed to fit in everything that would make this a real home. Compact appliances were a big help in the little kitchen. A 2-ft.-wide refrigerator, a 2-ft.-wide range, and a single-bowl sink all save counter space, while a single-drawer dishwasher allows for more storage space in base cabinets. For laundry, a dual-function washer/dryer in the closet takes up as little space as possible (see "Sources" on p. 21).

Three strategies help make this small house seem big

After combining multiple functions in a single space, the next-most-effective way to make a small house seem bigger is to maximize the ceiling height. I think that we have become so accustomed to 8-ft. ceilings that even a slight increase can deliver results. On this project, we were sandwiched between the city's 12-ft. height limit and a raised floor dictated by the type of foundation we used to save the oak tree (see "A Tree-Friendly Foundation" at right). Consequently, we had to hunt for additional headroom. Using pressure-treated floor framing allowed us to reduce the depth of the crawl-space, and exposing the rafters gained additional inches. The result is an 8-ft. 9-in. ceiling, which seems inexplicably generous.

To make the spaces feel more open, we ganged windows and doors, and ran them to the ceiling. Besides increasing daylight, this strategy breaks up the wall and opens the views, making the interior seem less confined. In the bathroom, a floor-to-ceiling glass-block wall provides both privacy and abundant light (see the right photo on p. 21). An 8-ft.-tall glass door also creates a grand entry to the modest house.

Finally, we added an exterior living area to expand the sense of spaciousness. A deck, defined on two sides by the house and on a third by the oak, is located centrally as the focus of the living room and the bedroom. The deck's use as entry access makes it an active extension of the house.

Using high-quality materials and getting adventurous with color

The star of the show is a red-cedar ceiling with matching exterior eaves. The exposed 4×6 rafters are Douglas fir, as are the windows, doors, and trim. We picked bamboo flooring for its durability and for its compatibility with the color of the maple cabinetry.

When it came to color selection, Suzie used her talents as a professional graphic designer. She chose interior and exterior colors that fit with the site

A TREE-FRIENDLY FOUNDATION

California live oak trees are protected in Berkeley, and new construction within the drip line of one of these trees is prohibited. Working with a structural engineer, a licensed arborist, and the local building department, we came up with a plan for protecting the tree's root structure. The solution was an above-grade beam foundation with no excavation other than individual piers located to avoid major roots (see the drawing below). This strategy allowed us to keep the root structure intact and to incorporate the tree into the design of the deck. The live oak now acts as the focal point of the deck while providing much-needed shade from the afternoon sun.

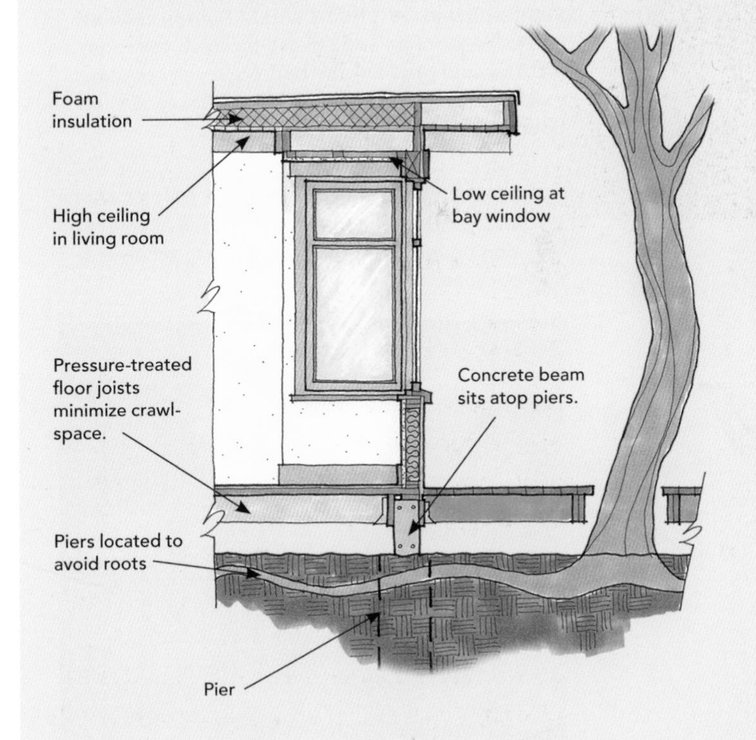

SPACE CAN BE IN THE DETAILS. Built-in cabinets maximize storage, and tall ceilings give the room a lift. The cool green of the bedroom wall recedes, making it seem farther away. Photo taken at C on floor plan.

A KITCHEN TUCKS INTO A CORNER OF THE MAIN ROOM. Downsized appliances and base cabinets on legs don't overpower the space. Photo taken at D on floor plan.

MAKING THE MOST OF 540 SQ. FT.

TWO PRIMARY ROOMS arranged in an L-shaped plan eliminate space-hungry hallways and divide the house equally into public and private realms. Most of the windows are focused on the outdoor space, creating a sense of transparency and spaciousness.

SPECS

- Bedrooms: 1
- Bathrooms: 1
- Size: 540 sq. ft.
- Cost: $400 per sq. ft.
- Completed: 2006
- Location: Berkeley, Calif.
- Architect: Hopkins Studio–Architecture & Design; John Hopkins, principal; Jonathan Heuer, associate
- Builder: Paul Cerami, Cerami Builders

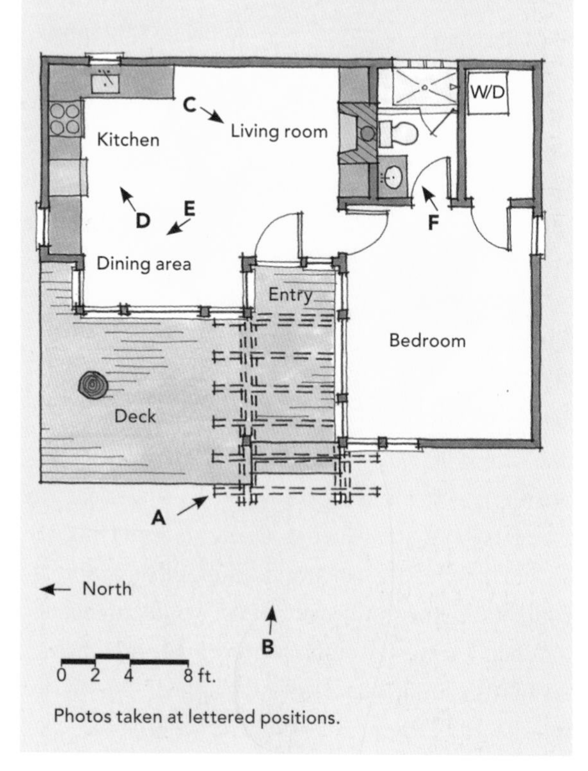

Photos taken at lettered positions.

and complement the natural materials. Surfaces are painted contrasting colors to delineate different areas within the main living space; in the bedroom, four subtly different tints of apple green are arranged to look the same on walls that receive different amounts of daylight. The exterior colors complement the wood deck and trellis and help tie the house to its garden setting. These kinds of color and material selections inject energy into a small space.

What does Billie think about her new home? Above all, she loves being close to her daughter and grandchildren, yet she also enjoys the privacy of her own place. She particularly likes the live oak tree, the wood ceilings, and all the tall windows. Billie also has been surprised by how well suited the small house is to her; she actually welcomed the chance to reduce "the amount of material possessions I have around." Another plus: "It's a breeze to keep clean!"

EXPLOIT THE VIEW OF THE GARDEN. Ganged together for maximum impact, tall windows overlook the deck and take in afternoon sun. At the right, a built-in desk provides a compact home office. Photo taken at E on floor plan.

A WALL OF DAYLIGHT IN A TINY BATH. Facing east, the glass-block wall in the shower is a cheerful wake-up call every morning. Photo taken at F on floor plan.

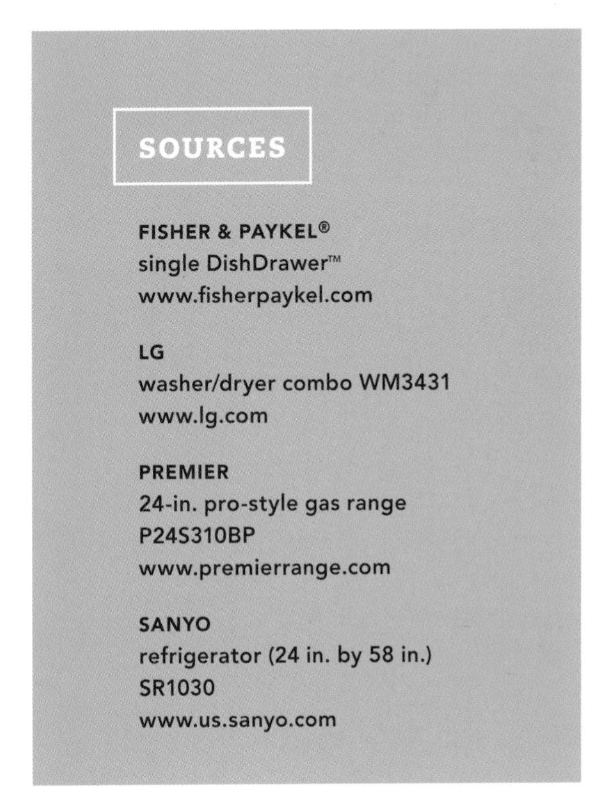

SOURCES

FISHER & PAYKEL®
single DishDrawer™
www.fisherpaykel.com

LG
washer/dryer combo WM3431
www.lg.com

PREMIER
24-in. pro-style gas range
P24S310BP
www.premierrange.com

SANYO
refrigerator (24 in. by 58 in.)
SR1030
www.us.sanyo.com

A House That's Half Porch

BY AL PLATT

Designing a vacation house is different from designing a primary residence. Primary residences meet the needs of everyday life, which generally demand lots of storage and privacy. Vacation homes are special places that may imply a way of life only dreamed about in the real world. Dreaming rarely involves storage; it more commonly involves things like lounging on an oversize porch, in front of an oversize fireplace, with a beautiful view of the mountains. But despite the differences in designing vacation and primary homes, there are similarities as well.

Quality, cost, or size: Something's usually got to give

For every project, whether primary or secondary residence, there are three interrelated variables: size, quality, and cost. Most people understand this relationship immediately. Everyone has a quality threshold below which he or she would not do the project, and most people also have some notion of a cost limit. In most cases, the variable most easily modified is size, especially for a vacation house. The objective is usually to build no more house than necessary and to build it as well as the budget permits.

The owners of this house, Beth and Steve Womble, wanted a small retreat with generous areas for

THREE PORCHES, ONE HOUSE. A screened porch for entertaining features a Tennessee-stack fieldstone fireplace (photo on the facing page, taken at A on floor plan). The long, covered porch (photo above, taken at B on floor plan) acts as a sheltered entry, an exterior hallway, and a place to enjoy the sunrise with morning coffee. A deck at the rear is a wonderful place to enjoy sunsets over the Blue Ridge Mountains.

informal gatherings and meals but with limited storage and overnight guest accommodations (see photo above). Because this vacation house isn't far from their main residence, most guests live close enough that they don't spend the night.

Achieving the lowest possible cost wasn't the main objective; making a comfortable and lasting building for themselves and their children was. However, limiting the size and simplifying the shape were tactics we used to save money, which then was spent on better-quality finish materials and the craftsmanship required to make the most of them. No drywall was used. With age and wear, the all-wood interior will look even better in 25 or 50 years than it does today.

Size affects cost in a number of other ways, too. The small enclosed area of this cabin takes less energy to heat and cool, which is another important consideration for the frequent start-ups common to vacation houses.

Compact design forces discipline yet provides freedom

Among the many ways a small cabin can succeed as a retreat is the limit it imposes on accumulating stuff and the subsequent freedom it grants from taking care of that stuff. The Wombles have especially appreciated this simplification. For them, the cabin is a place to establish and enjoy a selective and evolving collection of furniture, art, crafts, books, and plants.

To be effective, a compact design must be thought out. For example, the kitchen, the stairs, and the entry porch are each to some degree unusual to make the most of the cabin's limited space (see the floor plan on p. 25). The kitchen is L-shaped, but in reverse of what's typical, with the working sides on the outside of the L rather than inside. Wrapping around the bath and laundry, it concentrates the plumbing above the only enclosed foundation bay. There is room for more people to work together, and they are more or less facing each other. The leg parallel to the French doors also acts as a buffet table: As dishes are prepared, they're lined up for serving.

The stairs occupy the other concentrated area of the cabin and encloses the HVAC return ducts. Winder stairs make sense here. They take less depth

(Continued on p. 26)

PUT MONEY INTO DETAILS RATHER THAN SQUARE FOOTAGE

Keeping down the size affords fine craftsmanship. Builder Tim Robinson of Homeworks was able to sweat the details, such as aligning the battens perfectly with rafters and windows and custom-cutting the boards of the loft railing to expose two Ws (for Womble, the owners' name).

Interior finishes are all natural: wood, stone, and tile. No drywall was used in this cabin. Using stock rather than custom cabinets in the kitchen allowed the Wombles to choose a higher grade of wood (cherry) while staying within the project's specified budget.

An important place to spend money is on frequently used items. Parts used as often (and vigorously) as doors, windows, and kitchen faucets should be chosen for durability, efficacy, and good looks, not for price. Photos taken at C, D, and E on floor plan.

WHEN YOUR HOUSE IS HALF PORCH, THE OTHER HALF BETTER WORK PRETTY HARD

At just less than 1,000 sq. ft. (in 2003), this cabin cost about $200 per sq. ft. But with almost 800 sq. ft. of livable porch, the price drops to around $120 per sq. ft., including site work, well, and septic.

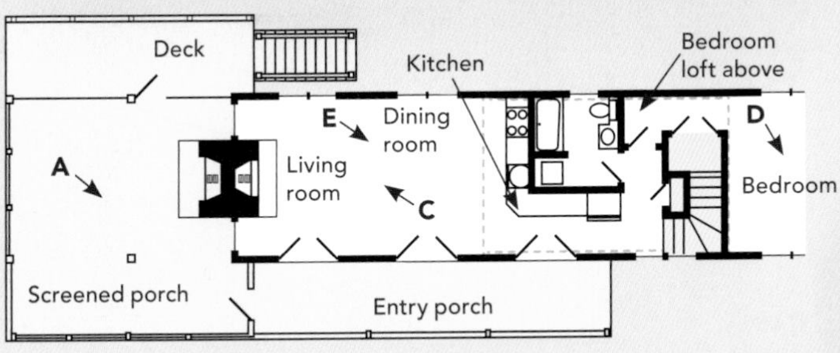

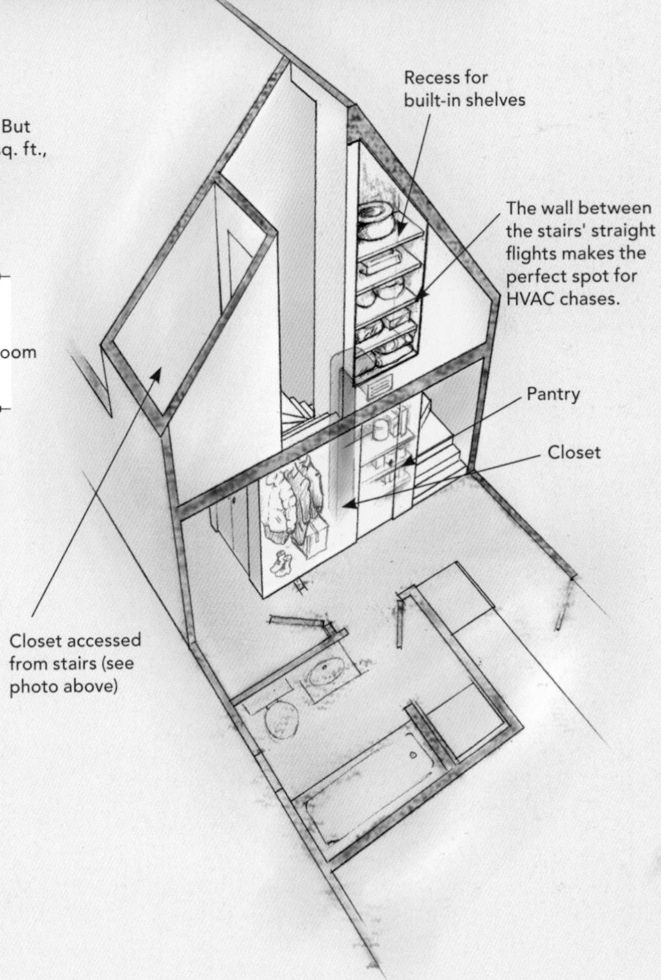

FIFTY SQUARE FEET OF PURE UTILITY

In addition to the stairs, this core contains a pantry, HVAC duct chases, an upstairs built-in shelf, and two closets. Winder stairs save floor space by eliminating a normal stair tread, and the wall between the stairs' straight flights makes the perfect spot for HVAC chases. On the lower level, the stairs wind around a built-in shelf unit for blanket and board-game storage. Below the winder, clothes are hung on three levels. Because this house is a getaway cabin, storage for clothing wasn't a high priority: no formal attire necessary.

on the floor plan by converting landing platforms into stair treads. The price is a wider footprint; the geometry is such that the central wall they wrap around must be wider than standard 2×4 interior walls to meet code (and safety) requirements. By exploiting this apparent drawback, both return ducts were concealed, and a pantry, clothes closet, storage closet, and a built-in shelving unit were added.

The porches serve several functions

The exterior spaces include a large screened porch with a fireplace, the covered entry porch, and an uncovered deck. The combined porches nearly equal the enclosed area of the cabin, and they are used in multiple ways.

The long, narrow entry porch shelters three pairs of French doors and serves several purposes beyond its entrance function: It is a hallway to bypass a busy kitchen, it provides room for the serving line for buffet-style meals set up in the kitchen, and it becomes a depository for the overflow of things that would otherwise clutter the interior living space. A breakfast table, plants, visiting dogs and dog bowls, ice chests, groceries, wet shoes, umbrellas, coats, hats, and fishing gear all find a home here, which helps preserve the interior space and condition of the cabin and the tranquility of the owners and their guests.

The big screened porch is as much a living room as it is a porch. In the mountains of western North Carolina, this porch and its fireplace are usable year round. The Wombles spend many winter days with a blanket, enjoying the fire, the view, and the low afternoon sun. In fact, it's now a Christmas tradition to spend a day on the porch.

Guest Friendly and Cost Conscious

BY GENE DESMIDT

In the summer of 2000, my wife, Sharon, and I were driving back to our home in the Bay Area from a remote piece of property that we own in northern California. We were exhausted from the dusty, unpaved roads, the dry heat, and the dogs drooling in back. This was no way to unwind. We decided to look for a vacation retreat that was closer to home and preferably on some water.

After looking at nearly a dozen houses, we found a piece of land that once had a resort hotel on it. Long ago, the hotel burned to the ground, and now the land had two overgrown building sites less than 50 ft. from a small lake. We bought it on the spot.

Big bites reduce small budget

After buying the land, we had $150,000 to complete the project. Right away we found out that a good chunk of it was going into the ground. Because we wanted to build close to the water, we couldn't install a traditional septic tank and leach field. Instead, we would have to install a sewage-treatment system complete with a pump to convey effluent to a leach field 1,000 ft. behind the house. That lightened the checkbook by $30,000.

Next, we learned that getting electricity to the site would cost $7,500 for the pole, the line, and the transformer. Now that our budget had been reduced by almost 25%, we had to make some hard choices about what kind of house we could build. Clearly, the house had to be small and composed of modest materials without fussy finishes. It also had to be easy to build because seasoned carpenters are tough to find in Lake County. Sharon and I figured we could get what we needed in 875 sq. ft. If we could keep the house to $125 per sq. ft., we could do it.

A FREESTANDING ISLAND SEPARATES the kitchen from the living room. Photo taken at B on floor plan.

In my work as a contractor, I typically build expensive houses. The company motto is "Perfect is close enough." But for my own house, we changed it to "Close enough is perfect."

Saving money starts with the plan

Before learning that we needed a sewage-treatment facility, our plan was to build three small structures with curving fronts next to one another, facing the lake. But curved walls cost a lot more than straight ones. With the help of our beloved architect, Helen Degenhardt, the early plan evolved into a rectangle with a shed roof. A house doesn't get much simpler than this, but a couple of twists energize the plan (see the floor plan on p. 31). The two primary rooms—the master bedroom and the living room/kitchen—are separated by a foyer that is akin to an interior courtyard. Accordion doors fold back,

BOARD-AND-BATTEN ROUGE. **Lipstick red and set to party, the author's vacation house features a shed roof with 6-ft. overhangs sheltering the patio. Photos above and on the facing page taken at A on floor plan.**

linking the foyer with the patio (see the photo on the facing page). On warm summer evenings, we swing open the doors and live out there.

We wanted the interior of the house to be visually open, from the bedroom to the foyer to the living room/kitchen. But we also wanted the option of complete privacy when the living room doubles as a guest room. The solution: insulated barn doors that open up each space or completely close off each one. The bath is off the foyer, accessible from the master bedroom and the guest bedroom.

Being as close to the ground as possible was important to us, and choosing a concrete-slab foundation and floor fit right into that goal by keeping the floor just a few inches above grade. The slab also saved us the cost of forming concrete stemwalls, floor joists, and an 18-in. crawl space with all the necessary vents and access hatches. We left the concrete (pigmented dark green) exposed in the entry foyer and in the bathroom. Both have floor drains to catch the runoff from the bathroom shower or from dripping swimmers just back from the lake.

We prefer, however, not to walk on concrete all the time. So the master bedroom and living room have hardwood floors atop the slab. By the end of the project, we were relieved to see that our cost-conscious approach worked. The house ended up costing $110,000 and change. That didn't include about $5,000 worth of building materials that I had been gathering over the years for a project like this. And it didn't include the time that I spent swinging a hammer and managing the subcontractors. But 90% of the work was done by locals. And it's fair to say that if the house had been any larger or any more complicated, we couldn't have done it.

I BUILT THIS PLACE FOR A SONG

In addition to keeping the house simple and the materials modest, we stretched the budget by developing some details that streamlined construction and others that will cut down on the future maintenance.

1 DOUBLE-DUTY SIDING

Our house is in an earthquake zone and therefore required shear walls to secure it to the foundation. Shear walls typically are composed of plywood or oriented strand board (OSB), so builders sheathe a house with one of those products and then cover the sheathing with another layer of siding. This redundancy adds another layer of expense.

I found a source for 4-ft. by 9-ft. lap-jointed fir plywood, 5/8 in. thick, that was designed for exterior exposure and rated for shear walls. We used it for both shear walls and siding, and gave it a board-and-batten look with 1× battens nailed over each stud. That detail covered the lap joints in the plywood; gave us the look of an informal, rural building; and didn't require any extra blocking for the battens.

2 SAVING WITH 2-FT. SPACING

Because so many building materials come in dimensions that are multiples of 2 ft., we framed the house to take advantage of them. All the studs are 2 ft. apart. The rafters are 4 ft. apart, bearing on studs placed directly below them to carry their loads. This kept our lumber costs to a minimum and allowed us to use standard-size windows rather than expensive custom sizes.

3 FLASHING WINDOWS IN PLYWOOD SIDING

Our plywood-as-siding detail presented us with a dilemma. Without the typical layer of siding over the plywood, we had to get creative about flashing the tops of the windows. As shown in the drawing below, a strip of foil-faced bituthene wraps across the intersection of the plywood and the wall framing. Above it, a flashing behind the rabbeted 1×4 head casing tucks into a ¼-in. reglet in the plywood.

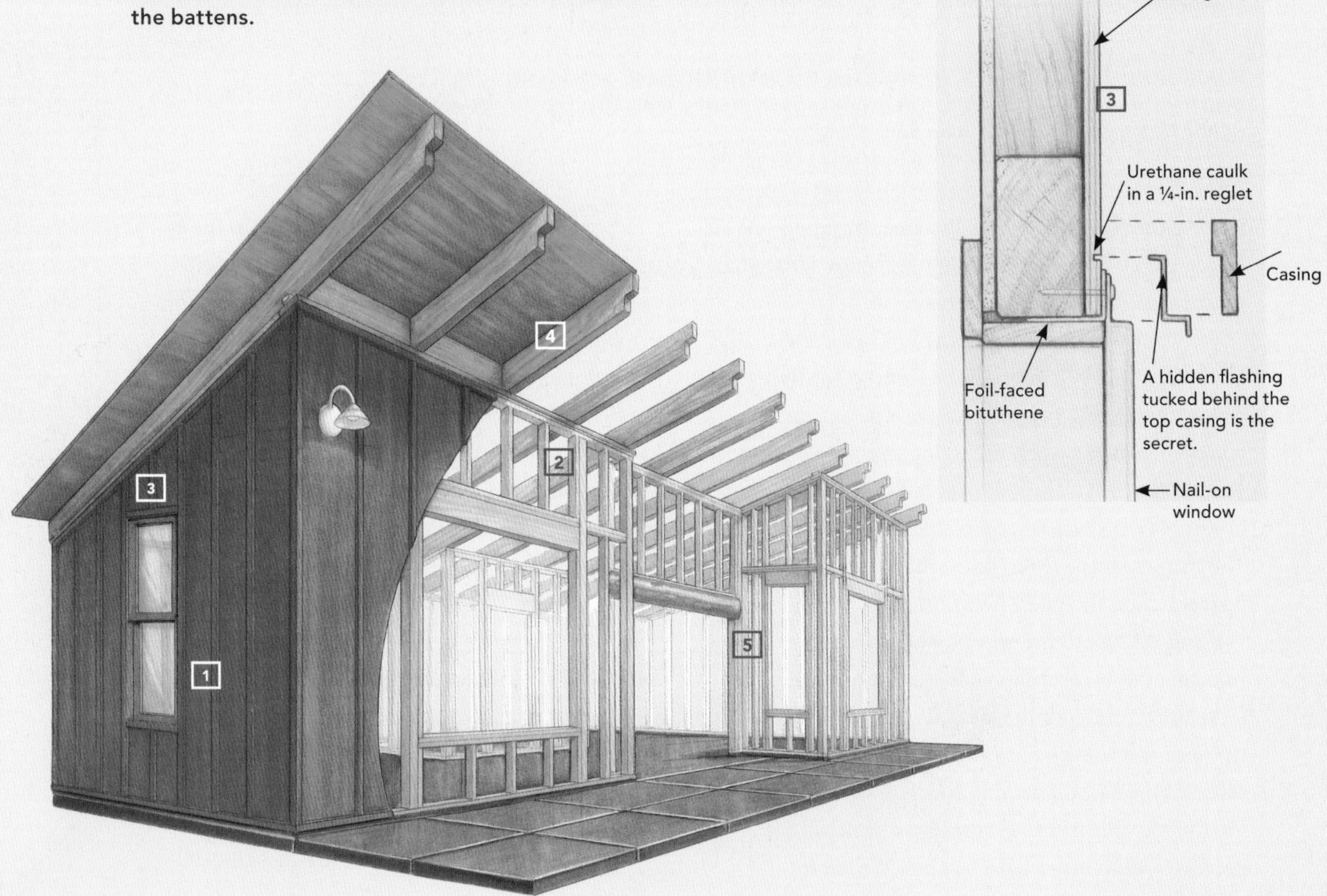

4 ROOF AND CEILING

The shed roof is built on as few rafters as possible. We used 3×12s, some up to 32 ft. long, spaced 4 ft. apart. These sticks are unwieldy to move around, so we used a little trick to help position them properly: 2×4 cleats atop the walls fit into notches in the rafters, locking them together in the right alignment. A prepainted 2×8 beneath the cleat acts in part as a top plate and as both interior and exterior trim.

The roof deck is ¾-in. plywood, joined at the unsupported edges by plywood clips at 1-ft. intervals, eliminating the need for more expensive tongue-and-groove plywood. Roll roofing over 15-lb. felt keeps out the weather right now. When we can afford it, we'll install a standing-seam copper roof. A 4-in.-thick layer of foam insulation concealed from below by knotty-pine boards completes the ceiling.

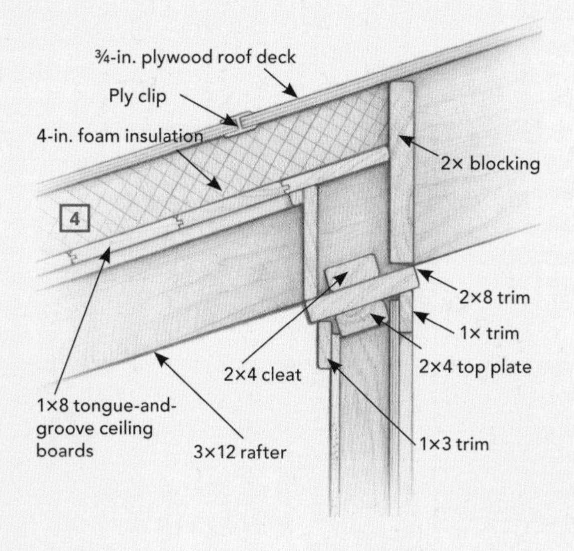

5 ACCORDION DOORS SWING WIDE TO THE LAKE

When the weather is warm, we want the house to blend right in with the patio. So we put a big opening between the two, along with four 30-in.-wide doors that can be folded out of the way. We didn't want sliders, and the hinged systems I've seen were out of our price range. So we made our own.

As shown in the photo below, we hinged together pairs of standard Simpson® door blanks with four pairs of stainless-steel 4-in. ball-bearing hinges. Experience has taught me over the years that gravity always causes the top hinge to droop when the doors are heavy. To keep these doors from sagging, we added an extra hinge toward the top of each door. Barrel bolts at the top and bottom of each door keep them secure in the closed position.

SPECS

- Bedrooms: 1
- Bathrooms: 1
- Size: 875 sq. ft.
- Cost: $125 per sq. ft. (doesn't include owners' involvement)
- Completed: 2002
- Location: Lake County, Calif.
- Architect: Helen Degenhardt
- Builder: Gene DeSmidt

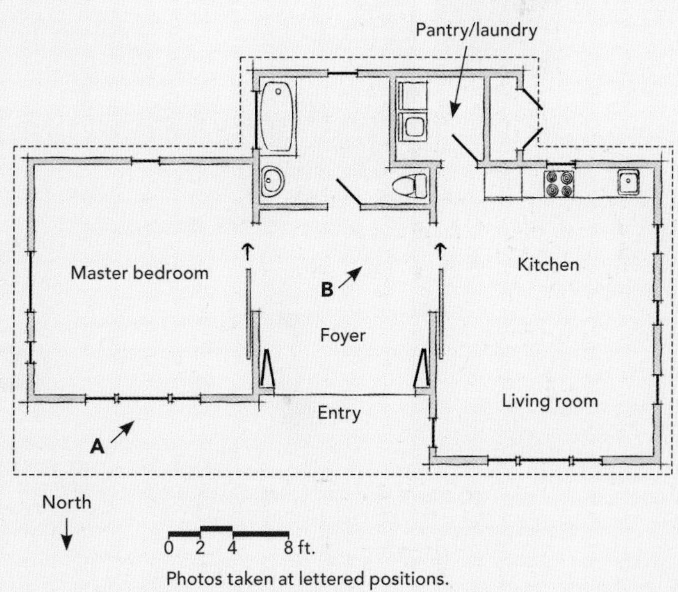

Photos taken at lettered positions.

ANOTHER TIME, SAME PLACE

In the vintage postcard shown below, five cabanas lined up like turtles on a log overlook the lake. Behind them, the lodge dining room occupies the spot that has become the site for the author's house.

The concrete bulkhead that supported the original cabanas was still in excellent shape 80 years after the demise of the old lodge. The bulkhead now supports a pair of colorful cabins—the Banana Cabana and the Grape Escape—which serve as guest sleeping quarters. Photo below taken at C on site plan.

Guest-cabin cabanas sit atop the seawall foundation of an old resort.

BUILD A GUEST HOUSE ON A LAKE AND THE GUESTS WILL COME

We have lots of friends who join us for weekends. After a year of tucking guest beds on couches, in cars, and in tents, we decided the best way to give us all a little privacy would be to build a couple of tiny sleeping cabins.

The long-gone lodge, the Laurel Dell, included a concrete bulkhead at the water's edge. It was still in great shape, so I designed two 8-ft. by 12-ft. cabanas cantilevered over the bulkhead and took the plans to the building department. Application denied: Zoning wouldn't allow us to build over the water.

At about the same time, my wife, Sharon, was on eBay looking for old postcards of the lodge. She found one that revealed five cabanas with decks hanging over the water (see inset photo on the facing page). Vintage postcard in hand, I went back to the building department and showed it to the head inspector, asking her if we could "grandfather" our cabanas. She and the zoning department were convinced, and our permit was approved (and we sent her a dozen roses).

We framed all the cabana walls in my shop in Oakland, and then trucked them to the lake. It took three people one day to install the walls and rafters. I spent many more weekends with my son Danny, putting down deck boards, building the railings, and trimming out the cabin interiors (see the top photo at right).

The floors cantilever so far beyond the bulkhead that we had to install piers uphill to keep the joists from lifting. As a result, the floors are a little bouncy. But so far, nobody who's stayed in the little purple and yellow cabins has complained about it.

DOWN THE HILL FROM THE MAIN HOUSE. The small guest cabins are out of conversational earshot, but are close enough to hear the dinner bell. Photos taken at D and E on site plan.

Living with Only What You Need

BY BRYAN J. HIGGINS

My wife, Chris, and I moved from Boston to Portland, Ore., with the dream that we might work downtown and live nearby, within walking distance of our offices. We eventually found a condominium located in a neighborhood sprinkled with Victorian houses, brick office buildings, and even a Carpenter Gothic church that became a science-fiction bookstore.

We loved the neighborhood and our 20-minute walk to work. But the reality of living in the condo started to wear thin. I'm an architect, and Chris is an engineer. We really wanted the opportunity to shape our own house.

Then we got lucky. A tiny 25-ft. by 50-ft. lot, just a Frisbee® toss from the condo that we were living in, came on the market. The piece of land was too small for the multifamily projects that have dominated the neighborhood in recent years. The city was willing, however, to allow a single-family house to be built on the lot.

The catch: We had to juggle tight setbacks, height restrictions, zoning issues, and design guidelines to get the approval of the city's design-review board, yet we still had to come up with a livable house. Here's how we did it.

SMALLER HOUSE, BETTER MATERIALS. Window bays and a shed dormer create a pleasing composition of shapes on the outside and expand the usable space inside. Cedar siding, wood windows, and a copper roof are some of the upgraded details. Photo taken at A on floor plan.

Keep the plan basic to maximize living space

City setbacks reduced the first-floor footprint of the house to 16 ft. by 38 ft. In a house this small, it's critical to keep the circulation space to a minimum. So we based the house on a simple diagram: circulation stairs in the center with living spaces on each side (see the floor plan on p. 37).

The lot is oriented north–south. The south side faces the street, and the west side overlooks our neighbor's beautifully landscaped yard. Taking

advantage of this sweet view, we put our living spaces and the majority of our windows on these two sides of the house (see the photo on p. 35).

To the east, an existing house sits 2½ ft. from our property line. Because of this proximity, we made the east side of our house the service side, with the bathrooms, stair landings, and kitchen all along this wall.

Dual-function rooms make the house flexible

We designed each space with an eye toward possible changes in the future. We also thought a lot about what kind of furniture should be in each room, both for flexibility and for compactness.

ABOVE: WARM WOOD AND CRISP EDGES. Instead of moldings or baseboards, orderly reveals border the intersections of wood and drywall, creating shadowlines that frame the work.

LEFT: SMALL HOUSE WITH A BIG CEILING. With its timber-frame rafters and lofty ceiling height, the Higgins house avoids the claustrophobic feeling that can curse a small house. Photo taken at B on floor plan.

THIS PLAN STARTED WITH THE STAIRS

WITH A MODEST 16-ft. by 38-ft. footprint, this house doesn't squander unnecessary space on hallways and corridors. For efficiency's sake, the stairs occupy the center of the house, with living spaces on each side. Modest bump-outs on each floor gain precious space and add visual interest to the exterior.

SPECS

- Bedrooms: 1 to 3
- Bathrooms: 2
- Size: 1,100 sq. ft.
- Cost: $240 per sq. ft.
- Completed: 2003
- Location: Portland, Ore.
- Architect: Bryan J. Higgins
- Builder: Don Young & Associates

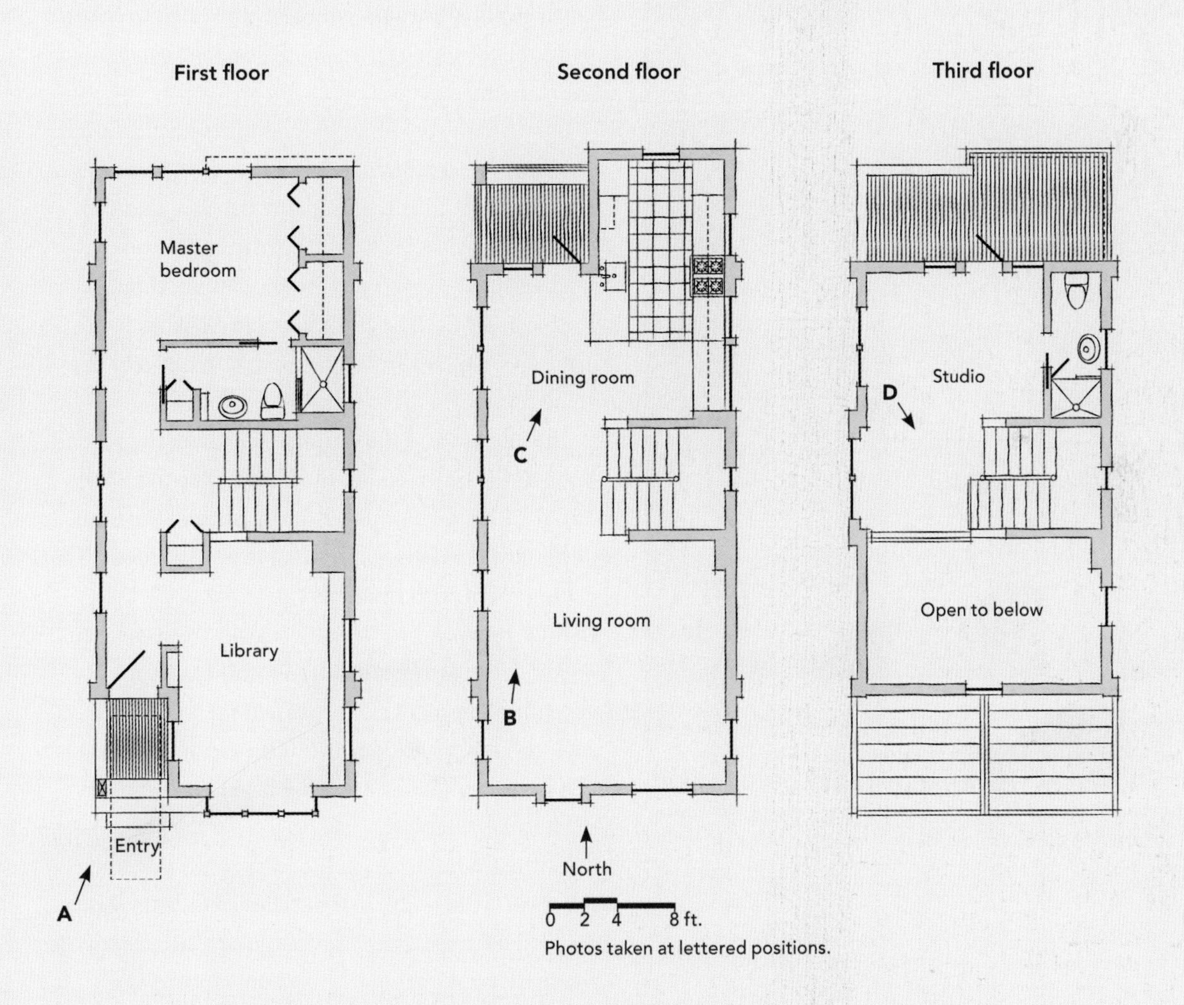

Photos taken at lettered positions.

TREETOP STUDIO. The west-facing dormer is home to a drafting table and a window that looks out on a cluster of trees. With its own full bath and a deck to the back, the studio doubles as a first-rate guest room. Photo taken at D on floor plan.

The first floor contains the master bedroom and bath on the north side of the house. The bedroom has modular shelving and drawers in the closets. This storage eliminated the need for chests of drawers, allowing the room to be smaller.

Pocket doors, which slide into a cavity in the wall, are an advantage when space is tight. We put two of them in the bath off the master bedroom; they improved circulation by getting rid of a dead end so that Chris and I aren't running into each other in the morning. With a second door, guests easily can access the bath from the hallway.

The east wall of the library is almost entirely built-in bookcases, with a couple of small windows high on the wall. This room could be converted to a full-fledged bedroom by turning the desk alcove next to the stairs into a closet.

Incidentally, the library's signature detail, the bay window, projects 16 in. toward the street from the front of the house. That puts the window into the code-required setback from the street. Because it is a cantilevered bay with no foundation, though, the bay is allowed by code. This kind of small annexation of available space can be a big help in a small house.

The kitchen and the dining area are on the second floor, at the north end of the house. Like the library bay, the kitchen bumps out 12 in. beyond the foundation wall, adding some space to a small room. The dining room, also small, has an expandable table that for everyday use seats two; away from the wall and with the top expanded, the table easily can accommodate eight people. When the weather is nice, though, we eat our meals on the deck, which is just large enough for a small table and a couple of chairs.

Our main living space is on the south side of the second floor, overlooking the street. This plan enabled us to get the most out of the available square footage by not having the front entrance in our living room.

The roof steps up as it moves back from the street, reflecting the height of the house next door. The ceil-

DAYLIGHT AT COUNTER HEIGHT. The galley kitchen features awning windows in the east wall that let in morning light and provide cross-ventilation. Photo taken at C on floor plan.

ing steps up along with the roof, reaching its highest point above the loft (see the photo on the facing page). This space on the third floor includes a second full bath and a small deck off the back of the house. On a site with almost no outdoor space, we thought that it was important to be able to step outside on each floor.

The loft is currently the design studio. But open the futon couch, and the loft becomes a guest bedroom. As our family grows, the loft eventually could become the master bedroom.

Victorian influence with modern, high-quality trimmings

We kept the shape of the house similar to others in the neighborhood, with comparable roof slopes, shallow eaves, Victorian proportions, and asymmetrical window placement. That's where the similarity stops, however. Chris and I both like crisp, uncluttered details, so we didn't apply gingerbread to the house. Instead, we chose flat, sage green window casings and water tables played against coral-colored beveled siding. Rather than classic Victorian double-hung windows, most of ours are awning style, which is great for keeping out rain while allowing some ventilation.

Interior details are equally minimal, with gray trim and mostly white walls serving as a backdrop for varnished or oiled wood. The shadowline reveals along the stair's skirtboard are typical of this approach (see the right photo on p. 36).

Because we were building a small house, we could afford some high-quality, long-lasting materials and mechanical systems. We used clear cedar trim and siding, wood windows, and a standing-seam copper roof. The roof and copper gutters cost $6,200, but they should last 100 years or more.

Inside, we were able to afford some of the built-ins important to the success of a small house, such as custom bookcases and desks. In addition, the white-oak floor is heated by a boiler-fired radiant-heating system (see "Radiant Heat Under Wood Floors" below). On a winter day, it's a real pleasure after the walk home from work.

RADIANT HEAT UNDER WOOD FLOORS

One reason we moved to the Northwest is the moderate climate. That climate was key to our choosing a hydronic radiant-heating system, even though it was about 30% more expensive than a forced-air furnace. The system provides a savings in monthly gas bills, which compensates for its higher initial cost. Our heating bills show at least a 15% savings. Because our house is small, it was nice not to have to gobble up space for ductwork and chases. We also like the evenly distributed heat.

However, a radiant-heating system cannot cool the house the way a forced-air system with an integral air-conditioning unit can. When it gets hot, we just open the windows and let convection currents cool the house.

Our system consists of a hot-water tank, an expansion tank, three-zone valves, thermostats, and several hundred feet of tubing that distribute the heat. The system, installed by a heating subcontractor, cost $11,300 (in 2003).

Radiant heat is most efficient when installed in a concrete slab. It is, however, becoming more common in wood construction. Metal plates affixed to the underside of the floor help distribute heat evenly. We are pleased with the way the system performs.

PROS

Even heat distribution, no blowing or moving air, concealed in floor, no need for duct space, no visible vents, low noise, can keep thermostat lower because of even distribution, lower energy costs.

CONS

Slow response time, travels in direct path upward, cannot heat around corners, higher initial cost, provides for heating only, ventilation is separate.

The Small House Done Well

BY KURT OFER

Right away, I could see that this project wouldn't result in a big house that followed a 10-Dumpster® teardown. The owners of a large farmstead here in upstate New York wanted the firm my wife and I own to expand a tiny outbuilding into a small house. The site was a real challenge: The building was situated near a busy road in front; behind, the ground rose abruptly up the hillside. The owners also insisted we save a 40-ft. cedar tree that grew only a few feet from the structure, which immediately limited our options. This project would be a challenge.

But despite this peculiar context, there are lessons here for anyone who is building a small house or addition, including this key issue: How do you make a 1,200-sq.-ft. space an interesting place to live? Instead of using an open plan, we tried to create a sense of separation between the main spaces so that each room became a destination with its own views, light, and character. Of course, we wanted the new design to fit in amid the surrounding farm buildings, so the scale and the details were important, too. Sometimes smaller projects are more suited to a surgical approach than to a bulldozer and a chainsaw.

SEAMLESSLY BLEND THE OLD AND THE NEW. **Although the exterior style remains faithful to the surrounding farm buildings, the interior, illustrated by the living room (see the photo on p. 44), manages to feel contemporary and traditional at the same time.**

FROM AN OUTBUILDING TO A HOUSE THAT BELONGS THERE

The project's purpose was to create a small house by adding onto an old outbuilding [1]. Seen from any angle, the new construction was to match the scale and overall feel of the original. A small bridge [2] made an interesting way to connect the old and new structures while preserving a large tree. From the exterior, the bridge windows [3] help it float visually between segments of the house; frosted glass maintains a measure of privacy.

Each room has its own character that makes the interior feel bigger. Stepping up the sloped site, the living room perches balcony-like above the kitchen [4]. Wrapping around the gable end, a line of windows gives the dining area [5] a unique sense of place.

ARRANGING THE PLAN ACCORDING TO THE SITE

The original building stood on a level spot at the bottom of a hill, close to a busy road. Rather than flatten the hill to accommodate the house, the author incorporated the new living room into the elevation. To minimize noise, the new deck was located in back; closets and small windows also help buffer road noise.

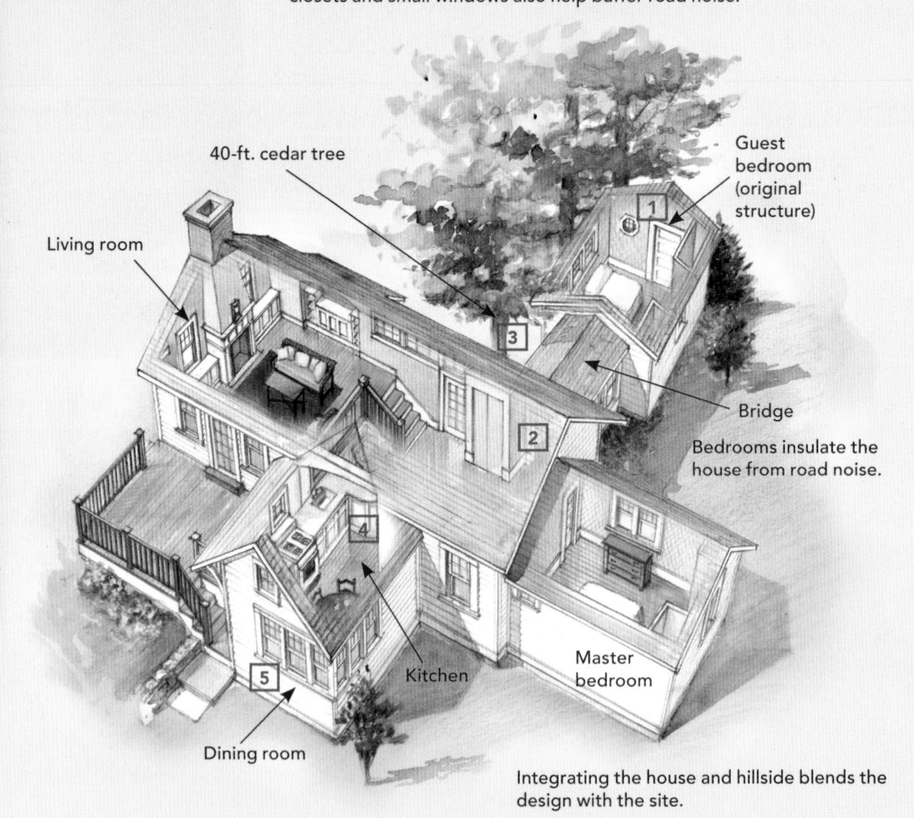

Integrating the house and hillside blends the design with the site.

Don't overwhelm the original structure

When many homeowners think about enlarging a house, they often want an addition that's much bigger than the existing building and thus run into a potential problem: how to preserve the character of the original and keep the addition from engulfing the house. Choosing to preserve the overall scale lets the house remain integrated in its surroundings while still making more living space, a point that became central to our work on this project.

Because scale also was important to our clients, we used a cruciform-like plan (see the drawing on p. 42) that allowed us to distribute the rooms into gabled boxes that matched the scale and detail of the existing buildings. The small boxes also were instrumental in establishing a sense of separation between rooms that's essential to making the interior of a small house seem bigger and more engaging. Instead of an open, undifferentiated plan, each major room has three windowed walls with a different view and sense of place that changes from room to room.

The character of the house's interior also is affected by ceiling heights. From room to room, the ceiling heights change: high in the kitchen, living room, and master bedroom and low in the hallways between. This constant variation gives a small interior a complexity that makes it seem larger.

Form Follows Function

BY DARYL S. RANTIS

For many years, the Chicken Hill area of Asheville, N.C., was best known for a large cotton mill that employed many in the close-knit hillside community. When the mill closed in the 1950s, the neighborhood fell on hard times, but lately, it's become a hot spot for artisans who value its quirky charm and proximity to Asheville's River Arts District.

When a local builder came to me with an idea for an artists' enclave on a small Chicken Hill site, I wondered how we'd fit six houses on a 2-acre parcel of steeply sloping land. The three-story homes we came up with are a response to the steep site, the small lots, and the tight budget. In addition to providing privacy and 1,300 sq. ft. of living space, each home's height provides sunset views over the French Broad River and the Patton Avenue Bridge. The design also minimizes the size of the foundation and the roof, which are among the most costly, energy-intensive parts of a new house.

Unfortunately, the housing market went bust before we could finish all the houses, but we're hoping to build the rest of the neighborhood in the near future.

Emphasis on privacy

Privacy for the new residents and the abutting landowners is one of the challenges when you're developing infill projects, so we paid very close attention to how we sited the house and to how we positioned the windows.

In the kitchen, we moved the window that would ordinarily be right over the sink to a spot higher on the wall. The unconventional placement shields the kitchen from neighbors without sacrificing natural daylight. We used a similar tactic in the dining room.

The living room's west-facing patio door is the biggest expanse of glass in the house. The deck it accesses is nearly 12 ft. off the ground. At this height, you get a great view, and you're also hidden from passersby.

We made an exception to privacy considerations with the basement patio door. This ground-level entrance provides outdoor access to the basement artist's studio, which makes bringing in materials and removing finished artwork much easier.

Vertical floor plan

The main floor includes a connected kitchen, dining, and living area to encourage an uncluttered lifestyle and to allow family members and guests to interact during meal preparation. A pair of bump-outs—one in the dining room and one for the main staircase—provide extra living space and break up large expanses of wall on the exterior.

The upstairs, which has a pair of bedrooms and two full baths, is accessed by a staircase near the front door. A window on the landing provides natural light and aesthetic balance for the front elevation. The finished basement is a large, open space with 11-ft. ceilings. It's meant as an artist's studio, but it also could be a third bedroom, a home office, or an in-law suite.

Designing a small house often involves trade-offs for space. For example, I originally planned a half-bath on the main level. The builder decided the half-bath encroached too much on the living space, so it was eliminated to keep the main floor wide open.

A mix of styles

The house is best described as a mix of modern and Craftsman styles. It has the clean, contemporary aesthetic of urban architecture while paying respect to the traditional wood buildings of western North Carolina.

Low-maintenance, inexpensive fiber-cement panels cover much of the exterior. The fiber cement is contrasted by locally harvested cypress that gives the house its warmth and beauty.

The interior has simple trim details and modern European cabinetry that breaks from traditional Craftsman style. At the same time, wood beams and

(Continued on p. 50)

MAKING THE MOST OF A STEEP LITTLE LOT

This tall, narrow house is a good example of architecture influenced by the site. The unique foundation shape and clipped rear corner were a necessity for setback requirements. Bump-outs on the upper floors gain living space in spite of setbacks.

SPECS

- Bedrooms: 2, plus art studio
- Bathrooms: 3
- Size: 1,300 sq. ft.
- Cost: $167 per sq. ft.
- Completed: 2009
- Location: Asheville, N.C.
- Architect: Daryl S. Rantis; project architect, Diane Meek; architectural intern, Robert Stenhouse
- Builder: William MacCurdy

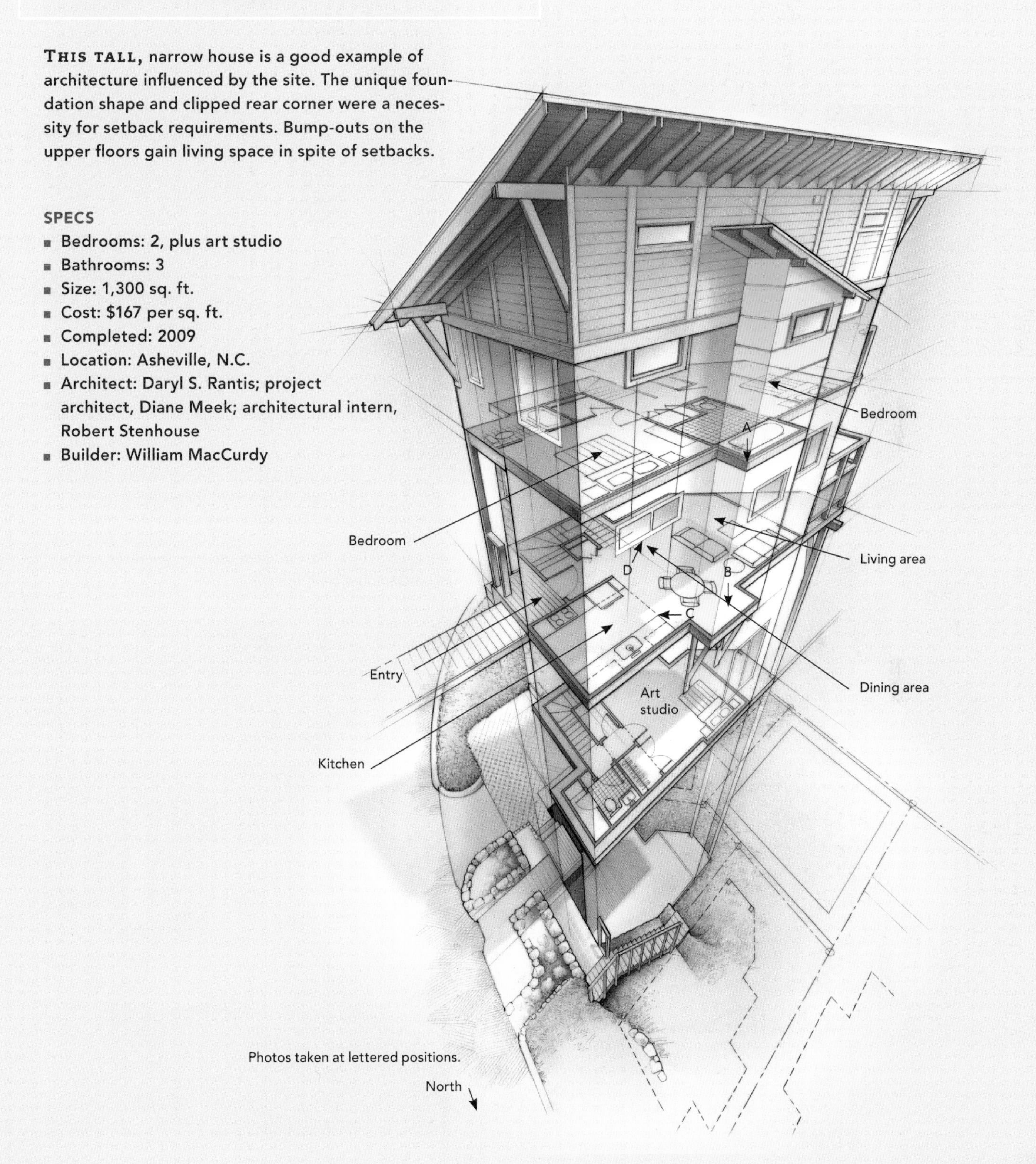

SIMPLE YET STYLISH

By combining warm, natural materials like native-hemlock joists with modern fixtures and details, the home is an inviting mix of styles that appeal both to modern and traditional sensibilities.

KEEP IT SIMPLE. The combined kitchen, dining, and living areas feature unadorned cabinets and minimal trimwork. The intent was to create simple details that would complement any decorating style. Photo taken at C on floor plan.

WARM AND INVITING. A freestanding gas fireplace provides a focal point for the living and dining areas. The furred section of wall behind the stove hides an angled flue necessary for sufficient clearance for combustibles. Photo taken at D on floor plan.

MORE WITH LESS. A two-story bump-out provides extra room in the master bath and the dining area. The cantilevered space also provides some visual interest on an exterior wall that otherwise would be rather boring. Because it doesn't touch the ground, setbacks are unaffected. Photos below and on the facing page taken at A and B on floor plan.

floors in the living areas pay homage to the home's Craftsman influence and provide a warm, inviting interior. Interior colors, tiles, and built-in cabinets are unassuming and complement most furnishings, allowing homeowners to personalize the space.

To keep down costs and to make the home affordable for the greatest number of buyers, the builder decided to forgo photovoltaic and solar hot-water panels, but we made the roof pitch and orientation ideal for adding solar at a later date.

At approximately $167 per sq. ft. for construction costs (not including the lot), the house is targeted to middle-income buyers, one of the few strong housing markets left in our region.

SIDING IN SHEETS

Sold in sheets, HardiePanel® siding is good looking and inexpensive, but because it doesn't have natural laps, keeping the building watertight can be a challenge. Although I considered installing the 4-ft. by 10-ft. panels over an airspace, rain-screen style, there just wasn't enough in the budget for the additional time and material. Instead, I installed the panels directly over properly lapped housewrap.

For the vertical seams between panels, I used Fry Reglet (www.fryreglet.com) reveal panel trim. This aluminum extrusion has a built-in channel that breaks up the monotony of the smooth surface and finishes the vertical seams. The same company makes a similar transition for horizontal seams, but I found it less expensive to have a local metalwork shop make an aluminum Z-flashing that we used to weatherproof and finish the tops of the panels. Generally, the siding is fast and easy to install, but the window and door openings are a little fussy to detail. With 40 sq. ft. of coverage per panel, it's a trade-off that's easy to justify. —William MacCurdy, builder

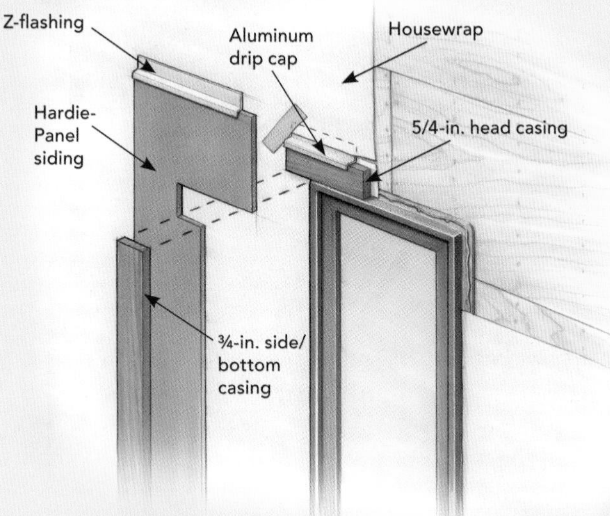

FLASHING DETAIL

Live Tall on a Small Footprint

BY MICHAEL MCDONOUGH

Because of my preference for smaller, smarter houses, I have kept a healthy distance from most developers. When I was asked to design homes for a development in picturesque Black Mountain, N.C., however, I received a pleasant surprise.

The Village of Cheshire is a skillfully developed neighborhood that encourages the building of small homes nestled among some of the most beautiful scenery in the world. When the developer, Caldwell Sikes Ragan, told me that most of the houses would be small and that one steep section would have houses limited to a 500-sq.-ft. footprint in an effort to minimize impact on the landscape, I realized that his commitment to responsible development was in line with mine.

Using these restrictions, I designed a handful of homes that afford the level of comfort my clients want on a footprint no bigger than a two-car garage. The two projects here show how I worked with Ryan McLellan of Copperwood Builders to use the landscape, a gracious entry, and a vertical mechanical scheme to create compact, three-story homes that feel spacious and uncluttered.

Homes spill into the landscape

I knew that a strong connection to the outdoors was going to be essential for these small homes to feel spacious. So I incorporated decks, porches, and balconies into each of the three floors.

By tucking the first floor into the sloping sites, both it and the middle level take advantage of grade-level exterior spaces for entries and patios. On the upper level, I cantilevered bedroom balconies that overlook the landscape. Brackets that support the balconies and roofs that shelter the homes' decks, patios, and entries add character and minimize the scale of the tall homes' exteriors.

Because much of the first floor is tucked into the hillside, there were limited opportunities to locate the homes' entries here. It made much more sense to enter the home to views and lots of natural light, given the strong outdoor connection that I was hoping to attain. I could still have grade-level entries on the second floor, but the foyer would eat up much of the limited floor space. The solution was to locate the entries on a stair landing between these two levels.

Having the landing also act as an entry foyer meant that an essential element would do double duty, an economical use of space. Although the actual size of the foyer may be limited, it feels large because it opens to the rest of the house. Your eye moves immediately up or down, and windows offer welcoming sunlight.

(Continued on p. 55)

EIGHT IDEAS FOR A LOW-IMPACT HOME

IN THE VILLAGE OF CHESHIRE, unique design guidelines overlay a cluster of lots, limiting each house to a footprint of 500 sq. ft. This restriction minimizes disturbance to the steep wooded sites and inspires a distinctive building form. The homes are taller than they are wide.

1 ENTER BETWEEN LEVELS to promote movement and to save floor space.

2 CARRY LOADS WITH BRACKETS to add visual interest and to minimize impact to the site.

3 USE BIG WINDOWS TO ADD architectural detail and to let light into the house.

4 EXTEND OVERHANGS TO PROTECT materials, provide shade, and ground tall facades.

5 CONNECT THE INTERIOR and exterior with balconies, patios, and porches.

6 INHABIT THE ROOF VIA DORMERS to add space inside and visual interest outside.

7 USE STONE AND PLANTS NATIVE to the site to weave the home into the landscape.

8 LEAVE THE CAR AT THE CURB for a more natural setting.

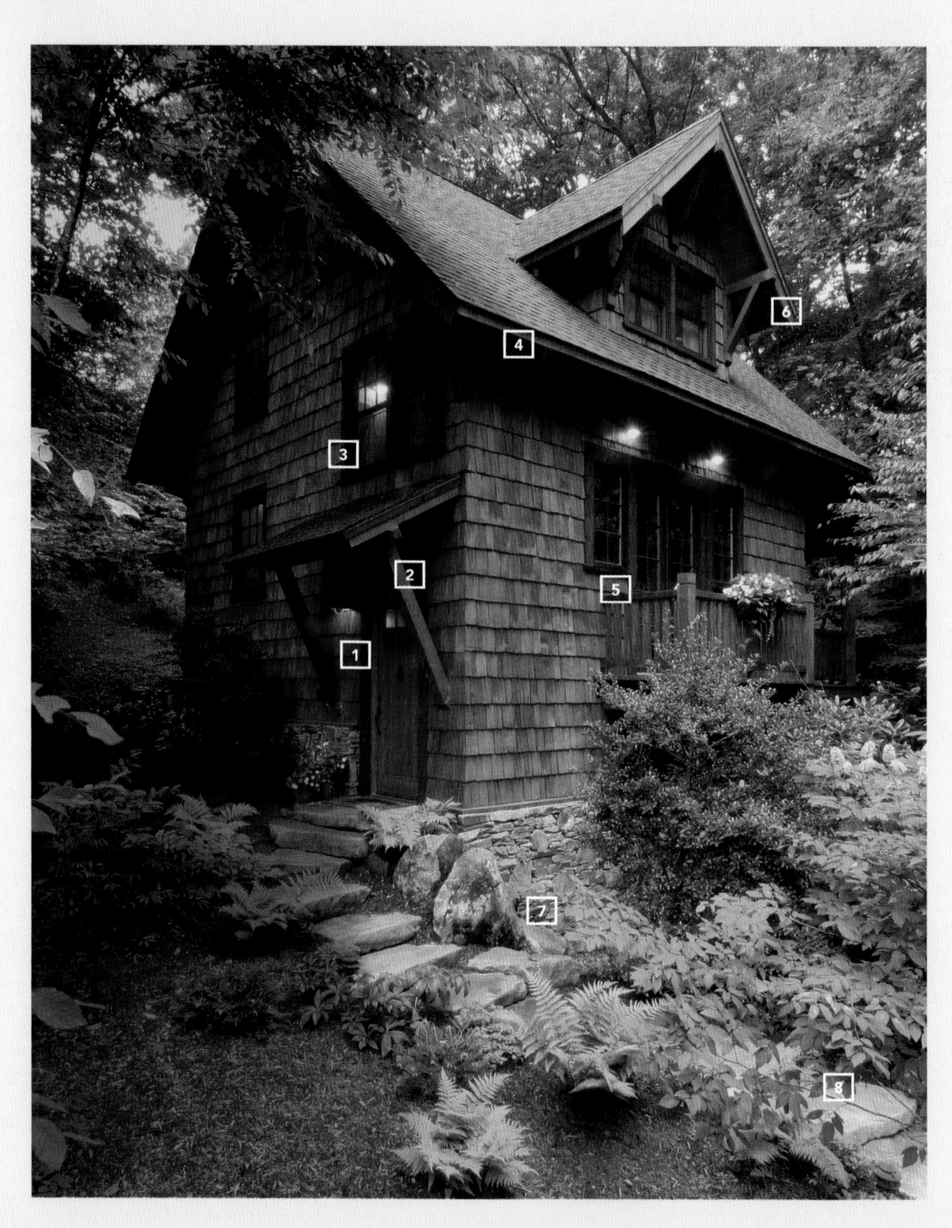

USE STAIRS INSTEAD OF HALLWAYS

In contrast to the iconic American ranch, where walls divide rooms and hallways define movement, these houses use floors to divide spaces and the stairway to establish a vertical flow. The living, dining, and kitchen areas occupy the main level, while sleeping, working, and bathing are done on the upper and lower levels. Situating the entry between levels makes for easy access to the main floor while allowing the lower level to flow easily to the outside.

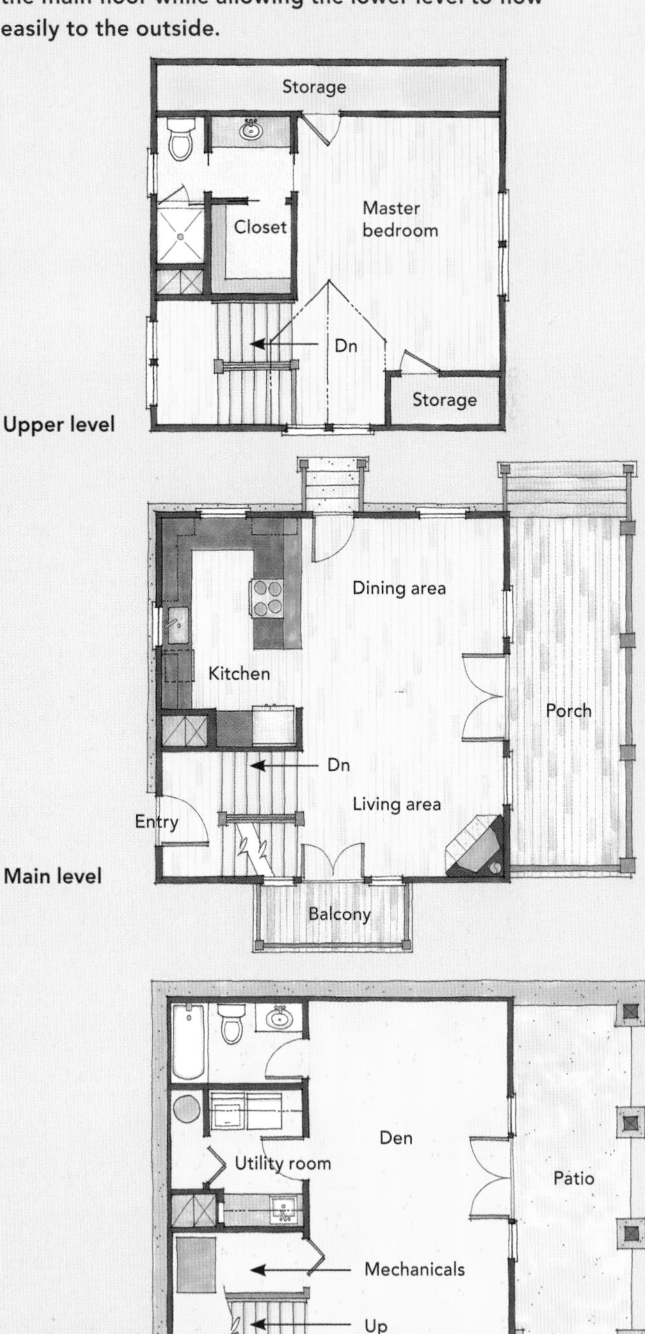

COMPACT COMFORT. Inside the house, it's the details that make the small space work. The TV, for example, stays tucked behind doors in the fireplace mantel when not in use.

TAKE IT OUTSIDE AS MUCH AS POSSIBLE. Sloped building sites create both challenges and opportunities. For small homes that rely on outdoor living spaces to feel more open, these sites offer multiple grade elevations. On one side of the house, the grade level allows the entry to be located between levels. The lower grade on the other side accommodates a patio off the den under a large deck that expands the living room.

LOWER LEVEL SPILL-OUT. Below the covered porch, a pebble-stone patio adjoins the den that doubles as a family room, guest room, and home office. The exposed deck framing adds a sense of spaciousness.

Obviously, these homes are not for everyone, especially those averse to stairs, and building smaller doesn't always translate to a smaller budget. While building and living in a small, vertical home is challenging, it comes with subtle rewards. Among my first clients was an unlikely retiring couple who embraced the challenge of purging unnecessary belongings, living with less, and keeping fit with daily movement up and down stairs. They are never more than a few steps from a window or door to a balcony, a porch, or their wooded surroundings.

COMPACT, INSIDE AND OUT

TO MINIMIZE THE SPACE REQUIRED FOR MECHANICALS, the author stacked baths, kitchens, and utility rooms near the stairs, as seen here in plans from a second Cheshire design. A compact chase concealing vertical plumbing, electrical, and HVAC shares the openings in the floor decks with the stairs. Short horizontal plenums connect the rooms.

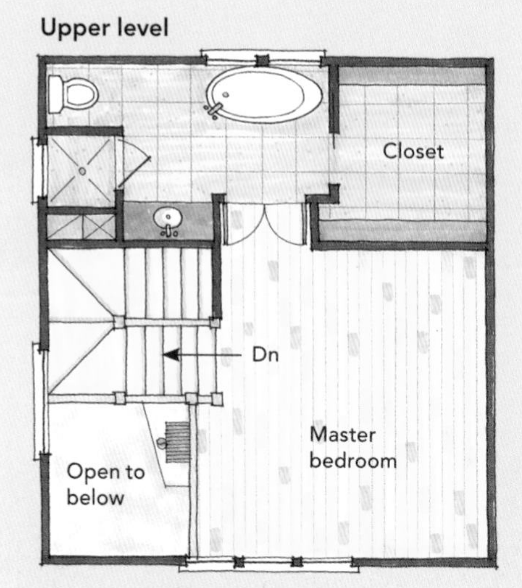

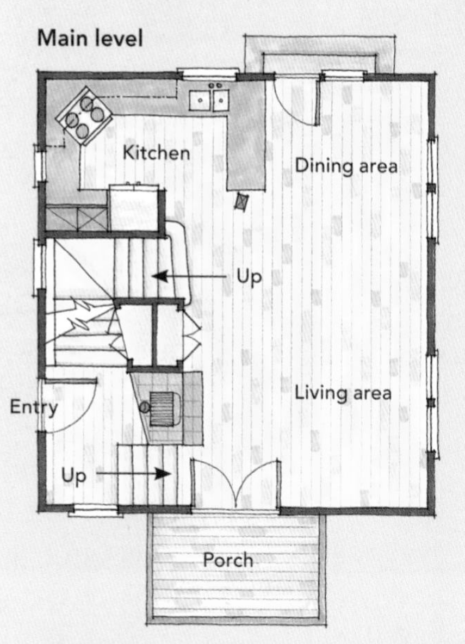

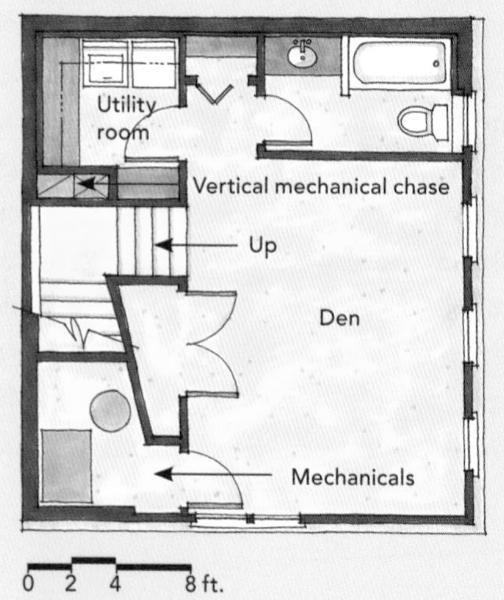

BY DUNBAR OEHMIG

Payback Time

When I tell people what it costs to heat and light the house my company recently built in Burlington, Vt., I don't think they believe me, and I can see why they're skeptical. With natural-gas and electric bills totaling $767 in 2010, this home's energy costs less than half of what you'd expect to pay for utilities in the same house built to code-minimum standards.

Even more surprising is that this house cost only about $16,500 more than the same house built to code minimums. If energy costs stay the same, the energy upgrades should pay for themselves in a little over 16 years. Of course, the payback will be quicker if energy costs rise as predicted.

Tight shell reduces heat loss

The SIP (structural insulated panel) construction and the attention to air-sealing by our crew and our insulator created a supertight house. The final blower-door test by the LEED℠ certifier came in at 150 cubic feet per minute at 50 pascals (150 cfm50). At the time, it was the tightest house (by a factor of two) ever tested by the certifier.

In most weather, the supertight shell means the heating load is met before the boiler shifts to a more powerful but less efficient firing mode. For domestic hot water, the Prestige modulating, wall-hung boiler

NARROW HOUSE, NARROW KITCHEN. The home's narrow footprint is a natural fit for a galley kitchen. The cabinets are hickory with slate-look PaperStone® countertops.

from Triangle Tube has a built-in 14-gal. indirect tank that operates in an on-demand mode when its storage capacity is exhausted.

A heat-recovery device captures the warmth in the drain water coming from the second-floor bath and uses this otherwise wasted heat to warm cold water going to the hot-water tank. Extra effort went into routing the pipes so that they'd provide hot water quickly without the energy use and heat loss of a recirculation system.

To supply the house with fresh air, there's a Venmar® Eko heat-recovery ventilator (HRV) with a high-efficiency ECM blower. Stale air is drawn from the kitchen and baths, and fresh air is supplied to the bedrooms and to the living areas.

Durable materials keep maintenance costs low

To minimize exterior maintenance, we used aluminum-clad windows and cellular PVC trim, and we installed the fiber-cement siding over an airspace. Often described as rain-screen siding, this assembly reduces peeling paint and discourages rot.

A green roof assembly from Hydrotech outside the third-floor office uses a lightweight growing medium over a filter fabric and root barrier. Underneath is a liquid-applied roofing membrane. Plants were selected for drought tolerance and hardiness.

BIG ANNUAL ENERGY SAVINGS

MADE FROM A SANDWICH OF OSB and Polyiso™ insulation, the 6½-in.-thick structural insulated panels (SIPs) provide an R-value of 38 without the conductive heat loss (thermal bridging) of conventional framing.

- **Energy costs 2006 code minimum (estimated) $1,775**
- **Energy costs with $16k upgrades (estimated) $911**
- **Energy costs 2010 (actual) $767**

ENERGY-SAVING INGREDIENTS

- Supertight SIP shell made from oriented-strand board (OSB) and 5½ in. of polyisocyanurate insulation.
- Triangle Tube high-efficiency modulating, condensing boiler with 14-gal. indirect tank for domestic hot water (www.triangletube.com).
- Wastewater heat-recovery device (www.gfxtechnology.com) that warms the cold-water supply before it reaches the indirect hot-water system.
- Fluorescent and LED lights throughout the home. Commonly used lights are also dimmer controlled.
- Venmar Eko heat-recovery ventilator (www.venmarces.com) with intake registers in the kitchen and bath, and fresh-air registers in the bedrooms and living room.
- Energy Star® appliances that reduce energy consumption up to 70% compared to conventional models.

SPECS

- Bedrooms: 3
- Bathrooms: 2
- Size: 1,500 sq. ft.
- Cost: $240 per sq. ft.
- Completed: 2009
- Location: Burlington, Vt.
- Designers: Sam Gardner, Jim Kemp, Stephanie Lind
- Builder: Red House Inc.

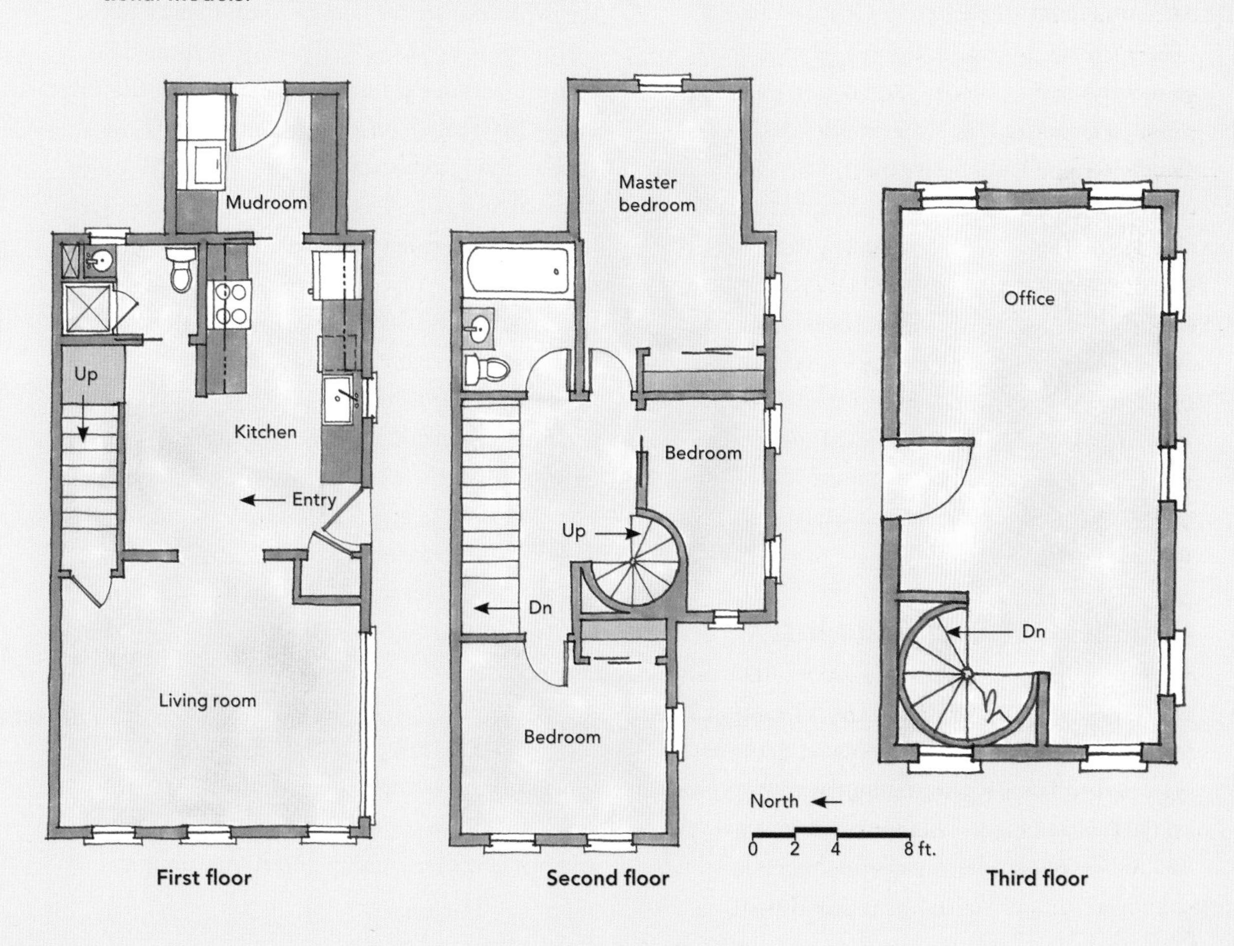

The Ever-Evolving House

BY DUNCAN MCPHERSON

There's no question that vacation homes are a luxury. As an architect in Asheville, N.C., I often work on such homes. Our firm believes in building small, sustainable houses, so we strive for sustainability regardless of function. But the clients for this project offered us a refreshing take on the second-home concept. Their dream was to create a central gathering place where both sides of their family would eventually live full-time.

First, the couple wanted a small family retreat that could serve as a vacation rental. Later, they planned to move from California to North Carolina to build their retirement home. The family retreat then would serve as their primary residence during construction of the house. This home will be modest in size, with minimal need for guest rooms, because the retreat will serve as a guest house. The house we designed needed to fulfill all these requirements and to be sustainable.

Carving out a hillside lot

In the initial design stages, we often look to the land and surrounding region to guide us. This was particularly important for this project because the owners wanted their home to have a minimal visual presence on the land and to maintain the environmental values and restrictions of an organic farm that sits nearby.

The highest portion of the 17-acre lot has stunning views overlooking the adjacent South Toe River; however, for the sake of their neighbors in this very tight-knit community, it was critical to the owners that we minimize the house's visual impact on the surrounding hillsides. To this end, we located the house downslope from the ridgeline and at the forest edge. This location offered greater privacy as well as protection from strong northern winds. We also oriented the house to take advantage of winter views along the river valley and to allow for a walkout basement.

Respecting the environmental goals of the organic farm and the neighbors was another driving force in our design process. We needed to minimize the physical impact and instill a sense of respect for the land during construction and after. This required extra attention to soil quality and erosion control as well as the exterior materials and finishes we selected. The builder was diligent in using silt fencing and monitoring auto and foot traffic to minimize erosion.

Fun, income, and the future

Designing for multiple functions in one house is challenging. We started with the home's initial goal and primary use: a family retreat. Accommoda-

A FAMILY RETREAT FOR EVERY STYLE OF LIFE. What began as a family getaway and vacation rental, will later become a temporary retirement home and finally a guest house. Photo taken at A on floor plan.

tions and storage for travel paraphernalia such as suitcases and coolers was important. The hallway to the bedrooms contains the laundry area, the storage cabinets, and a large countertop surface for all the things that often end up on the floor.

Sleeping and living areas needed to be separate for privacy and sound control, so we configured the house with bedrooms at the north end and living spaces at the south. The living spaces, which connect to outdoor spaces, are filled with daylight from windows on three sides and provide a strong visual connection to the outdoors. The home office and entry separate the living and sleeping areas.

Simple features within this framework ensured the house could function well as a vacation rental. We added locking doors to one master-bedroom closet inaccessible to renters. A lockable home office was important for both husband and wife so that they could work from home during extended stays and safely leave their computer equipment in the room while they were away.

The materials and details inside and out needed to be durable. Muddy shoes, towels, bathing suits, fishing poles, and gardening tools are all common castoffs from activities at the house, so designing enough utility space was essential to maintaining the property well and accommodating a family on vacation. Because the owners lived across the country, the house needed to be fairly self-sufficient from a maintenance and utility standpoint, including the landscaping.

To maximize the house's flexibility as it evolved, there needed to be room to expand without the expense of adding on. The house was configured on a slope to allow for a walkout basement that later

(Continued on p. 64)

PRIVACY AND VIEWS, IN AND OUT

The home now serves as a family retreat and vacation rental, but that will change. When the owners retire and relocate, they'll live here as they build their main house on the same site. Ultimately, this home will serve as a guest house. Besides serving these present and future functions, the house needed to embrace the landscape, to provide privacy for those using it, and to minimize its visual impact on nearby homes. After locating the home downhill from the ridge, the architects broke the house into three sections: entry foyer and work area, living area, and sleeping area. Canting the sleeping wing away from the slope embraced the southern exposure and allowed for a walkout basement and a carport/covered patio. An entry foyer provides a visual and sound buffer between the two wings. A screened porch on the southeast end of the house catches gorgeous evening light. Photo taken at B on floor plan.

SPECS

- Bedrooms: 2
- Bathrooms: 3
- Size: 1,538 sq. ft., main level; 450 sq. ft., unfinished walkout basement
- Cost: N/A
- Completed: 2008
- Location: Celo, N.C.
- Architect: Samsel Architects
- Builder: Richard Kennedy, Sunspace Homes

Main level

B

Entry

Laundry area

Master bedroom

Guest bedroom

Office

D

Kitchen

Dining area

C

Living room

Screened porch

A

Lower level

Carport

Future Pilates studio

Mechanicals

North

0 2 4 8 ft.

Photos taken at lettered positions.

LOCALLY GROWN. River rock from the site anchors the woodstove. Locally harvested cypress and maple add warmth. Photo taken at C on floor plan.

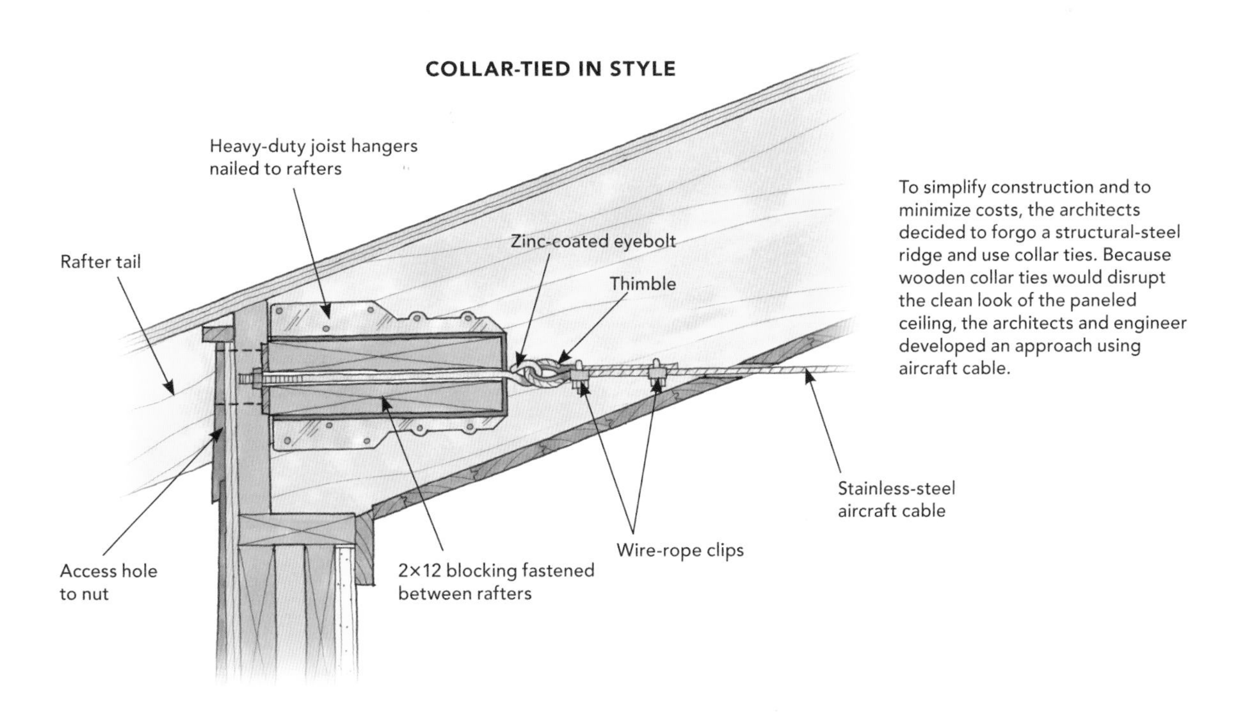

To simplify construction and to minimize costs, the architects decided to forgo a structural-steel ridge and use collar ties. Because wooden collar ties would disrupt the clean look of the paneled ceiling, the architects and engineer developed an approach using aircraft cable.

AN ENTRY AND A BUFFER. The entry foyer provides ample room for removing shoes, coats, and gear when coming in from outdoor activities. It also keeps the living and sleeping areas visually and aurally separate. A home office tucks away behind sliding doors. Photo taken at D on floor plan.

could serve as a utility storage area or a future Pilates studio as well as additional living and sleeping space.

Smarter often means smaller

The homeowners were savvy to the economic and environmental benefits of energy efficiency and, being from California, were also highly sensitive to water conservation. We based many of our design and budget decisions on those two factors.

The first step was to optimize the efficiency of space. The open living area and double-duty hallway in the sleeping wing made possible a smaller, more energy-efficient building. Having the interior connect directly to two outdoor living spaces expands the usable area most of the year.

Creating an airtight building envelope was our next priority. We achieved this primarily by using spray-foam insulation throughout the house. Built to perform 25% better than code minimums, the building envelope minimizes demands on the heating and cooling equipment. We included a controlled fresh-air intake to the return duct of the air handler that runs on a simple timer and a motorized damper to ensure good air quality.

Rainwater from the roof is captured in three underground cisterns (totaling 3,750 gal.) that provide irrigation for the landscaping and garden. These cisterns, along with a pervious driveway, patio, and walkways, minimize any storm-water runoff from the home as well. High-efficiency faucets and showerheads as well as dual-flush toilets minimize water use; the piping is set up to accommodate a future gray-water system.

A year after the house's completion, its multiple functions have performed well for the homeowners. They have been using the house so often that there is rarely time to rent it out, and the family's recent addition of a grandson has rendered the lower level a good decision.

Downsizing for Comfort

BY CHRISTOPHER STAFFORD

I've always been interested in promoting low-impact, environmentally conscious building in the United States, but my work as a building consultant overseas wasn't helping to change the situation at home. I wanted to demonstrate that you don't have to make serious changes to your lifestyle to be a responsible citizen.

At about the same time, my wife, Sakura, and I began assessing our own housing needs. We lived in a large house (about 3,400 sq. ft.) outside Port Townsend, Wash.; between the two of us, we often made three trips daily back and forth to town, which took its toll in time and fuel. Also, we are getting older, and we wanted to be closer to activities and services. We saw the potential of an in-town lot that had been on the market for a while and snapped it up.

Downsizing can be an economical path to fewer headaches

Murphy must have a law that says if you build the space, you will buy more stuff to fill it up. Of course, talk is cheap, and it's easy to tell people to consume less. Actually doing so isn't that easy. We had to think of downsizing this way: What's the smallest space we could live in and still be comfortable? After all, couples sail the world in boats with interior spaces that could fit inside many suburban kitchens.

SMALL, ENERGY EFFICIENT, AND ENERGY PRODUCTIVE. Combining responsible building and comfortable design, the house features photovoltaics and rain-collecting cisterns. Photo taken at A on floor plan.

LIVING ALFRESCO. A deck outside the kitchen expands the interior on sunny days and connects house and studio. A bench and trellis at the perimeter further define and personalize the space. Photo taken at B on floor plan.

SEVERAL PATHS TO DAYLIGHT. The upstairs-bathroom lighting scheme is augmented by one window in the shower area and a reflective skylight tube in the ceiling. A glass-block shower wall lends a little privacy without sacrificing any natural light. Photo taken at C on floor plan.

And Manhattan apartment dwellers live comfortably in small efficiencies that have the same square footage as some suburban living rooms.

We whittled the new plan down to 1,550 sq. ft. and imagined what it would be like to live in a house of that size. Would it be large enough for our needs? With a master suite and a guest bedroom upstairs, as well as a kitchen and a living/dining area down, we finally decided that 1,550 sq. ft. would be plenty.

After living here for the past two years, we've discovered that our home's smaller size fosters more intimacy and accessibility. We don't miss a thing, not even the extra space that we don't have to clean. Storage is not an issue, either, because we jettisoned most things we weren't using. The one-car basement garage holds the remnants resulting from our indecision.

An adjacent 700-sq.-ft. building houses studio-office space, which helps accommodate the occasional party or visiting family. It has a three-quarter bath and easily can become an accessory dwelling unit or an in-law apartment if needed. Oriented strand-board (OSB) floors, simple details, and a heating/plumbing system shared with the main house kept down the cost.

The house and the studio are connected by a deck, which also makes our home seem larger. Surrounded by benches, planters, and a trellis, the south-facing deck has the spatial qualities of a room that's moved outdoors—and it's a great spot for Sunday breakfast.

Materials should have a low environmental impact

When I started to think about the details of the house, certain materials such as the new, safer alkaline copper quaternary (ACQ) pressure-treated lumber and decking certified by the Forest Stewardship

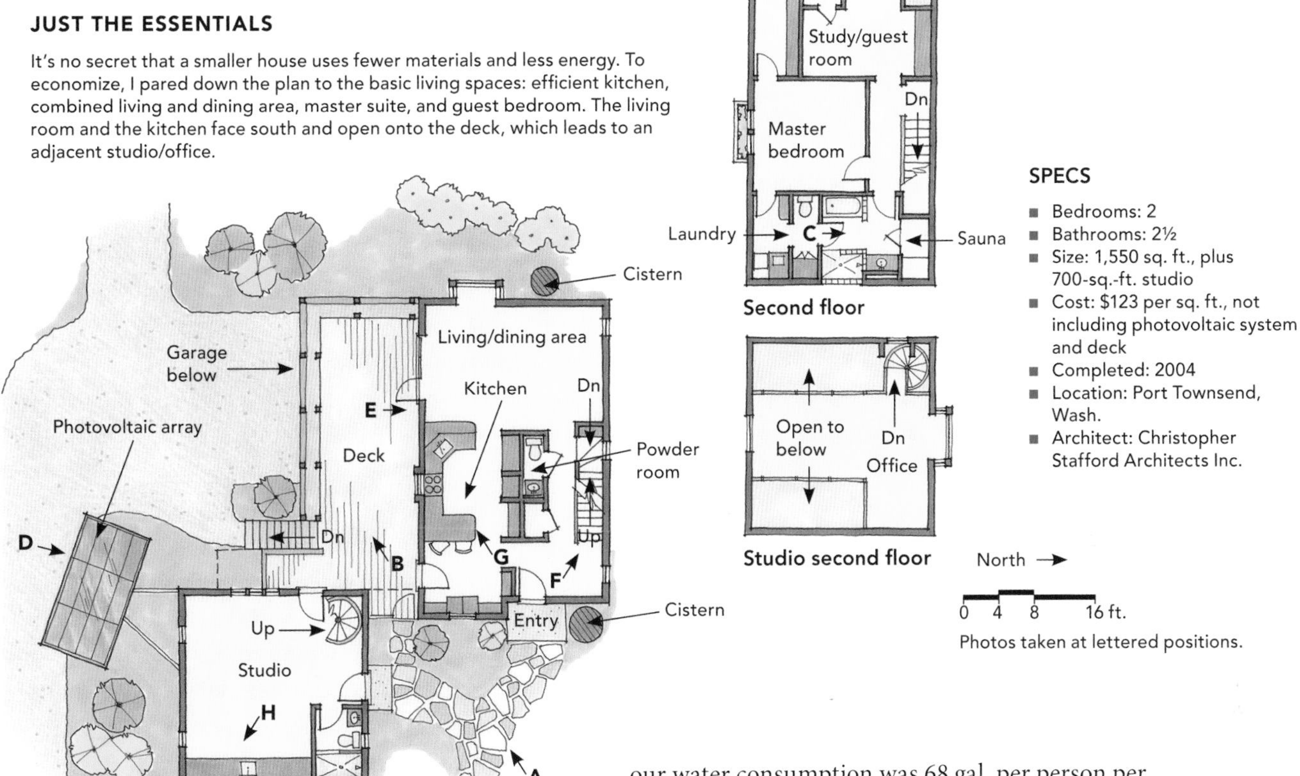

JUST THE ESSENTIALS

It's no secret that a smaller house uses fewer materials and less energy. To economize, I pared down the plan to the basic living spaces: efficient kitchen, combined living and dining area, master suite, and guest bedroom. The living room and the kitchen face south and open onto the deck, which leads to an adjacent studio/office.

Photos taken at lettered positions.

SPECS

- Bedrooms: 2
- Bathrooms: 2½
- Size: 1,550 sq. ft., plus 700-sq.-ft. studio
- Cost: $123 per sq. ft., not including photovoltaic system and deck
- Completed: 2004
- Location: Port Townsend, Wash.
- Architect: Christopher Stafford Architects Inc.

Council® (FSC) were a given. I also chose reclaimed lumber for the hardwood floors on the first level, fiber-cement siding because of its long life span, and a metal roof made of 26% recycled material that is itself recyclable. To reduce the potential for products that off-gas, I used natural-wool carpets (instead of synthetics) upstairs and low-VOC paint throughout the interior. The kitchen cabinets (www.ikea.com) also are made of nontoxic materials.

A less-obvious material choice was fly ash, a waste product of coal-fired generators, which we used as a replacement for half of the cement in all the concrete footings and foundations. Often touted as a green material, regular cement actually creates its own weight in CO_2 during the quarrying and manufacturing process. By using fly ash to replace 50% of the cement in the foundation's concrete, the embodied CO_2 released to the atmosphere is reduced by half.

We've also been able to cut our water usage with low-flow fixtures and efficient appliances. In 2006, our water consumption was 68 gal. per person per day (pppd), a rate that's 32% below the national average and local water-department goals of 100 gal. pppd, according to the American Water Works Association. A large factor in reducing our water consumption is two cisterns made from galvanized drainage culverts (one holds 1,000 gal.; the other, 800 gal.). Both collect rainwater from the house's roof for landscaping needs.

Photovoltaic array minimizes electricity bills

Acting as our own general contractor, we built the house and studio for $123 per sq. ft. The money we saved by building smaller was invested in renewable-energy systems. Purchased from Power Trip Energy Corp., a local solar supplier/installer, a grid-tied Sharp® 175-watt, single-crystal, photovoltaic 12-module tracking array is mounted on an 8-in.-dia. by 12-ft.-tall steel pole with a Xantrex™ inverter (www.xantrex.com). The tracking array generates approximately 28% more energy than if the same array were stationary—energy that's gained predominantly during long summer days.

ABOVE: GREEN CAN BE STYLISH. A corrugated polycarbonate panel over an aluminum railing gives the entry hall a modest, modern look. Ceiling fixtures use dimmable halogen lamps. Photo taken at F on floor plan.

ABOVE RIGHT: SAVE MONEY WHERE YOU MAKE MONEY. The two-story studio/office was kept to its barest essentials to economize. The flooring is plain OSB, the floor joists are exposed, and the trim is minimal. Photo taken at H on floor plan.

RIGHT: BRIGHT AND FRUGAL. Big enough to handle a large dinner party, the kitchen gets lots of daylight from neighboring spaces. Compact-fluorescent fixtures contribute to the home's low energy usage. Photo taken at G on floor plan.

The combination of a small house, compact-fluorescent bulbs, energy-efficient appliances, polyicynene insulation, and a heat-recovery system reduces overall energy consumption by 23%, compared with similar houses in our neighborhood (according to my research). When purchasing our appliances, we looked only at Energy Star–rated models and balanced their initial cost, durability, noise level, and performance to make our decisions. For instance, our Kenmore® front-loading washing machine uses 77% less energy and 67% less water than top-loading washers, based on manufacturer data. Its only downside is that the washing cycle takes a little longer.

Solar hot-water system heats the air and the bathwater

Our solar hot-water system consists of three 20-tube collectors from Thermomax Industries (www.solarthermal.com) and is designed to provide all the hot water for household use and for seven kick-space heaters (five in the house and two in the studio). The Toester™ (www.turbonicsinc.com) heaters are somewhat noisy and have a slow recovery time. When hot water from the solar collectors in the 120-gal. storage tank hasn't reached 120°F, a downstream on-demand propane boiler (Takagi Mobius T-M1; www.takagi.com) makes up the difference.

PAYBACK IS AS MUCH ALTRUISTIC AS FINANCIAL

Generating your own energy is a highly attractive idea these days. At first glance, it's a win-win situation for both the environment and your wallet—or it will be someday.

Our photovoltaic system cost $14,300 in 2003 (prices have risen since then). Seeing a financial return on our investment will take a long time, partially because of our location. Our electricity costs are a rather low 9¢ per kilowatt-hour. Also, the Pacific Northwest climate doesn't lend itself to bright, sunny days all year long. If your electricity costs are higher, your payback time will be shorter; annual solar gain and local rebates can add to your return.

Nevertheless, over the past 12 months, our grid-tied photovoltaic system generated 2,700 kwh, equal to 35% of the electricity that our house and studio/office used. If today's electricity rates are used to calculate a payback time, then factoring in utility and state incentives, we will recoup our investment in 25 years. The equipment has only a 20-year rated life expectancy. However, a safe assumption is that energy costs will increase in the near future, so we still expect to see a return on our investment.

The solar hot-water system's payback is similar. It cost $10,900, and the manufacturer, Thermomax Industries, rates the Solamax® collectors with a 10-year life expectancy. Although our estimated payback is 15 years, steadily rising fuel prices will shorten our payback time.

No, we're not going to get rich by generating energy, but we are making a difference, however incremental, and that's what counts. As more people embrace this technology, the law of supply and demand will cause prices to drop—and the benefits to all will grow.

If you'd like to estimate your potential gains and costs with solar energy, check out these Web sites: PVWATTS (http://nrel.gov/rredc/pvwatts) and Find Solar (www.findsolar.com). The sites feature easy-to-use solar estimators as well as links to solar-energy installers and engineers in your area. Photos taken at D and E on floor plan.

For the solar collectors to work, the house needs to be airtight and well-insulated. Nontoxic polyicynene insulation eliminates voids and encapsulates the house with 5½ in. (R-19) of insulation. The small insulated attic is the return-air plenum for the Venmar HEPA 3000 whole-house ventilation system (www.venmar.ca), whose 55%-efficient heat exchanger warms incoming air. Washington State's energy code requires whole-house ventilation systems; our upgraded version adds the heat exchanger and the HEPA filter for heat recovery and improved air quality.

Building Better Affordable Homes

BY KEYAN MIZANI

Portland, Ore., is known for dense, vibrant neighborhoods. A key component of the vitality of our community is the preservation and development of affordable housing. Affordable homes give people with lower incomes the opportunity to live in a community with rising property values. Despite having to work with a limited budget, I believe affordable housing must be well designed and well built; it must look good and be built to last. Being cost conscious is essential. However, that should not mean cutting corners, because short-term savings and gains often can result in greater long-term costs. This holds true whether designing multifamily or single-family homes.

This multifamily row-house project is for first-time homebuyers earning 80% or less of area median income, so it was important to avoid passing on higher future operating and maintenance costs. The nonprofit developer, Portland Community Reinvestment Initiatives, was committed to creating attractive, high-quality, efficient, durable homes, and it invested time and money on design and planning to do it well. Working as a team, the developer, our firm, an interior designer, and a general contractor collaborated to select lasting design, materials, and building systems that met a modest budget.

Crack apart the row house

Typically long and skinny, traditional row houses are built side by side, which can result in some undesirable conditions, such as dark interiors, long shotgun-style floor plans, small yards accessed only from the rear, and less overall privacy. We decided to make the most of the project's corner site by turning one unit 90° to the other so that each home would face a different street.

With this diminished connection, the homes have a greater sense of individuality, and they blend more seamlessly with the adjacent single-family homes. A sticking point for buyers of multifamily homes can be the common wall. People worry about a lack of sound separation. Turning the units perpendicular to each other minimized their attachment, and we increased privacy further by placing only utility and service elements on the shared double wall.

Each home has a surprisingly spacious yard. Parallel to the long axis of each house, the yards are easily accessed and can be viewed from multiple rooms. The building shape also results in greater access to daylight, which we took advantage of by including generous windows for bright, well-ventilated interiors.

A ROW HOUSE REDEFINED

TRADITIONAL ROW HOUSES typically have a production look and are devoid of details that give them the custom feel of single-family homes. These row houses are different. The extended rooflines were intended to help relate the structure to the older, adjacent 1½-story homes in the neighborhood. At roughly 1,600 sq. ft., each unit is not larger than the surrounding houses, but the height and area of the whole building exceeds that of its neighbors. The lowered rooflines and exterior variation, as well as the L-shaped overall plan, soften the building's appearance. The facade proves that the smart design and rich details that add visual appeal and protection are not reserved for big-budget buildings.

1 **THE ROOF PLANE** is extended below the truss line to break up the monotony of rectangular buildings with otherwise simple roof shapes. Lowering the height of the eaves also decreases the perceived size of the houses.

2 **FIBER-CEMENT SIDING** over a vented rain screen ensures maximum durability, little maintenance, and greater appeal than vinyl, with minimal cost difference.

3 **RAIN CHAINS, INTRICATE PORCH RAILINGS, AND TRIM DETAILS** suggest an enhanced level of design and custom building.

4 **RECESSED PORCHES**, complemented with strategically placed bump-outs, create welcoming entryways.

5 **DEEP OVERHANGS AND WIDE RAKE BOARDS** protect the facade, create contrasting shadowlines, and add visual interest to simplified building shapes.

OPEN FLOOR PLANS INCREASE THE IMPACT OF A FEW FINE DETAILS

ALTHOUGH THE ROOM SIZES ARE MODEST, the open plans create a sense of spaciousness and allow for overflow of rooms when needed. Generous windows open the interiors to views and daylight. The homeowners enjoy quality fixtures, materials, and finishes throughout the entire first floor.

[1] **CORK PLANK FLOORING** is a renewable resource that is easy to maintain, helps ensure good indoor-air quality, and has an attractive appearance.
Source: Wicanders® (www.wicanders.com)

[2] **NATURAL LINOLEUM** is used in bathrooms and the laundry room for its resilience in wet areas. Colorful, playful patterns make the most of the material.
Source: Marmoleum® by Forbo (www.forbo.com)

[3] **GLASS- AND CERAMIC-TILE BACKSPLASHES** add a punch of color in kitchens and bathrooms, with minimal cost impact. These materials provide a layer of detail often missing from affordable homes.
Sources: United Tile® (www.unitedtile.com), Daltile (www.daltile.com)

[4] **PLYWOOD CABINETS** have bamboo facing that will outlast cheaper options and add a rich appearance to the simple cabinetry.
Source: Cutting Edge Custom Cabinets; www.cuttingedgecc.com

SPECS

- Bedrooms: 3 per unit
- Bathrooms: 2 per unit
- Size: Unit 1: 1,620 sq. ft.; Unit 2: 1,555 sq. ft.
- Cost: $120 per sq. ft.
- Completed: 2010
- Developer: Portland Community Reinvestment Initiatives (PCRI)
- Architect: eM/Zed design architecture + planning
- General contractor: Terrafirma Building & Development
- Interior designer: Kismet Design

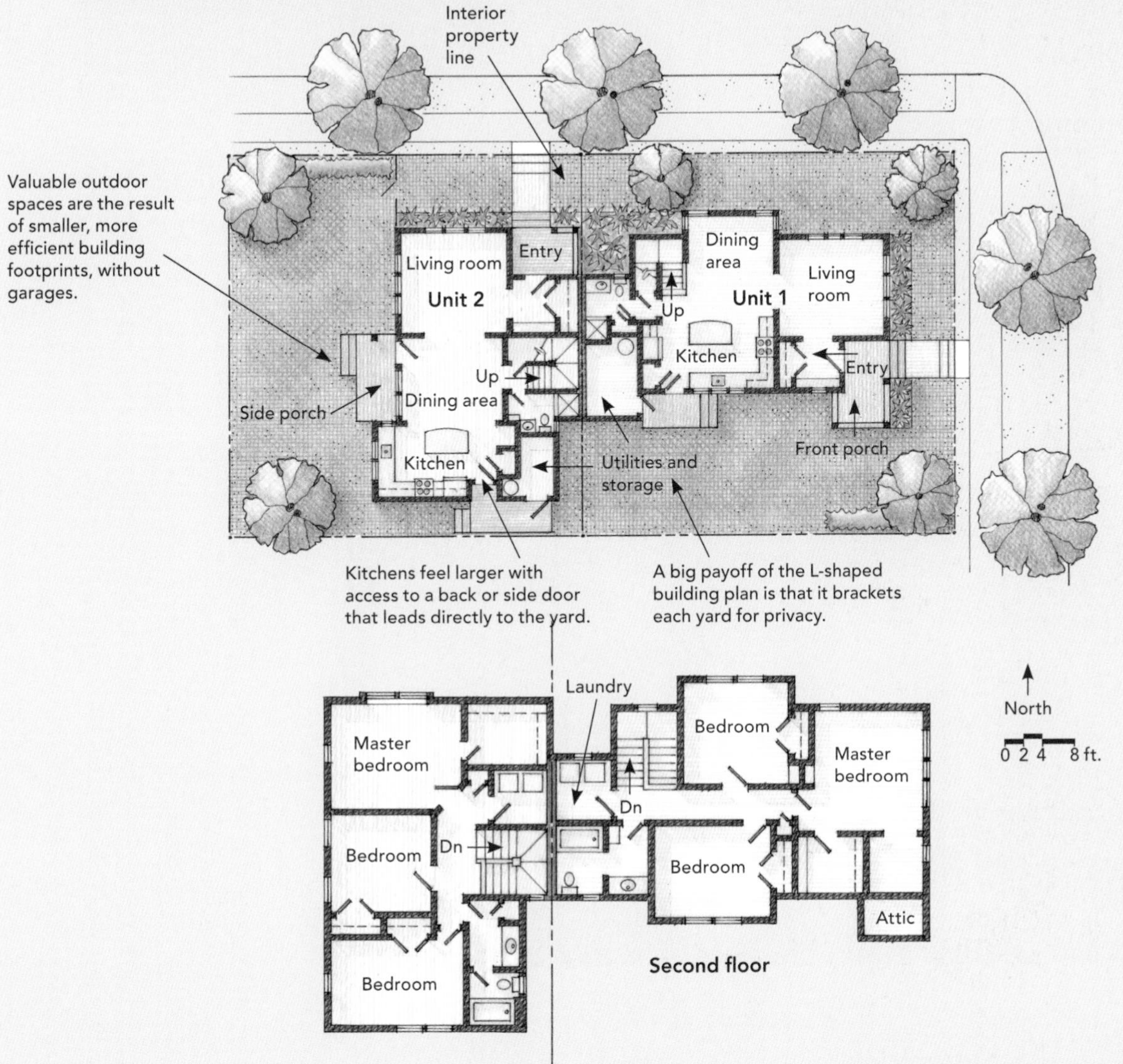
Interior property line
Valuable outdoor spaces are the result of smaller, more efficient building footprints, without garages.
Living room
Entry
Unit 2
Up
Dining area
Side porch
Kitchen
Dining area
Living room
Unit 1
Up
Kitchen
Entry
Front porch
Utilities and storage
Kitchens feel larger with access to a back or side door that leads directly to the yard.
A big payoff of the L-shaped building plan is that it brackets each yard for privacy.
Laundry
Master bedroom
Bedroom
Dn
Bedroom
Dn
Bedroom
Master bedroom
Bedroom
Attic
Second floor
North
0 2 4 8 ft.

TIME AGAIN TO CUT COSTS

THE ECONOMIC DOWNTURN and the availability of a surprising number of discounted, foreclosed homes in the Portland area have provided more affordable options for first-time homebuyers. Even with the requirement that buyers for our project not earn more than 80% of median family income, the pool of potential buyers has shrunk significantly. To sell more easily, the homes need to cost even less than we thought when we started. The question is how to do this without compromising quality of design and long-term durability and energy efficiency.

The most likely answer is reducing square footage. Space savings could be gained by tightening the floor plan and combining the laundry and second-floor bathroom, and/or by substituting a half-bath for the full downstairs bath. The exterior storage rooms could be eliminated, too.

Although the bump-outs were needed to relieve a tight footprint, there could be fewer of them. Each jog adds complexity and cost to a number of building components: foundation, framing, roofing, siding, and drywall.

Make it look good

Each unit has an efficient, rectangular footprint, capped by roof trusses. However, several strategies were used to avoid the boxy, unvaried appearance of a basic two-story rectangle with a trussed top. Carefully placed bump-outs allow the narrow plans to expand where necessary and to create visual interest outside; recessed porches create welcoming facades. Side porches and stoops offer connections to the yards. All these elements work together to disguise and embellish the homes' basic rectangular building blocks.

We kept exterior materials simple for cost and durability; they include fiber-cement lap siding and factory-primed flat trim. When a restrained palette is used, enrichment relies on careful building proportions, well-placed windows, and special details such as custom porch railings.

Design for efficiency

Our team selected the most affordable and effective energy-saving strategies early in the design process so that they could be woven into the core of the design rather than needing to be added later, which is always more expensive.

We specified 12-in. raised-heel trusses, which have a greater depth at the edge, to allow full perimeter roof insulation. These trusses have only a relatively small cost impact. The roofs were insulated to R-49. The R-26 walls were insulated with 1 in. of closed-cell spray foam, bulk-filled with blown-in fiberglass, and finished with airtight drywall.

A high-efficiency air-source heat pump by Carrier provides heating and cooling and was a logical choice for our climate, where this technology works effectively. Locating all of the ductwork inside conditioned spaces significantly reduced heat loss and enhanced the efficiency of the heat pump. A Marathon electric water heater has an energy factor of 0.94 and is warranted not to leak for as long as the buyer owns the home.

Most light fixtures are fluorescent, but few need to be on during the day thanks to our daylighting strategy. Window head heights are 7 ft. to allow light farther inside. As a result, high windows in areas requiring privacy and/or furnishable wall space still admit plenty of light.

Year-Round Cottage in the Woods

BY DAVID BAIRD

A good part of my childhood was spent wandering these Vermont woods and fields. The property, which my parents bought in 1955, is crisscrossed with stone walls, and at one time my brother and I built forts out of them. Years later, when it came time to build my own home on this land, I knew I would use many of the same stones.

Once I'd finally settled on a building site—a knoll tucked into the woods facing a field frequented by deer and fox—I spent weeks imagining the house from every direction. I didn't want to disturb the hilltop or the surrounding foliage. I wanted the house to match the site, not to dominate it. And it had to look like it has always been there.

Eventually, I had a form. There would be a stone cylinder supporting an elevated terrace and three stone columns to carry the roof on the south side of the house. Like northern Europe's stone-and-thatch country homes, which I've always admired, the house would have a steep, protective roof with low, deep eaves overhanging stone terraces. The eaves, sometimes only 4 ft. from the ground, would have arched openings carved back into the rooflines, creating deep-set windows, doors and dormers.

Rustic materials gathered from our own backyard

My brother and I cut "roads" into the woods and began scavenging rocks from some unsound stone walls. After spending two summers amassing a mountainous pile of stone, I began building the cylinder, which came to be known as the "round thing." My wife, Linda, had categorized the stone according to shape and size, and more often than not, she knew which stone I needed before I did. I was able to raise the round thing's walls only 12 in. to 18 in. a weekend, backfilling and tamping, and starting all over the following weekend. Eventually, it grew to 16 ft. in dia., rising to 18 ft. at the tallest point .

After four years, with one summer taken off to finish the design, we were ready to hand off our project. Garth Quillia of Kline Construction in Bethel, Vt., evaluated the plans, the site, and our approach to building and convincingly said, "No problem." One October morning, he showed up with a bulldozer and began to cut and pull huge white-pine trees from the surrounding woods, piling them in a field to be milled later for the interior beams. We were off.

UNDER THE BIG TOP. The steeply pitched roof extends over the native-stone terraces like an open umbrella, giving this 1,600-sq. ft. cottage a massive first impression while protecting it from Vermont's fierce winters. Photos taken at A, B, and C on floor plan (p. 82).

WELL-EXECUTED PLAN. The kitchen/dining area and living room (above) were designed to accommodate a group. The upstairs studio (left) was once a bedroom but has been transformed into a light, airy space. White-pine floors throughout most of the house are friendly and warm, evoking the sense of an elegant camp. Photos taken at G and H on floor plan.

A simple footprint with a twist

As we began excavating for the foundation, we soon realized that we were sitting on a bluestone ledge, and unless we blasted, a basement was out of the question. Instead, we would place our footings directly atop the ledge, pouring frost walls from 52 in. to only 6 in. in some places to accommodate the ledge. This same ledge wasn't so cooperative later. It shifted in direction and rose up, forcing us to create three levels on the first floor, and eventually to change the direction of the roofline.

To keep the roof over solid ground, I decided to bend it a bit, creating a shallow hip, then straighten it again after finding the wandering ledge (see the drawing on p. 81). Although complicated to frame, it is reminiscent of a 17th-century thatch roof.

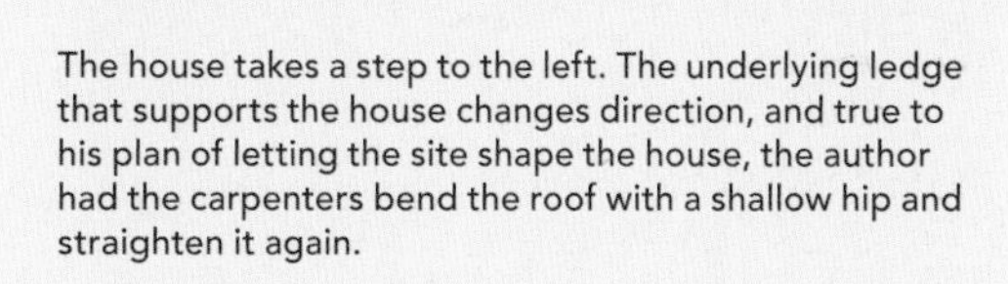

The house takes a step to the left. The underlying ledge that supports the house changes direction, and true to his plan of letting the site shape the house, the author had the carpenters bend the roof with a shallow hip and straighten it again.

COMFORTABLE, OPEN SPACES IN 1,600 SQ. FT.

THE EXTENSIVE ROOFLINE PROTECTS THE house and creates a transitional outdoor space off the dining area. The timber framing relieves much of the roof's massive weight from the outside walls, allowing the second floor to be cantilevered over a portion of the terrace and using as much space as the humble footprint permits.

SPECS

- Bedrooms: 2, plus studio
- Bathrooms: 2
- Size: 1,600 sq. ft.
- Cost: N/A
- Completed: 2000
- Location: Berlin, Vt.
- Architect: David Baird
- Builders: Peter Kline, Garth Quillia, principals

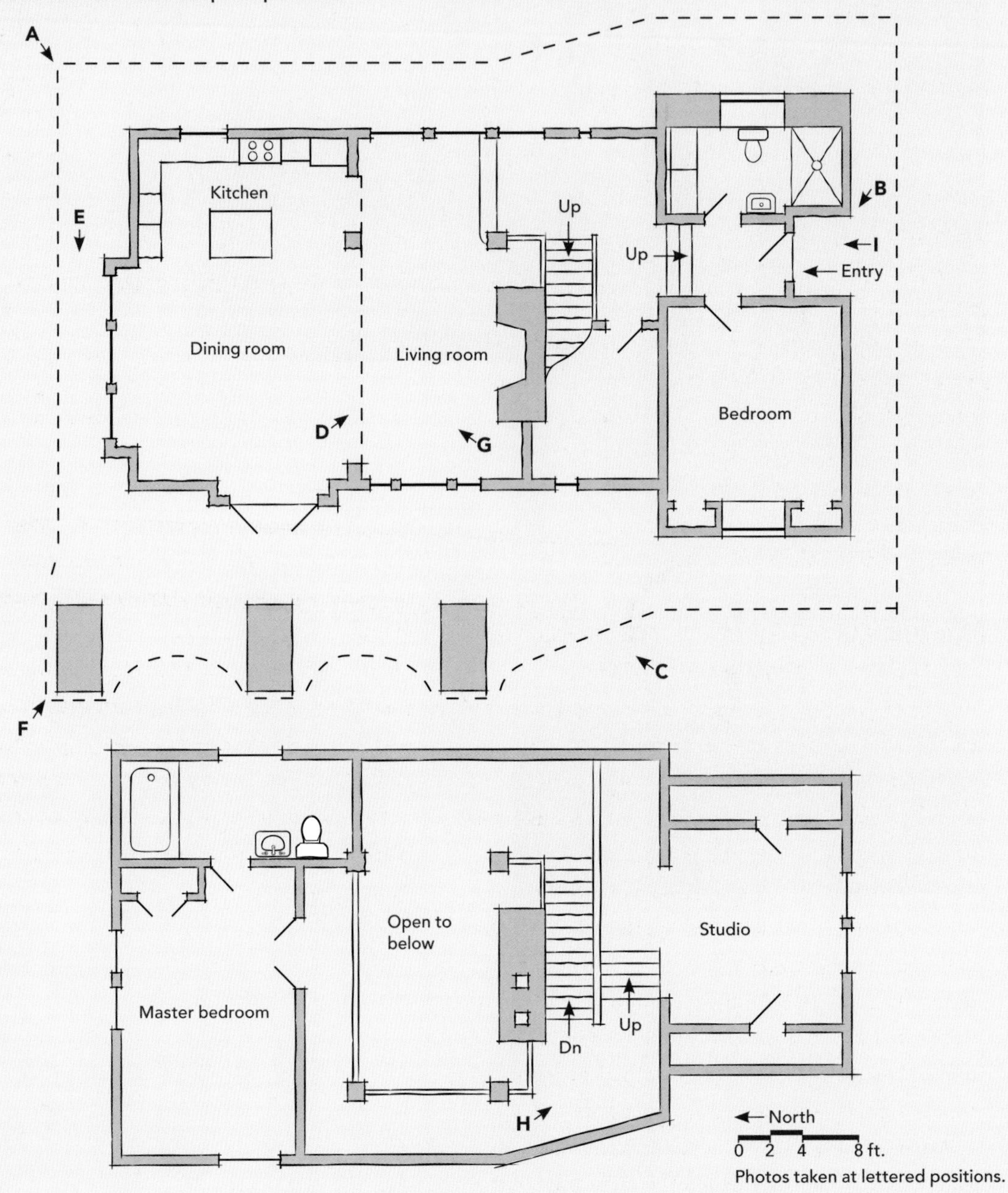

Photos taken at lettered positions.

Versatile space and feathering for an empty nest

The interior space is organized around a large central fireplace, historically the first drawn element in any house and the center of activity (see the photo on p. 79). We wanted it to be our starting place as well. The fireplace has proved to be a wonderful, warm presence that can be seen and enjoyed from almost every vantage point in the house. The chimney rises the full 18 ft. of our "pretty great" room, effectively linking upstairs and down.

The upstairs is organized around the chimney, with open balconies lined with book-cases overlooking the living room. The balusters and railings around the balconies are inspired by a 13th-century Flemish tapestry and animate the space from above and below.

Originally, the upstairs had two bedrooms and a master bath, with a third bedroom and a laundry/bath downstairs. We have two teenage children and designed the house with that fact in mind. Within three years of moving into our new home, both of our children would be moving on to their own lives, so we designed the upstairs bedroom to have a wall that could be removed. We have since converted it into a painting studio (see the left photo on p. 78).

A WELCOME SIGHT ON A STORMY NIGHT. The well-lighted front door is protected from the elements under a dormer carved into the deep eaves. The door's plywood core is sandwiched with 5/4 white pine and varnished to an antique patina, making it both inviting and stable. Photo taken at I on floor plan.

Invoking a sense of the past but mindful of present needs

We chose white-pine floors for most of the house, and tile for the downstairs entry and bath. The pine is friendly and warm, evoking the sense of an elegant camp. We even used it at the entry, where Garth and the crew created a site-built door in keeping with the sturdy nature of this house (see the photo above). We aren't concerned about the marks and scars left in the soft pine because those marks tell a story and add to the charm. We chose radiant heat for the entire downstairs because that kind of heat rises only so far, then dissipates. The high cathedral ceilings couldn't draw all the heat from the floors.

We live simply and weren't building a house for a large family, so we chose to eliminate some of the appliances we didn't need or use, such as a dishwasher, and put more of our budget into a commercial cooking range and refrigerator (see the right photo on p. 78).

Although we had a limited budget, we were lucky enough to find an intelligent, sympathetic builder who believed in what we were trying to do. He guided us, making suggestions and being creative with simple materials. As a result, we have a beautifully crafted home that will stand for a long time to come.

A Low-Budget, High-Impact House

BY CHRIS STEBBINS

A dozen years ago, Bill Brewer and Nancy Mannelli left the hectic city that Seattle had become and started a simpler life in Eugene, Ore. They bought a fixer-upper on a sloping double lot in a neighborhood of smallish old homes and big oak trees on the west side of town.

The extra lot naturally evolved into their garden, but over the years, Bill and Nancy kept eyeing it as a potential site for a new home. By 2003, property values had gone up enough to make the project feasible, if some important conditions could be met: The new house had to be a bit larger than the old one, with more natural light, and it couldn't cost more than their current mortgage.

As Bill and Nancy's designer/builder, I knew we could meet those conditions if we stuck to some ground rules. Their new house had to be simple in shape and had to use standard building materials efficiently; where possible, they had to do double-duty as both the structure of the house and its finished skin. Any splurges on finishes had to be played in conspicuous places. Finally, taking advantage of Bill's experience as a decorative painter, we had to have fun with color.

THE BASIC BOX, PLAYED WELL. A partly sheltered deck makes an outdoor room that can be used in any weather (above). Upstairs, an open, airy den can be converted into a guest room with a sliding door/wall (on the facing page). Photos taken at A and B on floor plan.

Get the homeowners involved in the design

Instead of taking on this project in the traditional role of a designer/builder, I asked Bill and Nancy to have a go at being their own designers, with me as their guide. I wanted them to own the project from conception to completion.

Our design process began with sketches describing spatial relationships and quickly moved into cardboard models that Bill constructed to understand the volumes and shapes of the house.

We also took walks around town to identify desirable features in Eugene's eclectic neighborhoods. Then we talked about which details or strategies would deliver the greatest return on the time and materials that it would take to make them.

We started with something simple; it gradually grew more complex and layered with details and expenses that weren't really necessary. Then we pared things down. "Happiness is a place between too little and too much," according to a Finnish proverb. That drumbeat drove this project: Our goal was to arrive at a design that was just enough and no more.

AN AFFORDABLE HOUSE BEGINS WITH THE FLOOR PLAN

Keeping the shape of the house simple is part of the equation. At 24 ft. by 36 ft., the house takes advantage of materials that come in 4×8 increments. Locating baths along one wall cuts down on plumbing costs, and keeping hallways to a minimum gets the most from the available floor space.

LIGHT AND ROOMY

High ceilings and clerestory windows that run the length of the upstairs give the house a sense of airiness, even in Oregon's sometimes cloudy climate.

SPECS

- Bedrooms: 2, plus 2 offices
- Bathrooms: 2½
- Size: 1,728 sq. ft.
- Cost: $126 per sq. ft.
- Completed: 2005
- Location: Eugene, Ore.
- Designers: Chris Stebbins and Bill Brewer
- Builder: Chris Stebbins

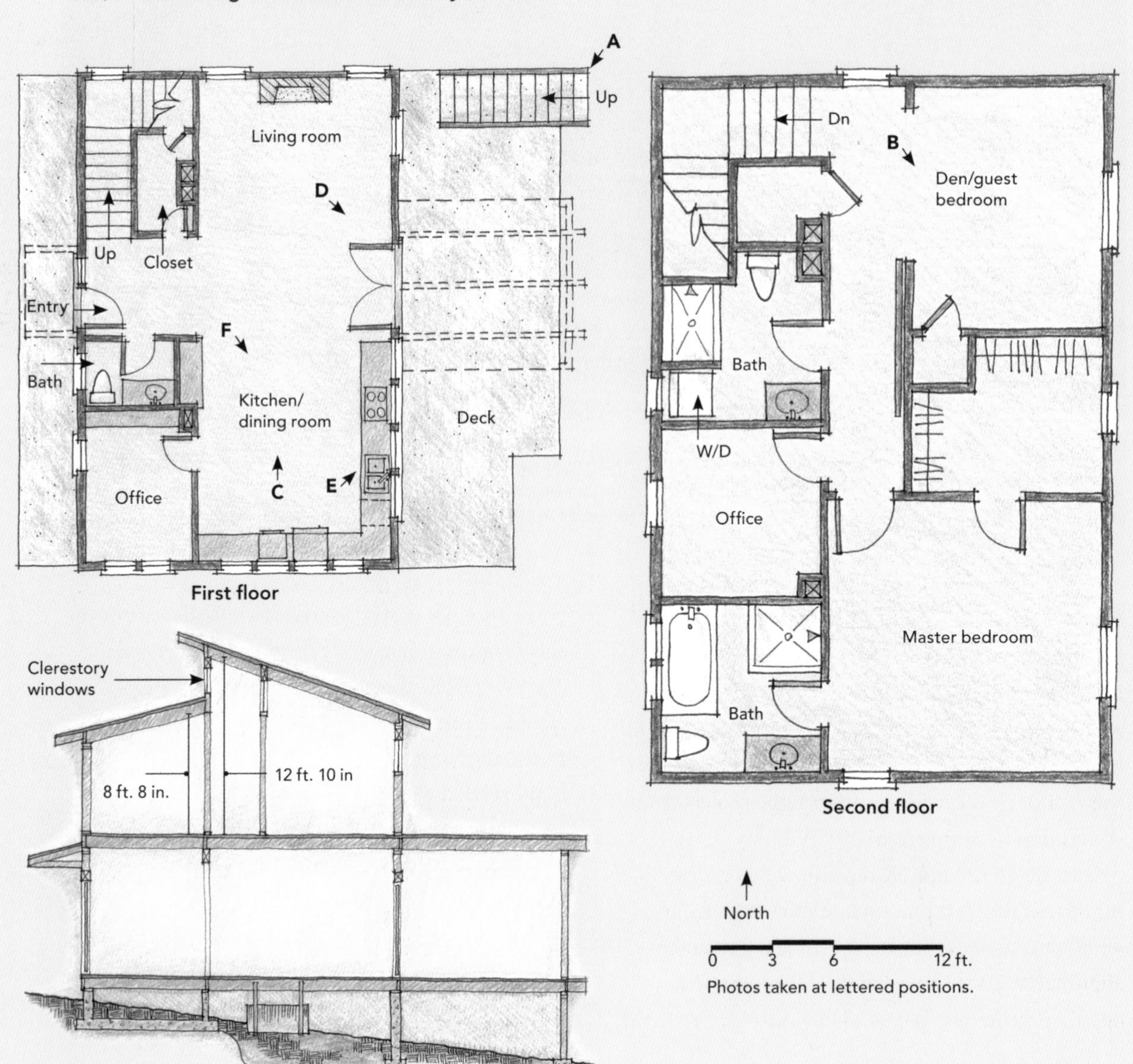

A DOUBLE-DOOR CONNECTION. The eastern half of the downstairs is one big room, with 9-ft.-tall walls and a pair of French doors that open onto the deck so that the two spaces can mingle in nice weather. Photos taken at C and D on floor plan.

Build multipurpose spaces into a simple package

The only hurdle in the design phase was Bill and Nancy's sentimental desire to have a bedroom for their college-age daughter when she comes home to visit. They also wanted a den, but the budget wouldn't allow for both if we tackled the design traditionally.

Instead, we compromised, creating a large, open space at the head of the stairs (see the floor plans on the facing page). It feels and functions like a den until you pull the 8-ft.-tall barn-type sliding door closed, turning the space into a private bedroom. Other dual-purpose spaces include the kitchen, which has a big table and doubles as the dining room, and an upstairs bath, which is also the laundry.

Eventually, the house took shape as a simple two-story 24-ft. by 36-ft. rectangle. It is topped with two shed roofs, allowing a daylight-grabbing clerestory over the upstairs spine of the house. The design minimized waste by sticking to 4-ft. modules, and we eliminated unnecessary framing members by aligning rafters, beams, joists, and studs. Windows and doors were positioned to fit within this efficient frame rather than the other way around, which can waste lumber.

Even though we were on a budget, we weren't willing to sacrifice quality. Every item we used will wear well and will survive design trends. For longevity, we treated the framing materials with a borate-salt solution to inhibit mold and dry rot.

Double-duty materials and some surprisingly affordable upgrades

The downstairs ceilings are 9 ft. to the bottom of the exposed 4×10 beams. This extra height added little to the cost of materials but went a long way

"The 9-ft.-high ceilings go a long way toward creating a sense of spaciousness."

IS IT A WINDOW OR A PASS-THROUGH? It's both, of course. Big windows overlooking the deck make it easy to hand platters back and forth (below). At the south end of the kitchen, a row of windows above the refrigerator/oven cabinets equalizes the light (left). Photos taken at E and F on floor plan.

toward creating a sense of spaciousness. We used wire brushes mounted on grinding wheels to remove grade stamps and mill marks from the beams and to give them a pleasingly rough texture. The 2×6 decking serves as both ceiling and upstairs floor.

We also saved money by using Breckenridge plywood siding (www.roseburg.com). It comes in 10-ft. lengths and has patch-free veneer faces that take paint well. Breckenridge costs more than other exterior-grade plywood, but because it serves as both sheathing and siding, it's worth the price in the long run.

The upper story is clad with Galvalume® (www.aep-span.com) siding. This corrugated metal breaks the house's tall facade into separate horizontal bands. Although Galvalume costs more than Breckenridge siding, it is virtually maintenance free and helps cool the house in the summer by reflecting heat.

Copper counters in the kitchen seem like a luxurious splurge in a budget-minded house, but at about $40 per sq. ft. (for the 16-oz. material used here), they were less expensive than other premium countertop materials.

Another affordable premium material is travertine. Because of the high cost of traditional hardwood stair treads and the labor that it takes to install them, we looked for alternatives. We found travertine tiles for less than $3 per sq. ft. They turned out to be easy to cut and forgiving to install as well as solid to the touch and lovely to look at.

Put a flexible outdoor space within easy reach

At 1,728 sq. ft., Bill and Nancy's house is not large. But because of its tall ceilings and long sightlines, it has a distinctly spacious feel. An important component of that feel is the concrete deck off the first floor. Big windows overlooking the deck make it a real presence inside the house.

The deck is large enough to host a party and small enough to have the intimate feel of a room. Concrete wears well here in the Northwest (often called the "Northwet" by locals) because it doesn't grow the moss that plagues wooden decks. Partly open to the sky and partly under a roof, the deck can be enjoyed in any weather, and the grill doesn't have to wait for a clear evening to be fired up.

MATERIALS MAKE THE DIFFERENCE

SPACE-SAVING SIDEBOARD. Shelves and a cabinet use a bit of the wall space between the powder room and the dining table.

STONE WORK. The travertine tile in the foyer gives way to a playful spread of colorful vinyl tile in the entry closet.

LOCAL COLORS. Olive green plywood siding below and corrugated-metal cladding above reflect the dominant colors of the site.

COPPER COUNTERS: FIELD NOTES

At about $40 per sq. ft., copper countertops are a good midprice alternative to slab stone. They have the benefit of minimal joints because the backsplash and the nosing are integral to the copper's profile.

Any seams would have to be butt joints (two pieces glued edge to edge), so I try to minimize them from the start. I lay out the counter by designing the seams to coincide with natural breaks, such as drop-in cooktops, sinks, or inside corners. I keep counter sections to 8 ft. or less because the material distorts easily at longer lengths.

I've resolved the butt-joint problem by turning the counter edges down ¼ in., as shown in the left drawing below. This design leaves a clean, soft joint that seals easily with clear silicone caulk. I cut a kerf in the ¾-in. plywood substrate at every seam to allow for the turned-down edge.

I glue the copper to the substrate with latex-based floor-tile adhesive spread with a ⅜-in. notched trowel. Once the glue has set up, I make the necessary cutouts for sinks or cooktops with a bimetal blade in a jigsaw. By the way, cutouts for electrical outlets in the backsplash need to be done before countertop installation and reinforced during the cut with a clamped-in-place wooden block to prevent distortion.

If the counter has an exposed end, I instruct the metal shop to fold down the edge to match the nosing profile. The shop solders the corner and smooths it out to eliminate sharp edges.

A light application of olive oil every now and then keeps copper counters relatively stain free. However, nothing can prevent acids from etching and discoloring copper. That is part of its great charm.

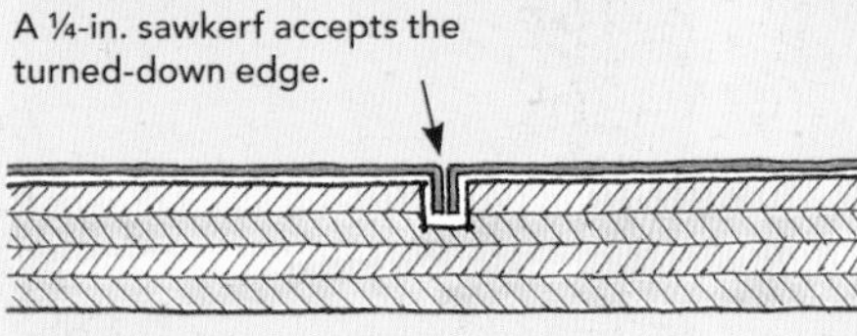

Strategic seams

To minimize seams, sections of countertop are arranged to meet in the center of drop-ins like stoves and sinks.

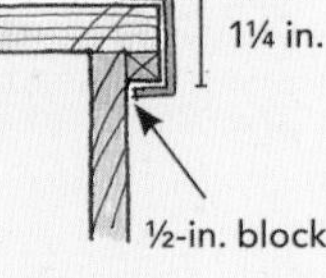

Plywood support

Beneath the copper skin, a plywood substrate provides the strength necessary for the countertop to span the cabinets.

From Luxury to LEED

BY JIM AND MARK PICTON

Like other building contractors, we have enjoyed the challenge of building big, fancy houses, and we are honored by the confidence and trust their owners have placed in us. In the best of those projects, the details were exquisite and demanding. Besides providing a good living, however, the single-minded, spare-no-effort pursuit of quality in big projects should leave us spiritually nourished and enriched.

In recent years, though, we began to feel a numbness as over and over, we saw materials thrown in Dumpsters because of design changes and skilled workers lose their edge as they tore out their own good work to accommodate the whims of busy globe-trotting clients. There also was something troubling when International Energy Conservation Code (IECC) minimum standards were dealt with as stumbling blocks to get around or over rather than as a starting point to improve energy efficiency. There's something unwholesome, too, about building heating and cooling systems sized to meet the demands of an inefficient envelope, then seeing a fuel truck routinely replenish a 1,000-gal. tank and being assured that for this client, fuel costs are "not an issue." Were all costs being considered? And to whom, besides the clients, might those costs matter? Might they include us? Might they include you?

LESSONS LEARNED: TECHNOLOGY IMPROVES EFFICIENCY

ALTHOUGH WE CREATED AN AIRTIGHT, superinsulated home that has an R-23 basement, R-40 walls, and an R-60 roof, this is by no means a passive house. We implemented technology to increase the home's comfort and energy efficiency while still taking advantage of as many of the site's natural offerings as we could. The house was sited and designed in regard to the lot's southern exposure. The home uses low-e, argon-filled windows (SHGC: 0.31; U-factor: 0.33) for energy efficiency. There is more window area on the south wall for solar tempering. In the lowest level of the south facade, the low-e coating was eliminated to increase heat gain in the insulated concrete slab. The entire home is insulated with 4 in. of rigid foil-faced foamboard outside the frame, and with cellulose blown in between the studs and the rafters.

- The 2-kilowatt, 10-panel Sanyo (http://panasonic.net/sanyo) photovoltaic system on the roof generates net metered electricity and is expandable to 3 kilowatts. The panels are mounted to the standing seams of the metal roof. They look good, but next time, we'll consider collectors designed for new-building integration for a more architectural look.
- A balanced whole-house ventilation system uses a heat-recovery ventilator to provide fresh air. This system should solve the indoor-moisture problem during the heating season in a superinsulated house and help conserve energy.
- The solar hot-water system is composed of two Schüco (www.schueco.com) flat-panel collectors that measure roughly 4 ft. by 8 ft. There is also an 80-gal. solar storage tank in the basement that feeds into the indirect-fired water heater supplied by the propane boiler. We have high hopes of using mostly solar-heated water in three seasons. In the future, we'll investigate the use of evacuated-tube collectors mounted on a wall for easier installation and maintenance.
- The 80,000-Btu gas-fired boiler heats the air in a high-velocity forced-air heating system. Next time, we'll downsize the equipment for the minimal heating demands of the home.
- An efficient wood-burning stove by Vermont Castings (www.vermontcastings.com) with a low emissions rating makes use of the site's abundant trees, a renewable fuel supply.

A new project, a new way

In response to these questions, we set out to build a house that made sense in terms of both the natural and built environment.

Fortunately, the U.S. Green Building Council (USGBC) was then field-testing its LEED for Homes program, which defines sensible building. We chose to enroll in the LEED program because it not only codifies, informs, and guides the green-building process but also provides tangible recognition for achievements in sustainable building. We thought that by becoming LEED certified, the home would help distinguish our achievements from those of builders who do not participate in such rigorous third-party vetting.

Plan early, and focus on efficiency

We would have liked to build a one-room bungalow with a ladder to a loft, but the smallest ground-floor footprint allowed under our town's zoning regulations is 900 sq. ft., or an 840-sq.-ft. main-floor living space. So we chose to build a simple Cape on a 28-ft. by 32-ft. footprint. The opportunity to place the highest values on simplicity, compactness, and practicality over all else was restorative. But the process of building this house didn't always offer such clarity.

We attempted to rely mostly on our own extensive knowledge as builders and realized quickly that going it alone wasn't the wisest decision. Visualizing the finished home, then working back from that vision through all the elaborate assembly details was difficult. We had to think through the details of the construction daily and make critical decisions hours or sometimes minutes before the crew needed direction, and that cost us time and efficiency.

What we should have done was to assemble a team of designers, consultants, managers, employees, suppliers, and subcontractors before the start of the project to solidify the plan, to refine the integration of technology, and to smooth the construction phase.

For example, we designed and ordered our high-velocity forced-air HVAC system before fully comprehending the thermal performance of the super insulated shell. We were committed to the only local contractor we thought could install such a system and ended up with the smallest conventional high-efficiency modulating boiler available, which still had twice the heating capacity our small house needs. It's not a disaster because a modulating boiler fires at different levels according to demand, and there is excess capacity for a future addition.

Keep your standards high

We weren't sure if we could count on using our usual subcontractors and suppliers to carry out the construction. However, we brought them into the green-building process wherever we could, and most responded with proficiency and enthusiasm.

It was still a job site, though, and things didn't always work out as we hoped. We had a couple of subs who did it their way regardless of instructions to do it differently or even to do it the way the manufacturer specified. Where it mattered, they had to do it over. Where it didn't matter, we corrected it ourselves and moved them down the list of preferred subs.

Hesitation or reluctance to embrace this new way of building isn't always a conscious decision. It was remarkable to see the effect routine and habit have on the construction process. Perhaps nowhere was this more obvious than when it came to our waste trail. We limited our entire waste volume to one 15-yd. container, which you can really do only if you have a fully committed crew. We did, and in fact, our crew acted as monitors to keep most of the subs from tossing all manner of recyclable waste into the container. We also spent a few sessions in the container ourselves sorting out items that didn't belong there. It's amazing how much of a difference in volume this kind of diligence can make.

Buy local; build more than a house

We believe that using local materials is one of the most important green principles, and we found it to be more enjoyable, more economical, and more accessible than we thought it would be. By keeping our money within the local community, we're contributing to our own economic environment, and it gives us a special reason to appreciate the materials that grow or are produced where we live.

The ash heartwood floor in this house, for example, came from trees in Vermont and was milled by Cole Brothers in nearby Woodbury, Conn. We have sold timber to Cole Brothers in the past, and buying their lumber seems like completing the circle.

Over the years, we have found that a lot of people aren't always aware of the social and environmental effects of materials sourced from around the world, and we were careful not to fall into the trap of green consumerism. For example, we should ask what cork, bamboo, or other exotic flooring has to do with environmental and economic sustainability in this country. How do we know that the American demand for a sustainably harvested rain-forest product does not ultimately increase the demand for illegally harvested rain-forest products? What about the energy used to transport those goods?

We think it is well to stop—after a search for locally produced 100% recycled-glass tiles has led to a village in Italy—and ask whether beach stones gathered by a grandchild and placed creatively on a bathroom surface might provide the same level of aesthetic joy while using far less jet-A fuel and diesel.

Sourcing materials with such awareness also made us take a closer look at the materials we had at our disposal. For example, we milled cedar decking from 1½-in.-thick siding salvaged from a house we renovated a couple of years ago. The floor tiles for the entry, hearth, and bathrooms came from another renovation, along with the Fireslate counters for the kitchen and the bathrooms. Preparing these materials took time and money, but if life-cycle costs are considered, the effort seems well worthwhile.

Change your perspective

Green building should be thought of as only part of an evolving ethic, not just as a specialty trade.

A LEED PLATINUM HOME BY THE NUMBERS

- Lot size: 13 acres
- Footprint: 896 sq. ft.
- Living space: 1,732 sq. ft.
- Bedrooms: 2
- Baths: 2
- LEED-H score: 89.5
- HERS rating: 30
- Energy Star rating: 5+ stars
- Construction cost: $266 per sq. ft.

Otherwise, as a trade or a simple building method, it might be implemented only during working hours and left on the job site, and that's not enough.

While green building has been criticized for its expense, we came to an important realization. We know the budget went up because of our program, but probably less of the increase was attributable to "green" issues than to the more-or-less expected cost of high-end custom building. If a house is designed properly, following LEED guidelines should not affect construction costs much.

While our praise for LEED runs deep, it does not come without some criticism. LEED has been faulted for not making energy efficiency more of a priority, and this flaw needs to be corrected. It's also worthwhile to reduce the prevalent interest in exotic methods and materials to achieve a LEED rating and to increase the focus on what helps to make a local community sustainable. We have most of the resources to build better homes right where we live. Maybe, in some way, our small home represents that idea.

LESSONS LEARNED: USE LOCAL MATERIALS

Even more important than limiting what left the job site was limiting what we introduced to it. As consumers—which builders are to the highest degree—we could see green building as just a new market that satisfies a new purchasing ideology without getting truly positive results. The conscious builder—and the one whose homes will have the least impact on the land and the biggest impact on society—is the one who invests in the most environmentally responsible materials that are produced locally.

- The exposed second-floor framing is made from locally sawn pine and was milled by Cole Brothers (www.colebroslumber.com).
- The house is outfitted with energy-efficient appliances at close to the highest levels available.
- Fluorescent lighting is used throughout.
- CitiLog™ (www.citilogs.com) sources much of its wood from reclaimed city and campus trees. CitiLog cabinets, which we have in our kitchen and bathroom, are made by Pennsylvania Shaker woodworkers.
- Fireslate countertops were reclaimed from a previous remodel. They serve as work surfaces in the kitchen and bathrooms.
- Very low-flow faucets and showerheads throughout the house reduce water consumption.
- The 1×8 white-pine boards used as wall paneling add a farmhouse feel to the home. These boards, like all the wood in the house, have been finished with products that are Green Seal certified (www.greenseal.org).
- The ceilings are covered with drywall that has recycled paper and gypsum. It was difficult to find such a supply within 500 miles. The drywall had to come from one particular U.S. Gypsum plant, and getting the company to guarantee that its product met our standards was tough. It took roughly 40 hours of research to source the drywall.

At Home on a Hilltop

BY CHARLES MILLER

Here are two ways to decide where to put a house on a piece of country property: One, find the perfect picnic spot and build the house there; or two, find the perfect picnic spot and build the house next to it, where the picnic spot can be appreciated from both inside and out.

Architects call the second approach "site repair." It recognizes the wisdom of preserving the qualities that made the site attractive in the first place rather than burying them under a building. In an unusual twist on the site-repair approach, a retirement home designed by architect Obie Bowman turned a sheared-off hilltop into a garden courtyard bordered by a lap pool (see the photo on the facing page).

House and garage corral the courtyard

Hal and Mary Weber retired from their careers in the airline business and left Atlanta to live in one of their favorite vacation destinations: the wine country of Northern California. The 40-acre parcel of land they acquired is hilly terrain between taller ridges to the east and west.

The developer of the eight lots in the subdivision cut roads along the crests of the hills, then lopped off the hilltops to create building sites. This precious commodity—a flat pad where much of the surrounding land approaches the angle of repose—became a de-facto picnic spot. Many people simply would follow convention and build a house on the level area. The Webers, though, chose to encircle the flattened hilltop with a house and a garage, creating a courtyard. The house spans the hill from one side to the other, in some measure restoring the hilltop's original profile (see the drawing on p. 104).

When visitors pull up the drive, the first thing they see is a long, one-story outbuilding—part garage, part storage shed, part woodworking shop—that shields the house from view. This part of the compound stakes out the eastern boundary of the courtyard (see the photos on p. 100). A portal through the entry building is framed in part by one of architect Bowman's signature elements: a stout tree-trunk lintel held aloft by heavy brackets. A V-shaped trough let into the top of the log is the rain gutter. The impact is that of a torii gate gone Western, an effect amplified by one of Hal's bonsai ginkgo trees flanking the tunnel-like passageway.

The house, which forms the western boundary of the courtyard, projects two distinct personalities. The courtyard side faces northeast, where its shed roof drops low to the ground, deflecting prevailing breezes (see the photo on the facing page). This caplike shed roof gives the house an almost contem-

AN EDGY MIX. Straddling a Sonoma ridge, this contemporary house is a mix of weathered boards, corrugated metal, and a plan that invites outdoor living. Photo taken at A on site plan.

plative quality, amplified by the broad shoulders of its simple triangular shapes. Weathered redwood siding, along with gunmetal gray corrugated-steel siding, echoes the muted hilltop colors.

Exuberance is the disposition on the sunny side of the house. It's two stories tall, with a long porch off the living room that is open to views of sunsets and distant vineyards. This is the kind of place that can take the sting out of all those 401(k) contributions.

Passage to the sunny side leads through a timbered breezeway separating the main house from the guest quarters. The breezeway spills into an outdoor dining area that includes a cooking alcove carved into the corner of the main house (see the top photo on p. 101). Lined with corrugated steel over a thick concrete counter, the alcove is home to Hal's built-in gas grill. The noncombustible metal lining adds a measure of safety to a built-in outdoor grill with an exposed flame. For nighttime cookery, the reflective lining of the alcove bounces light onto the grill from a pair of no-nonsense jelly-jar sconces (Roughlyte; www.stoncolighting.com).

PART GARAGE, PART GATEWAY. Long and low, a wall-like building that contains a garage, a woodshop, and a garden shed flanks the east side of the courtyard. A hefty log lintel marks the passage into the courtyard. Photos taken at B and C on site plan.

THE LEVEL SPACE IS BETWEEN THE BUILDINGS

Bordered by the garage to the east and the house to the west, the courtyard includes a garden and a lap pool.

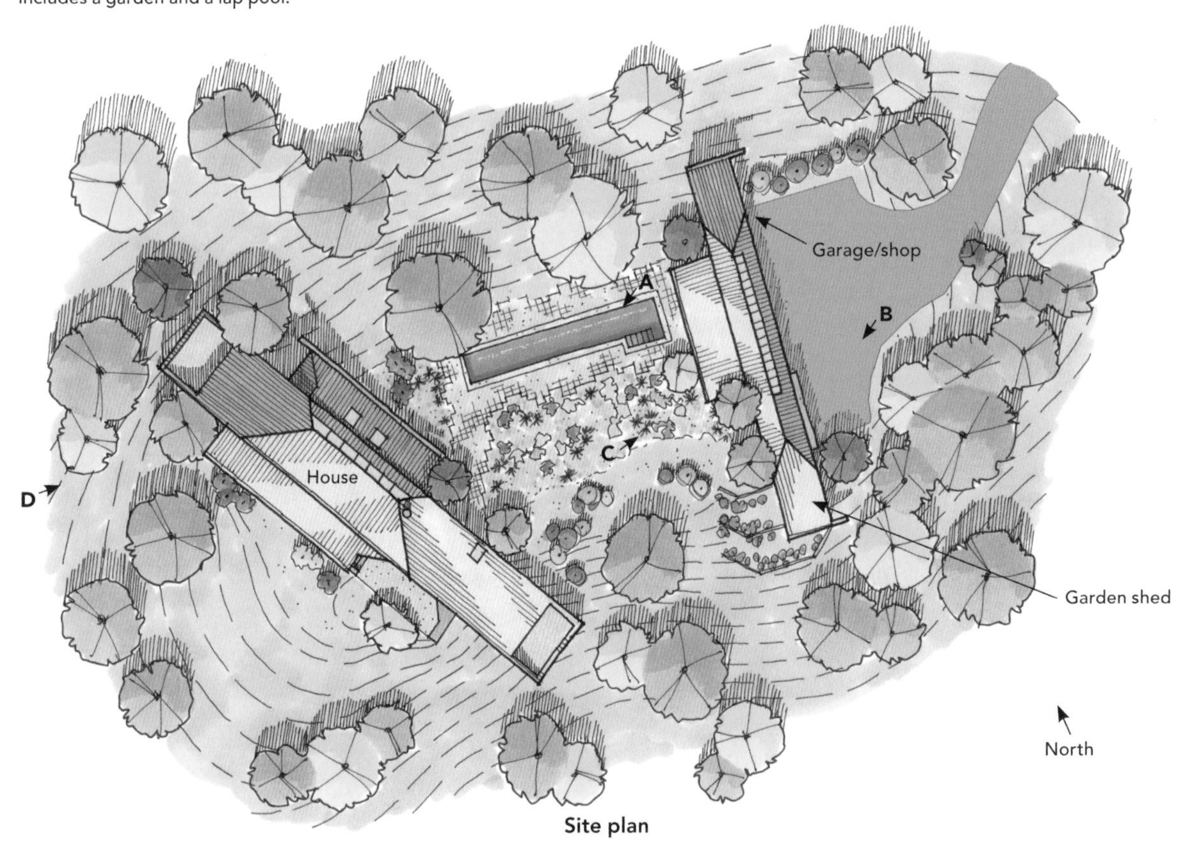

Site plan

Photos taken at lettered positions.

PORCH, PATIO, AND A PLACE TO COOK. Stretching along the southwest side of the house, a covered porch overlooks an outdoor dining area and layers of hills and vineyards receding into the distance. A gas grill is tucked into a metal-lined alcove carved into the corner of the house. Photos taken at D on site plan and E on floor plan.

THE CRYSTAL INSIDE THE GEODE. As the sculptural centerpiece of the house, the stainless-steel hood over the kitchen island draws both stovetop exhaust and attention (above). Bookcases made of 2×10s carry the library and the weight of the beam spanning the kitchen (facing page). A library ladder rides the track affixed to the beam. Photo above taken at G floor plan; photo on facing page taken at F on floor plan.

Inside, it's mostly one room

This house doesn't have many doors dividing the interior. Instead, lots of dedicated corners are sized to fulfill their functions without wasting space. A sitting area for watching movies or the fire shares a low-ceilinged space with a dining area and an alcove for the piano.

The center hall is a cathedral for book lovers. Hal and Mary are avid readers, and even though they were ruthless in weeding their library before the move, they knew that ready access to a wall of books had to be part of their new home. The 11-ft.-tall bookcases include a sliding ladder that rides on a rail for reaching the top shelves (www.putnamrollingladder.com).

The kitchen is on the courtyard side of the hall, overlooking the pool, and includes alcoves at each end for a home office and a pantry. Spotless black-granite countertops set the tone in the kitchen. Like a freshly waxed black town car, they are the gold standard for timeless elegance. Conversely, black-granite counters that bear witness to meal preparation need constant attention, like a town car let out of the garage. Although it's not quite a love–hate situation, Mary admits she wonders if she would choose black granite again.

Pool covers all the bases

Sonoma County requires rural houses to have enough water for fighting a fire. The minimum is 5,000 gal., typically contained in a holding tank. The shape and size of the Webers' building site made it tough to find a spot for a holding tank that wouldn't be an eyesore. Hal and Mary had been harboring a wish for a lap pool all along. It was the perfect convergence of need and desire: At 13,000 gal., the pool solved both.

A SIMPLE SHAPE THAT SUITS ITS SITE

Recalling the profile of the original hill, the main house and the guest house are joined at the breezeway. Decks, a patio, a covered porch, and a courtyard to the north face all points of the compass, providing sunny or shaded places to suit the weather or the mood. The main house—with its high-ceilinged hallway, long interior sightlines, and views to the outside—feels larger than its 1,838 sq. ft. would suggest.

SPECS

- Bedrooms: 2, including the guest room
- Bathrooms: 2½
- Main house: 1,838 sq. ft.
- Guesthouse: 340 sq. ft.
- Cost: $400 per sq. ft.
- Completed: 2002
- Location: Cloverdale, Calif.
- Architect: Obie Bowman
- Builder: Hawkes Construction

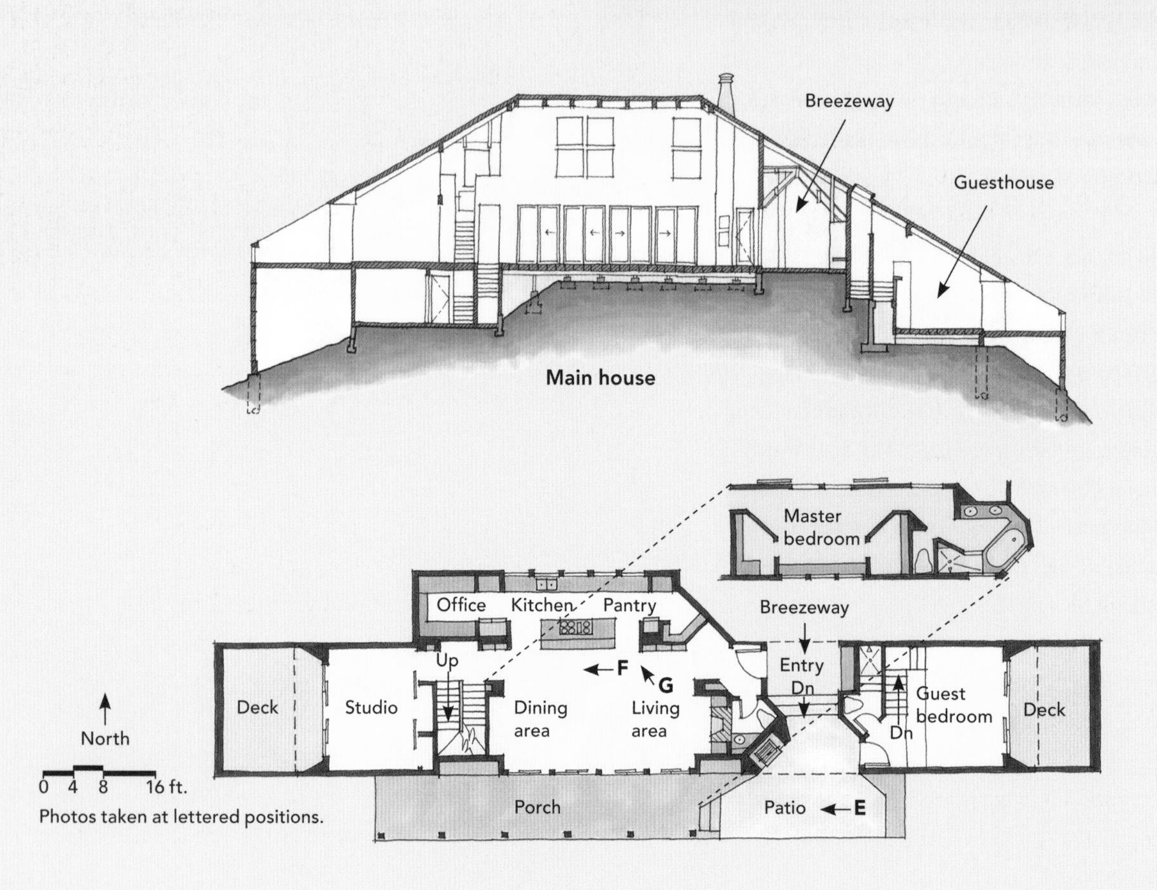

Photos taken at lettered positions.

Pointed at the Sun

BY CHARLES MILLER

"How big a house do you want?" asked the architects. "About 2,500 sq. ft.," replied the client. "OK, we're pretty sure we can get that down a bit," countered the architects. It wasn't the response that Arianne Dar, the client, expected. But the suggestion wasn't out of character from the architects offering it.

The firm of David Arkin and Anni Tilt, a husband-and-wife architectural partnership in Berkeley, Calif., is known to push the boundaries of sustainable building. For them, that means using materials that are in it for the long haul, catching the sun's energy and putting it to work, creating spaces that can be used for multiple purposes, and most important, designing a house that is no larger than it needs to be.

Arkin and Tilt refined the plan, eliminating redundant spaces and orienting the house for optimum solar exposure. The result is a 1,600-sq.-ft. home for Arianne and her teenage son and daughter that uses both active and passive solar strategies to gather electricity and heat.

HOME FOR AN ARTIST. An innovative solar-heating system is the foundation of an artist's small country house, where an equally smart plan accommodates both life and work. Photo taken at A on floor plan.

Flexible floor plan 101: No spaces go unused

The house is one of two narrow, rectangular buildings that are parallel to each other but offset a bit (see the photo above). It shares a roof with a 300-sq.-ft. apartment. Separated from the main house's ground floor by a breezeway (see the floor plans on p. 109), this little getaway is ideal for weekend guests. It's close enough to be a part of the house, yet far enough away to give everybody some privacy.

The kids' bedrooms are over the guest apartment, where they can be reached by way of the primary stairs in the center of the house or by exterior stairs

CATCH THE LIGHT, DEPOSIT THE ENERGY. Hard against an oak hedgerow, the curving roofs of the house and studio echo the gentle curves of the Marin Headlands to the east. Photovoltaic panels laminated to the studio roof supplement the home's energy needs. A solar array to the right banks the heat. Photo taken at B on floor plan.

along the west end. The outdoor stairs give the kids their own private entrance. If Arianne decides to divide the house into a duplex once her children have moved out, the stairs will join the apartment with the two upstairs bedrooms. These rooms open onto a wide space in the upstairs hall that functions as a study or as a small living room for the kids (see the left photo on the facing page). Each of the bedrooms includes a sleeping loft tucked in above the hallway. No space goes unused, and closets and shelves turn up wherever a wall that's deep enough is within reach.

The shop/studio is to the south and west of the main house, where it shelters the front yard from the prevailing wind without blocking the sunshine. Arianne is an artist who works with multiple materials, from paper to glass to welded steel. Her studio and shop share a single roof, with an open space between them. The walls of the shop can be opened to the outdoors to let in light and breezes. If Arianne decides she'd like to start keeping her car indoors, the shop and the breezeway are sized to be a garage and a carport, respectively.

MORE THAN JUST A WIDE PLACE IN THE HALL. Right outside their bedroom doors, the kids' living room includes space for studying and lounging, and has its own outside entry at the end of the hall. Photo taken at C on floor plan.

Electricity and warmth from the sun, even when it's foggy

When the fogbank rolls in, coastal California can stay under cloud cover for weeks at a time. Yet solar energy still penetrates this marine layer and is available for harvest. Instead of using a more-familiar flat-panel photovoltaic system, Arkin and Tilt put the newer thin-film technology to work.

Also known as amorphous film, this type of photovoltaic collector comes in sheets that can be adhered directly to metal roofing. Amorphous-film systems don't generate as much electricity as the flat-panel variety, but they perform better in cloudy or partially shaded conditions. Placed between the standing seams of this roof, the film blends right in. The system, which cost about $24,000 in 2006, produces 7 kilowatt-hours per day on average, supplying about half the electricity needs of the house.

The house is heated primarily by a solar water-heating system that is a lot like the old warm-

INSIDE A SAND-BED HEAT BANK

LOOPS OF CROSS-LINKED POLYETHYLENE TUBING course through what will eventually be a 2-ft.-thick layer of sand beneath the house's slab floor. The sand is insulated below and at the edges with 2 in. of extruded-polystyrene foam. Glycol heated by the sun shining on the collector panels courses though the tubing, heating the massive layer of sand and the rooms above it.

BAMBOO ALL OVER. An abstract forest of ceramic-tile bamboo canes, made by homeowner and artist Arianne Dar, forms the backsplash above the bamboo cabinets. She also made the cast-bronze fish-vertebrae door and drawer pulls.

rock-in-the sleeping-bag trick used by campers. But instead of a warm rock toasted in a campfire, Arianne's house sits atop a 2-ft.-thick layer of solar-heated sand (see the right photo on p. 107). As described in solar pioneer Bob Ramlow's book *Solar Water Heating* (New Society Publishers, 2006), the sand bed is wrapped at the sides and bottom with polystyrene insulation. Polyethylene tubing snakes through the sand, carrying glycol heated at the solar station.

The target is to heat the slab to about 75°F. It, in turn, will keep the temperature of the house in that range. In a typical installation, the heated sand bed accounts for about half the energy necessary to heat a well-insulated house. That's the theory; here's how it played out.

As it got into the heart of the first heating season, the house became colder and colder. Arianne had to rely more and more on the backup systems—a Rais® woodstove and electric baseboard heaters—to keep the house comfortable. Something was amiss.

It turned out that the glycol pump's temperature sensor wasn't turning off the pump when it was supposed to. As the sun set and the glycol cooled, the pump kept running, thereby cooling the sand bed. A new sensor solved that part of the problem.

The house's aluminum windows were the other heat-loss culprit. Even though they're dual-glazed, the windows lose heat through their highly conductive frames. Arianne has since installed curtains in the rooms most affected, and that has helped bring the performance of the sand-bed heating system up to expectations.

Arkin and Tilt estimate that the sand-bed heat bank added about $15,000 to the cost of the house. Besides heating the house, the solar panels also contribute energy to the domestic hot-water system. Arianne estimates that between the photovoltaics and the sandbed, her energy costs have been cut in half—to about $2,000 a year.

OFFSET BUILDINGS CREATE AN OUTDOOR ROOM

It gets breezy on the Bolinas Mesa. Prevailing westerly winds pick up nearly every day, turning the pages in your book whether you want to or not. Siting the shop/studio building to the southwest of the house buffers the breeze, making a calm zone in front of the house.

SPECS

- Bedrooms: 4 (house and apartment)
- Bathrooms: 3½ (house and apartment)
- Size: 1,900 sq. ft. (house and apartment)
- Cost: $350 per sq. ft.
- Completed: 2006
- Location: Bolinas, Calif.
- Architect: Arkin Tilt
- Builder: David van Dyke, Riverwood Construction

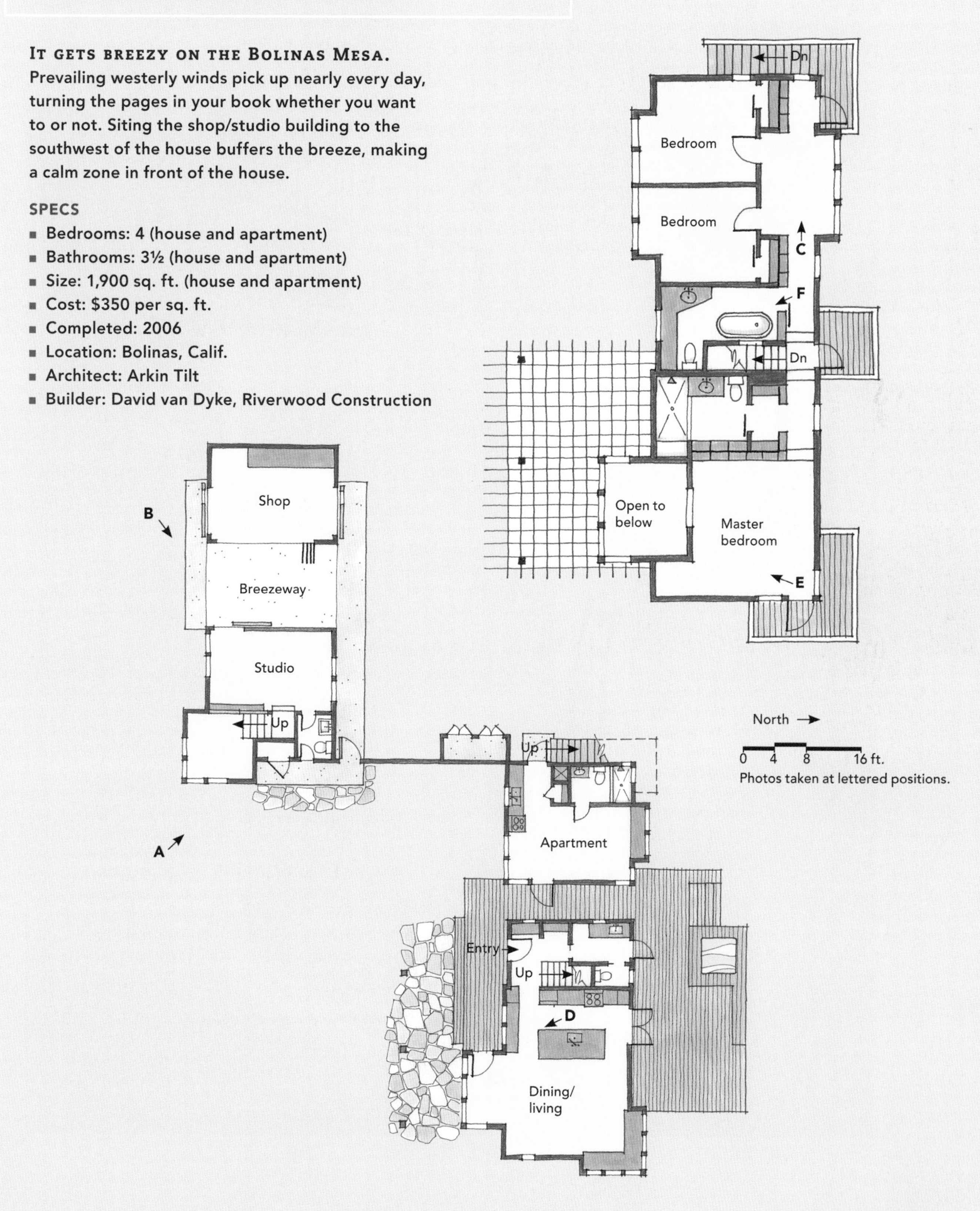

Photos taken at lettered positions.

TALL WINDOWS, SKYLIGHTS, AND TRANSOMS PULL LIGHT INTO THE HOUSE

THE DINING-ALCOVE WINDOWS FUNNEL LIGHT into rooms upstairs and down, and let the sunshine help warm the concrete floors (below). The view to the meadow sails right through two sets of windows, where it can be enjoyed from the master bedroom (see the top photo on the facing page). Photos taken at D and E on floor plan.

BROKEN GLASS MAKES GOOD. The concrete counter contains aggregate from defunct stop-light lenses and the occasional gear.

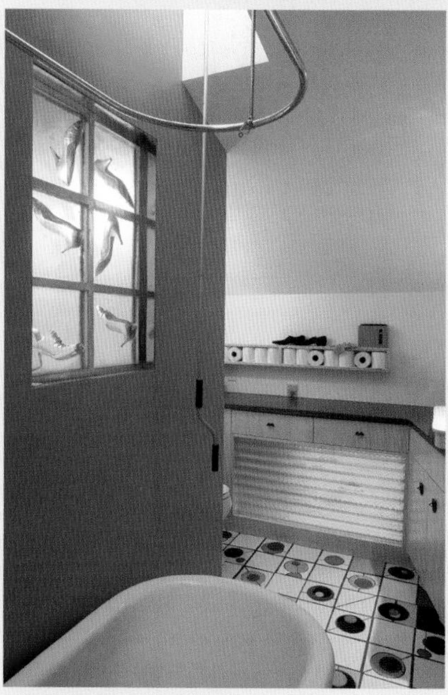

NO EXTERIOR WALLS, BUT THREE SOURCES OF DAYLIGHT. In the bath, a skylight grabs sunshine from above, while a grid of glass blocks admits light from the stairwell. Below the far counter, a panel of corrugated wired glass catches daylight from the transom over the front door. Photo taken at F on floor plan.

Combining daylight, art, and a hand-me-down sink

At the southeast corner of the house, the sun-space dining room is like a two-story-tall net that catches winter light and brings it deep into the living room and kitchen (see the photo on the facing page). The light plays across surfaces and fixtures spiced with an inventive mix of found objects, recycled stuff, and totemic Pacific Rim flora and fauna.

The kitchen island includes a stainless-steel sink from Arianne's childhood home, saved from the Dumpster during a 1960s remodel. Its satin finish, big bowl, and integral drain board have come full circle from the day they were deemed out of fashion. The island's countertop is concrete with glass aggregate made from stoplight lenses (see the inset photo on the facing page). It bears on a laminated bamboo cabinet.

Taking her cue from the bamboo, Arianne created a tile backsplash that evokes an abstract stand of bamboo canes rising from the counter behind the cooktop (see the photo on p. 108). The drawer and door pulls below are bronze, cast in molds that replicate fish vertebrae found on a local reef (see the inset photo on p. 108).

More custom castings appear in surprising places. In the kids' bathroom, a half-dozen glass blocks featuring high-heeled-shoe shapes tap-dance over the tub (see the bottom photo at left).

Daylight from the tall dining-room windows also makes its way into the master bedroom (see the top photo at left). At the foot of the bed, a bank of old industrial-steel sash windows overlooks the sunspace dining room and the meadow view to the south.

Living Lightly on the Mountain

BY TINA GOVAN

When Sam and Anne Eich began planning their retirement, they came to me with the desire to build a simple, affordable home in Tennessee's Cherokee National Forest. They wanted their new house to accommodate them, their dogs, and the occasional visit from their daughter. Like many heading toward retirement, they saw their new house as an opportunity to downsize, to simplify, and to learn to live with less. They wanted a house that focused attention on its setting. Anne wanted the feeling of living in a tree house, and a big screened porch was high on her wish list.

In response, I designed a house that is sensitive to the forested landscape, that brings in lots of light and views, and that is constructed of simple, durable materials that demand little maintenance for a couple longing for stress-free living.

A steep site leads to a creative layout

To minimize disturbance to the site, I broke the house into smaller pieces, each only 16 ft. wide. This way, the house could closely follow the contours of the land, and front-to-back grade changes would be minimal. This enabled most of the house to exist on a single level, which is important for older homeowners who would rather not be forced to navigate lots of level changes and stairways. The four main building blocks—the carport, the master-bedroom suite, the kitchen/dining/living area, and the den/guest wing—are each treated as individual "houses" gathered around a courtyard on one side and a screened porch on the other. The home reads as several small buildings rather than just one big one.

I also wanted the house to sit comfortably within its natural and built environments. Colors and

LIGHT IN THE WOODS. This small, day-lit house deep in the Tennessee woods brings one retirement couple closer to their natural surroundings. Photo taken at A on floor plan.

building materials were chosen to blend into the natural vegetation and to mimic the clusters of outbuildings you see on farms in the valley below.

Natural-lighting strategies have multiple benefits

Because the house is narrow, daylight can stream from one exterior wall to the other, so the entire house is lit by the sun when it is low in the sky. The lighting strategy, accomplished with an abundance of large windows, double doors, and few interior partitions, also helps with passive cooling; southwesterly breezes can easily pass through the house.

Having open interior spaces flanked by windows and doors also helps build a strong connection between the front and back of the house and among indoor spaces, expansive exterior views, and outdoor sitting areas. On the south, a large screened porch projects into the treetops. The north side, on the other hand, digs into the hillside, offering a striking sense of contrast in a mere 16 ft. It includes a patio sheltered by the mountain and accessed from the dining area by double doors. The house has an uninterrupted flow; you can easily move between living spaces and adjacent outdoor areas.

"The house has an uninterrupted flow; you can easily move between living spaces and adjacent outdoor areas."

LIGHT SHINES IN WHERE VIEWS EXTEND OUT. Lots of windows and double doors in the kitchen and dining space (above) offer nearly uninterrupted views of the sloping forest. Within the same large space, the living room (left) is washed in daylight that pours through a bank of large casement windows. Photos taken at D and E on floor plan.

SEVERAL BUILDINGS CREATE ONE FLOWING HOUSE

ARCHITECT TINA GOVAN'S WORK IS LARGELY INFLUENCED by the relationship between indoor and outdoor spaces. In designing the Eich project, she saw the house and site as one, weaving indoor rooms together with outdoor ones. Rather than treat the house as a single object, she designed it as several "houses," each with its own designated living space and tied to two key outdoor areas: a porch and a patio. The houses and adjacent outdoor areas sit on a single level, which allows for easier access throughout indoor and outdoor living spaces.

SPECS

- Bedrooms: 2
- Bathrooms: 2
- Size: 1,935 sq. ft.
- Cost: $125 per sq. ft.
- Completed: 2006
- Location: Butler, Tenn.
- Architect: Tina Govan
- Builder: Lester Rominger

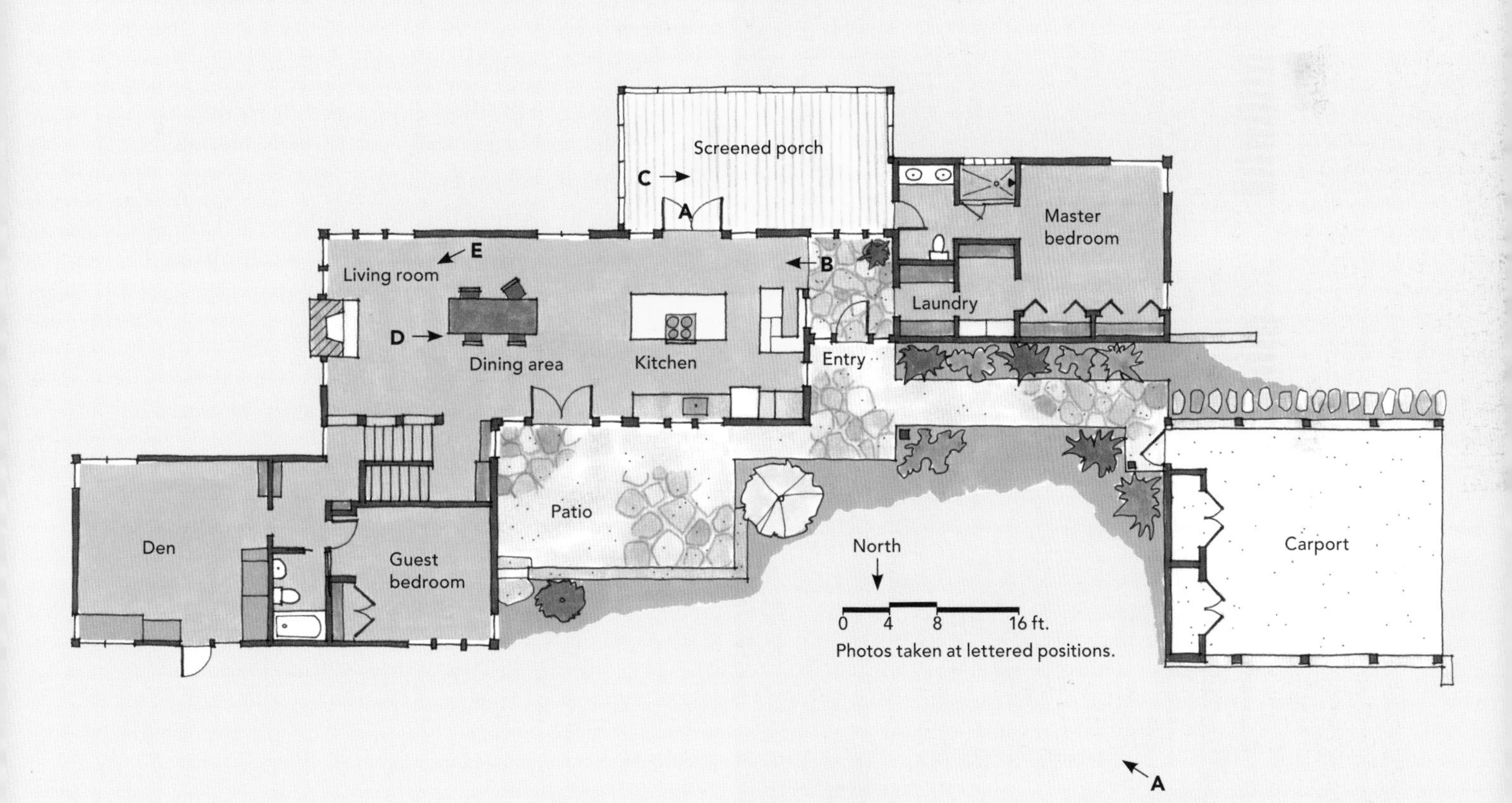

A simplified design keeps costs in check

The budget for this project was tight, so to keep down costs, we kept the structure of each house simple. Outside, we achieved texture and detail by offsetting each of the buildings, creating inviting outdoor areas and selecting simple yet attractive finishes. For example, the carport wall is a decorative assembly of plywood, posts, and staggered 2×2s that cast intricate shadows on the entrance walkway. Past the carport, a sunny courtyard garden and patio are revealed, enclosed by the mountain on one side and the house on the other. Paralleling a landscaped walk, the entry roof pulls away from the house to create a trellis, allowing light to pass through to the garden below.

The interior of the house is kept simple as well, with a focus on open, continuous spaces. Rather than solid, full-height walls, partial walls, built-ins, and furniture are used to distinguish spaces. This allows for a variety of flexible living areas and eliminates construction complexity that typically drives up building costs. Through simplified design details and material selection—ash floors, pine trim, and IKEA® cabinetry—we were able to achieve a level of detail, definition, and comfort that defies the cost of the house.

OUTDOOR SPACES INSIDE. The entry foyer (above left) is finished with stone tile and painted clapboard siding that matches the exterior cladding. Floor-to-ceiling glass lets in an abundance of light thanks to porch skylights (left). The space is intended to feel more like a breezeway between "houses" than a traditional entry, and it begs visitors to question whether they're inside or outside. Photos taken at B and C on floor plan.

A Duplex Grows in Brooklyn

BY JILL AND JOHN BOURATOGLOU

As a pair of young architects with two small children living in Brooklyn, N.Y., one of the most expensive real-estate markets in the country, we found ourselves in a housing dilemma: We couldn't afford $1.5 million for a brownstone, nor could we squeeze much more time out of the two-bedroom apartment we'd occupied since before the kids were born. Our solution was to look for a vacant lot somewhere in the city and to build our own house.

After squeezing two more years out of our small apartment, we found a long, skinny, irregularly shaped lot. The 25-ft. by 116-ft. lot was located on the edge of a brownstone neighborhood, adjacent to some commercial buildings that quickly were being converted to residential use. The neighborhood was about to blossom.

Duplex cuts the mortgage in half

With a tight lot, a tighter time line, and a tightening budget, we did as much ourselves as possible. Although we had designed lots of houses, we had never built one before. We researched and bought online many of the components and materials for our house (see "The House That FedEx Built" on p. 122). Besides the masonry, electrical, and plumbing subcontractors, the UPS® and FedEx® drivers were key members of our building team.

Installing the drywall, laying the tile, and painting the walls ourselves saved money in the short term. But it was our decision to design the house as a duplex that has helped with the mortgage. Plus, the rental apartment will continue to be a source of income after the mortgage is paid off.

Off-street parking in the city is worth its space in gold

Another major consideration in our design was parking. Many New Yorkers don't own cars because there is nowhere to park them affordably; those who do routinely pay $3,000 a year for off-street parking. By squeezing a garage into the plan, we were able to avoid a parking bill and raise the value of our house significantly.

To find space for a garage, we designed the house backward. Rather than starting with a floor plan and then working into a section drawing, we began with a cross section showing how far back from the street we could locate a garage below grade and still have a driveway that wasn't too steep (see the drawing on p. 118). Unfortunately, every inch that we set the house back ate up an inch of our backyard, which is another precious commodity in the city. Setting the house back from the street, however, ultimately benefited both our neighbors and us: It kept our house

(Continued on p. 123)

A CUTE LITTLE BUILDING WITH TWO HUGE ASSETS

TUCKED BETWEEN TWO "GROWN-UP" APARTMENT BUILDINGS on a skinny city lot, this house finds space for an underground garage by setting it back from the street below grade (see the photo on the facing page, taken at B on floor plan. Out back is a comfortable yard that's a haven for cookouts and playing with the kids (see the photo at right, taken at A on floor plan).

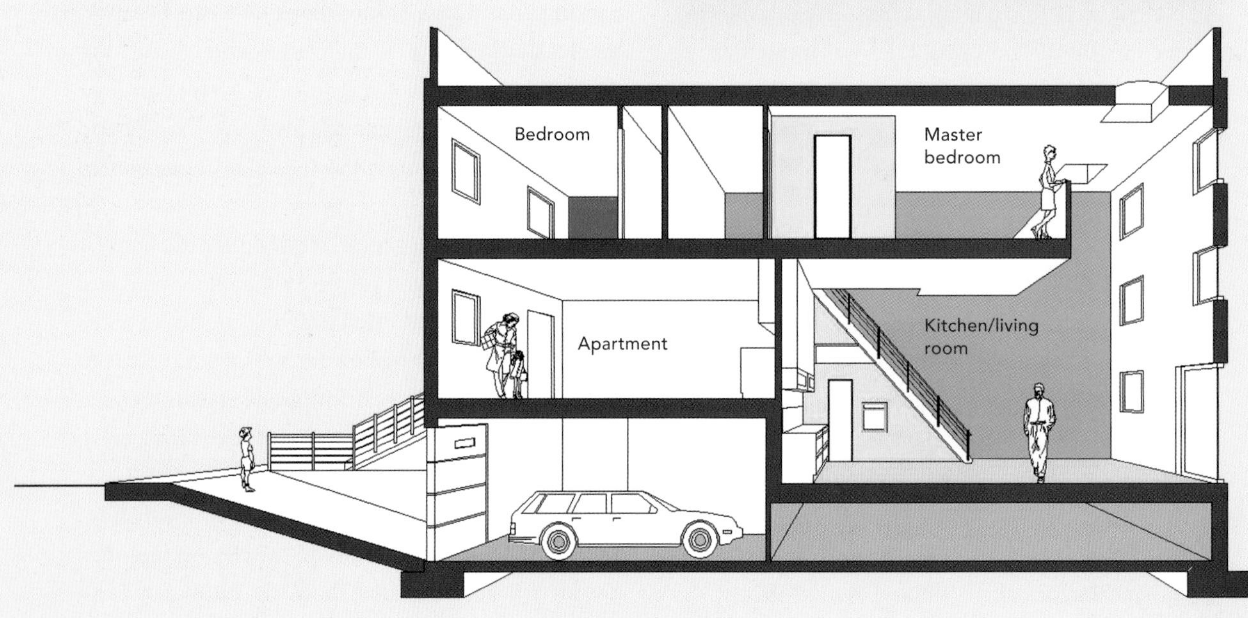

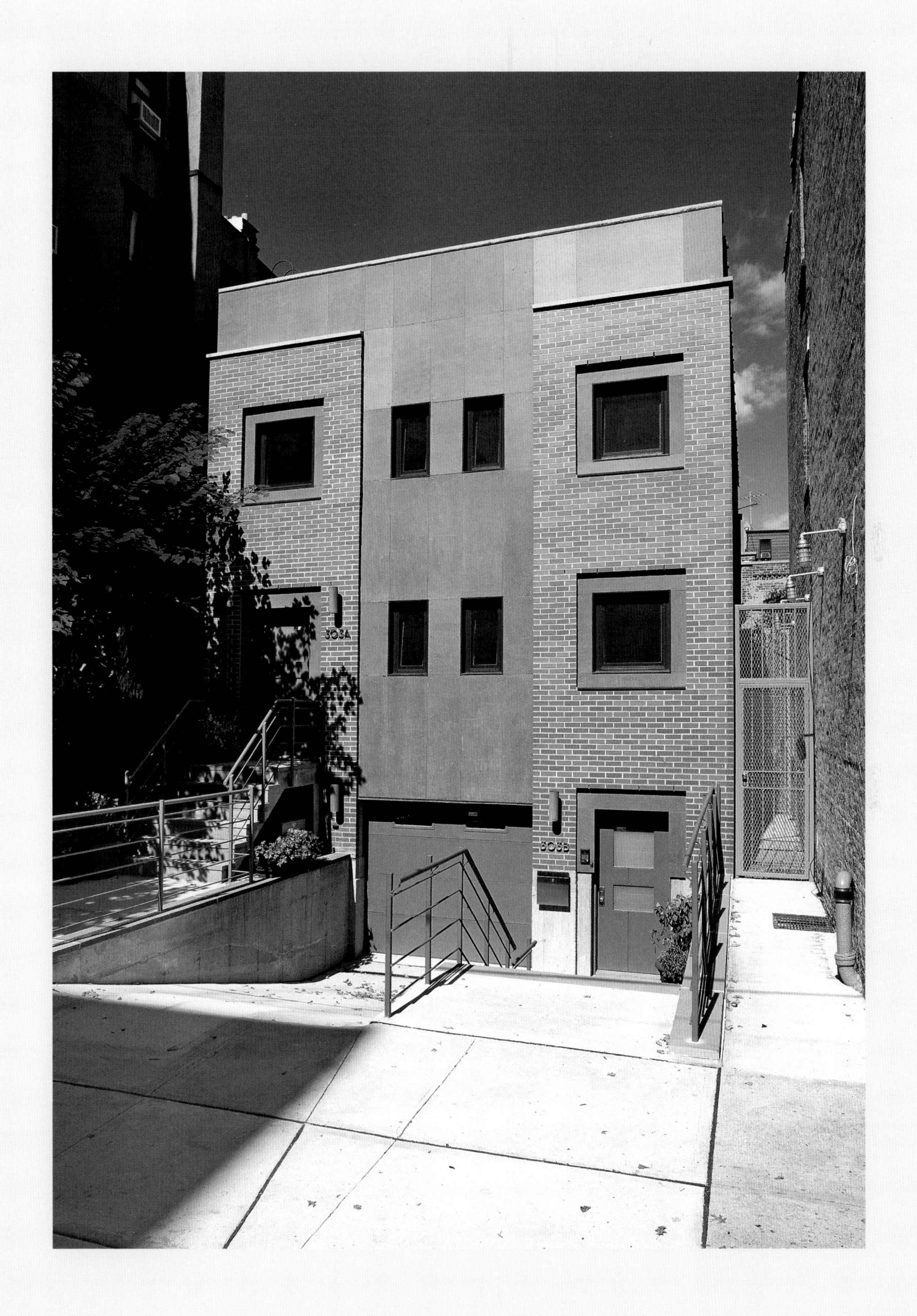
303A
303B

WITH COLOR ON BOTH SIDES, the white wall draws the eye toward the backyard view (top). Photo taken at C on floor plan. Rather than unifying windows, doors, walls, and floors with baseboard and casing, the authors chose to isolate them with metal drywall reveals (above). Square cutouts in the half-wall, which echo window placement, are for inevitable bulb changes in the hanging lamps (left). Photos taken at C and D on floor plan.

THE HOUSE ENVELOPS AN APARTMENT

Tucked above the garage and below the kids' bedrooms, a one-bedroom apartment occupies the front third of the house. Behind it, the open plan of the main-floor living area is defined by ceiling heights. This openness continues upstairs to the master bedroom/office, which is open to below over a half-wall.

SPECS

- Bedrooms: 3 (house) + 1 (apartment)
- Bathrooms: 2½ (house) + 1 (apartment)
- Size: 1,950 sq. ft. (house) + 500 sq. ft. (apartment) + 400 sq. ft. (garage)
- Cost: $135 per sq. ft.
- Completed: 2005
- Location: Brooklyn, N.Y.
- Architect: Bouratoglou Architect, PC
- Builder: John Bouratoglou and I.E.B. General Contracting Corp.

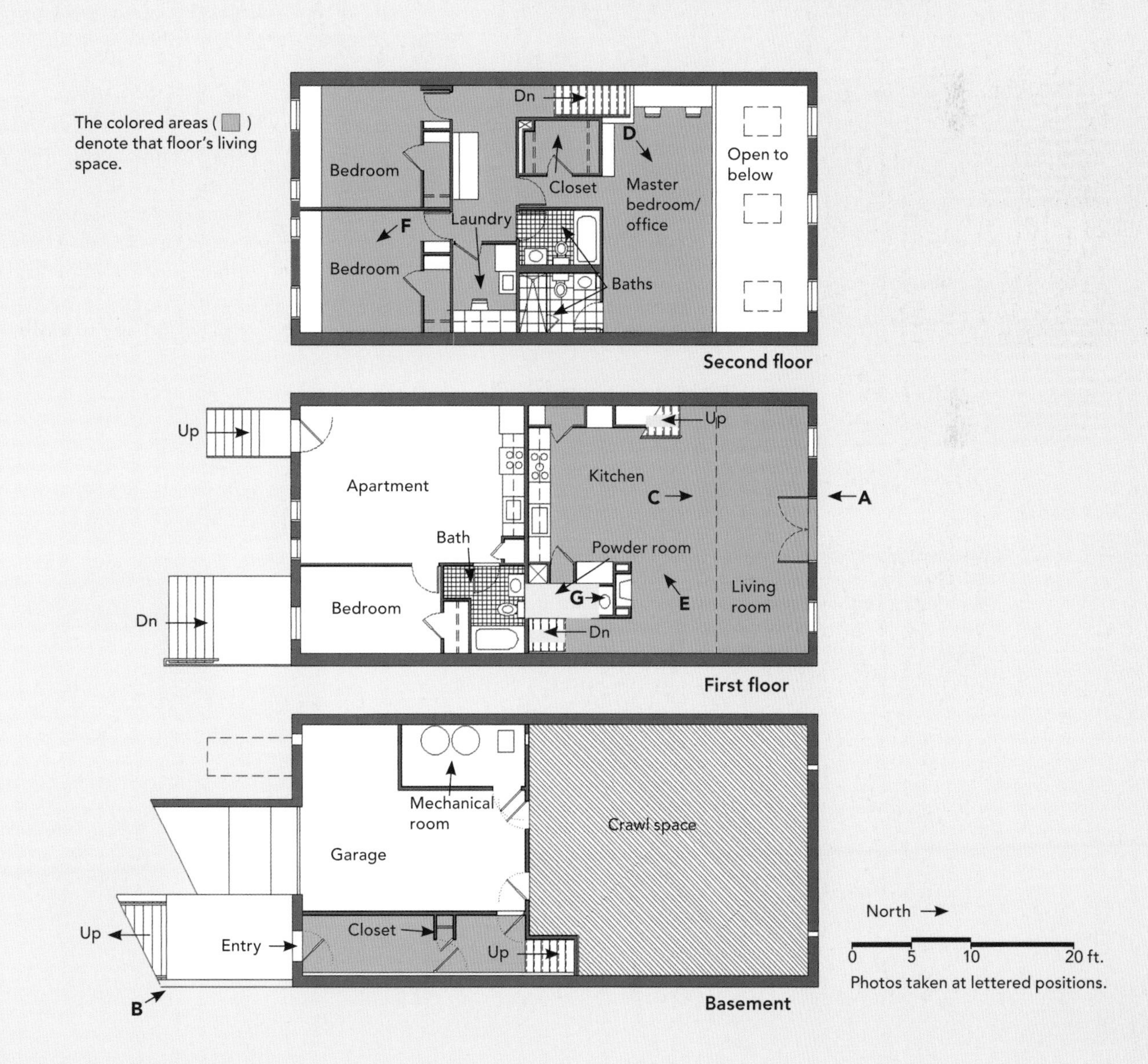

THE HOUSE THAT FEDEX BUILT

AFTER TEACHING CLASSES at New York City College of Technology, updating and revising the drawings for the house, making site visits, and being a mom, I found myself with 10 hours left in the day for material selections and purchases: from 8 p.m. to 6 a.m. Because local distributors weren't open during those hours, I turned to online retailers, from whom I purchased everything from the flooring to the fans. I found great prices, tracked the shipping online, and had everything delivered directly to the job site without ever leaving home.

While all the Web sites listed on p. 124 were useful, the Hakatai tile site (www.hakatai.com) was a pleasant surprise. It allowed me to design a custom blend of mosaic tiles for the first-floor powder room. I could choose the percentage of each color and see a diagram of the design online within seconds. I kept changing the percentages until I was happy with the mix (or until I could no longer tell the difference). When three cases of tiles arrived a few weeks later, I was impressed with the final result of my own custom blend. Besides mosaics, the Hakatai site offers the capability to custom-design murals, borders, and tile rugs. —Jill B.

COOLEST ONLINE FINDS. On Hakatai's Web site, you can blend glass tiles in customized mosaics, murals, borders, and tile rugs. Playful and useful, the ceiling fans in the kids' bedrooms also were found online. Besides fans, Farrey's sells lighting, hardware, and kitchen and bath products. Photos taken at F and G on floor plan.

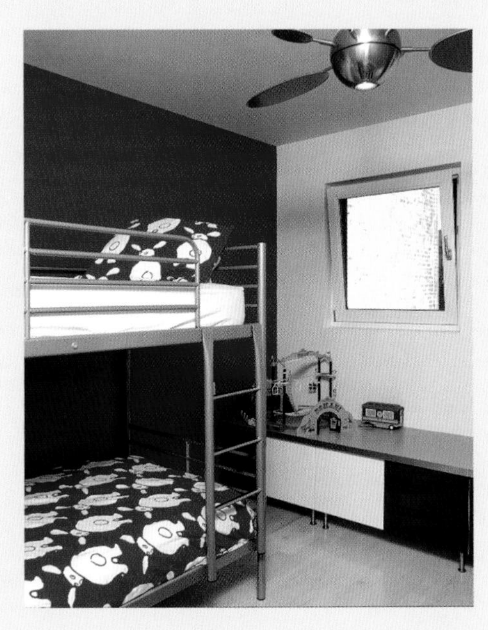

SIMPLE STRATEGY FOR A STREAMLINED LOOK. Recessing the appliances into the wall emphasizes their steel facades and hides their bulk. Cream-colored walls soften the black, white, and gray palette typical of modern design. Photo taken at E on floor plan.

from being monstrously tall, it allowed more natural light into the neighboring co-op apartment building, and it reduced the sightlines from our living room into our other neighbor's rear carriage house.

By keeping the ceiling height in the garage to a minimum (8 ft.) and by setting the apartment on top, we derived the ceiling height in the living room. Our front entrance is at the same level as the garage and leads into a mudroom, up a few stairs, and into a large, open, double-height living/dining/kitchen area (see the floor plans on p. 121). The master bedroom/office overlooks this main room, and three skylights aligned over three bays of windows bring

"Coloring the large walls channels attention to the view of the backyard."

in natural light and establish a connection to the backyard from both floors.

Modern materials, classical proportions

John grew up in Athens, Greece, and has been influenced greatly by classical architecture. Although not directly apparent in our home, the exterior proportions are derived from the classical model of the Parthenon. The front and rear facades are divided into three sections using the base, shaft, and capital proportions found in classical orders. We emphasized the proportions by framing them with minimalist materials, the same way the Parthenon's shapes are punctuated with white marble. Instead of white marble, though, we chose fiber-cement board in keeping with our "modern classical" scheme—and our limited budget.

Outside, the windows and their cement-board surrounds are recessed into the brick facade, creating shadows that reinforce the simple shapes. The interior approach is the same. Rather than using baseboard and casing to unify floors, walls, windows, and doors, we used reveals and aluminum J-channel to separate them. In the kitchen, appliances are recessed into the walls to highlight their facades while minimizing their visual weight.

Because the walls are 50 ft. long and 25 ft. tall, the modern architectural palette of black, white, and gray just wouldn't work on them. Coloring these large walls enlivens them and also frames a view of the backyard. Our color choices are typical of what you see when taking in this view: blue and green. The white is the whitest white we could find.

Although this house seems to be a jumble of architectural thoughts spanning from ancient to modern times, for us it's really a culmination. Our goal was to achieve the classical adage "The whole is greater than the sum of its parts."

SOURCES

CARPETING
www.interfaceflor.com

CEMENTBOARD
www.cbf11.com

CENTRAL VACUUM
www.centralvacuumstores.com

FANS
www.farreys.com

FIREPLACE
www.stovesdirect.com

FRONT DOORS
www.upstatedoor.com

GLASS SHOWER DOOR
www.abcshowerdoor.com

HOUSE NUMBERS
www.customhousenumbers.com

KITCHEN AND BATHROOM FAUCETS
www.irawoodinc.com

KITCHEN CABINETS
www.newformkitchens.com

LAUNDRY/CHILDREN'S CABINETS
www.ikea.com

MAILBOX
www.chiasso.com

WINDOW AND DOOR REVEALS
www.gordon-inc.com

WINDOWS
www.marvin.com

WOOD FLOORING
www.lumberliquidators.com

Privacy and Light on a Small Lot

BY DAVID HALL

When Sue Mason and Richard Roth decided to leave Anchorage and move south to the Lower 48 for their retirement years, they didn't stray far from the sea. Experienced mariners, they decided to build a home on a vacant lot they owned in Anacortes, Wash., gateway to the San Juan Islands. Minutes from Puget Sound, the 75-ft. by 100-ft. lot is tucked into an established neighborhood. After living on boats, Sue and Richard were accustomed to getting maximum use out of every available bit of space. That's exactly what we would have to do to squeeze a sunlit house, a two-car garage, a woodshop, and an outdoor room onto this small lot.

Like the proverbial ring of wagons creating a protected zone at its center, the house, the shop, and the garage encircle the yard (see the drawing on p. 127). The house fronts the street, while the two-car garage and the 600-sq.-ft. woodshop border the back of the lot, accessed by an alley. In between lies a sheltered courtyard. On sunny days, Sue and Richard swing open the folding doors in the dining and living areas to mingle house and yard. A fountain plays water music to muffle neighborhood sounds.

The fight for light

In the Pacific Northwest, famous for its cloudy days, sunlight is a powerful tonic. We used a variety of tricks in this house to give Sue and Richard their fair share. A 22-ft.-long ridgetop skylight (www.crystaliteinc.com) illuminates the home's oval core, which includes the kitchen and the master and guest baths.

PRIVATE YET OPEN. With a durable exterior and a surprising day-lit interior (photo, p. 125, taken at A on site plan), this shipshape small home offers both privacy and openness. Photo taken at B on site plan.

In the master bath, translucent fiberglass walls—2×4 framing sandwiched between flexible 1⁄16-in. fiberglass panels (www.dipcraft.com)—keep things bright while providing privacy (see the top right photo on p. 129). At each gable end, triangular clerestory windows admit morning and late-afternoon light deep into the interior.

The rooms that most benefit from natural light and views, such as the living and dining areas, are situated along the exterior walls. The walls of the kitchen, meanwhile, are peeled back, with the oval defined not by full-height partitions but by the arc of a two-tiered breakfast bar and the curved transition between the kitchen's rubber-tile flooring and the polished concrete of the open-plan dining/living space.

The expanse of south-facing windows in the living and dining areas combines with the dark concrete floors to create a passive-solar system, giving an assist to the radiant-heating system embedded in the floor. In summer, on those rare sweltering Northwest days, the folding doors can be opened wide to let in a breeze. Overhanging eaves provide shading from the sun. Year-round, the house is filled with natural light, augmented by the light reflected off the outdoor pool.

Spare detailing and marine-grade materials minimize maintenance

Sue and Richard have a collection of modernist furniture and contemporary art, and they came to the drawing board wanting a house that reflected their sensibility. It had to be open and uncluttered, with a presence and personality established by materials and structural components rather than by historical precedent.

The open-plan layout is emphasized by a high gabled ceiling running along the spine of the house. Beams from salvaged timbers provide structure and accent in the living and dining areas. The floors in the living, dining, and guest/office spaces are exposed concrete with a ground-and-polished finish. Zinc control joints help minimize cracking and add visual interest. The master bedroom—which is raised 18 in. above the ground floor to allow light into the cellar below—has oak flooring with radiant heating installed between the joists.

Marine-grade Douglas-fir plywood finished with four coats of spar varnish clads the gable ends of the house, the walls adjacent to the entries, and the bay window fronting the street. The amber warmth of the fir is heightened by its partner in exterior finish: gunmetal gray U-panel steel roofing (www.metalmart.biz), installed horizontally as siding with custom-fabricated battens. Although selected primarily for their aesthetics, both materials were relatively inexpensive at about $10 per sq. ft., leaving room in the budget for a standing-seam metal roof and folding window walls in the living and dining areas (www.quantumwindows.com).

Incidentally, the metal siding and roofing are coated with Kynar®-based paint. In my experience, it has proved to be the most durable, colorfast paint for exterior metal applications that are exposed to salty seaside air.

OPEN PLAN WITH A HARDWORKING CORE

Spaces that demand the greatest connection to the outdoors are arranged around an oval core, the nucleus of this house. All the rooms that require plumbing are here, as is the stairway to the basement. At the hub of the house, the kitchen enjoys long views through the west-facing gable-end windows and interior views of the front door, fireplace, and entertainment center.

SPECS

- Bedrooms: 2
- Bathrooms: 2
- Size: 1,960 sq. ft.
- Cost: $305 per sq. ft.
- Completed: 2006
- Location: Anacortes, Wash.
- Architect: David Hall
- Builder: Dykstra Construction Services

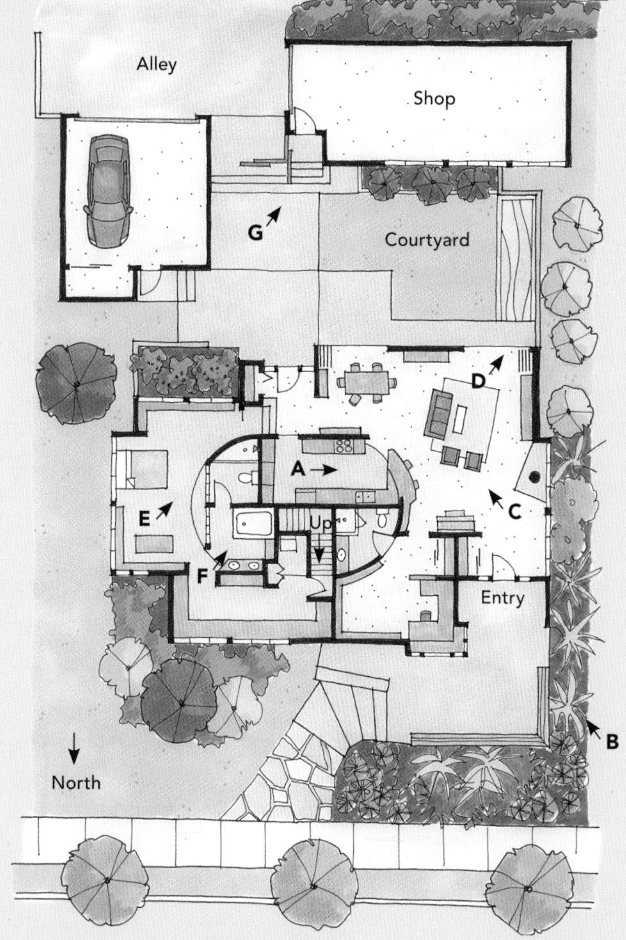

Photos taken at lettered positions.

OPEN PLAN OPENS UP. Under the ridgetop skylight, the kitchen spills smoothly into the living and dining areas, where a quartet of doors can be folded open to mingle courtyard and house on sunny days. Photo taken at C on site plan.

Galvanized wide-flange steel I-beams held aloft by galvanized pipe columns are the structural bones of the entrances and the sliding gate off the back alley. We left these rugged and simple steel elements exposed to lend their character to the modern style of the house. Commercial-grade aluminum windows and storefront entry doors (www.arcadiaproducts.com) complete the exterior palette. At the front door, the glass is frosted for privacy, and the aluminum frames are anodized gray so that they look at home next to the steel siding.

It may be landlocked in an Anacortes neighborhood, but Sue and Richard's house is nevertheless shipshape, marine-grade, and detailed for the long haul.

FOLDING DOORS AND FALLING WATER. The concrete retaining wall required along the southwest corner of the backyard created an opportunity for a lively water feature that can be enjoyed from both inside and out. Photo taken at D on site plan.

TWO KINDS OF PRIVACY. In the master bedroom, a bank of windows facing south overlooks a sheltered courtyard formed by the garage and the shop. The curving wall of the central core includes translucent fiberglass panels that admit light from the bedroom to the master bath, and vice versa. Photos taken at E and F on site plan.

CIRCLE THE OUTBUILDINGS

THE HOUSE, THE SHOP, AND THE GARAGE are arranged to create a secluded outdoor room with southern exposure between the alley and the street. Steel panels covered with Kynar-based paint are used as both roofing and siding on all three buildings. The galvanized posts and beams and the concrete steps, planters, and retaining walls are equally suited for long exposure to the elements without maintenance. Deciduous trees along the western edge of the yard complete the sense of enclosure. Photo taken at G on site plan.

Why Modular?

BY CHRIS ERMIDES

It isn't often that the term *modular* is used to describe a custom-built home. And why would it? Modular homes are designed from stock plans and made of factory-built modules finished with limited options for windows, cabinets, and millwork. What's more, they rarely illustrate the mindful design and impeccable craftsmanship found in custom homes. The point is that most modular-built homes aren't custom anything.

Cookie-cutter drawbacks aside, modular construction does have some benefits worth paying attention to. For example, there's less waste because offcuts from one module end up as part of another project. And the house never sees a drop of rain until it's weatherproof and finished. For these reasons and more, custom-home builders like Randy Lanou and his design/build firm BuildSense (www.buildsense.com) are finding ways to capitalize on the modular-built model without sacrificing design and construction integrity. Lanou calls the result a "hybrid" house: part modular, part site-built. This project in Durham, N.C., is a great example of how the two can come together in a way that benefits the builder and the homeowner.

Design starts with the limitations

House modules need to be transported via highway. Highway regulations in eastern North Carolina limit a module's size to 13 ft. 9 in. in width and 15 ft. 9 in. in height, a size, Lanou says, that can work for bedrooms, kitchens, and bathrooms, but not for large spaces with tall ceilings. Clients Scott and Vikki Metheny went to BuildSense looking for a custom home that was affordable, efficient, and modern. (Scott, a skilled carpenter, later joined Lanou's crew and became the contractor on record.) They wanted a large living room, a master suite, two additional bedrooms, ample daylight, and easy outdoor access.

Achieving these goals would be a challenge. With size restrictions in mind, Lanou used three modules, each for a separate part of the home. Kitchen, dining, half-bath, and laundry made up one module; the master suite and office alcove made up another. Two bedrooms and a full bath were in the third. Lanou arranged the modules and stitched them together with a floor and roof to give the Methenys the large living room they were looking for.

FACTORY BUILT. This affordable custom home combines modular units with on-site construction, shedding light on the strengths and weaknesses of factory-built homes.

Customizing can be a challenge

Modular manufacturers rely on Henry Ford's assembly-line model for their success. Each module moves down a line where stations are set up for specific parts of the process. Unlike custom homes, though, the modules moving along the line don't vary much from one another in terms of design. It's all about efficiency of labor and materials.

The rub in all of this is that most modular companies are adamant about working with their own plans drawn by their own team of draftspersons. Interrupting the staff designers' normal workflow can create problems. For BuildSense and the Methenys, this meant there were some discrepancies between the original drawings and the ones created at the factory. Before anything was approved, both builder and client reviewed each draft and made appropriate changes.

Small details can be missed. For example, no one noticed that a wall in the kitchen had been moved until the module was delivered. The mistake had to be corrected because custom cabinets already had been built.

Once the final plans were agreed on by all parties, the modular manufacturer was able to provide a specific and detailed price. Both Lanou and Metheny agree that the financial consideration is one of the most beneficial aspects of modular construction. You know what the price is, and you know exactly where you'll stand in the process once the modules arrive on-site.

All in all, both builder and client were happy with the process and the outcome. Their advice to anyone looking to use modules as part of their next project is twofold. As a start, take a tour of the factory, and pay attention to the products as they're being built. Second, understand the fabricator's process, the materials, the details, and the limits of transportation, and work with these parameters rather than against them.

MODULAR HOMES ARE MODELS FOR THE EFFICIENT USE OF MATERIALS AND TIME. Once the pre-built modules arrive on site, they can be assembled and tied together in as little as six hours, as was done in this 2,000-sq.-ft. home.

IN BETWEEN MODULES THERE'S ROOM FOR A LARGE, BRIGHT LIVING SPACE. The site-built floor, roof, and exterior walls complete the structure and yield a grand living space that connects the modules. Orienting the home properly on-site and incorporating high-performance windows not only add ample daylight but also contribute to the house's efficiency. Electricity bills, which include heat, total $50 a month.

THERE'S GOOD REASON TO FRAME IN THE FACTORY AND TO FINISH ON-SITE

LOWER COSTS

Modules are built from plans offered by the manufacturer, which is equipped to streamline the process in a way that optimizes efficiency. When houses are built in a controlled environment, costs can be controlled as well. Modular companies can be extremely accurate in pricing their part of the project. Stripping away too many components offered by the factory can alter the cost benefit, however. For this house, all cabinetry, floors, and wall finishes were done by the builder on-site. The total cost for the house—about 2,000 sq. ft., including the porches—came out to $143 per sq. ft.

SAVE TIME

Once manufacturers have code-approved plans in hand, modules can be built frame to finish in a few days. Site work and foundation work are done simultaneously. Customizing the modules slows the process. These modules didn't run through as rigorous a schedule, but there was still a time benefit. Due to a backlog with the manufacturer, the foundation was finished months before the modules were built. But once the modules arrived on-site, they were craned in place and tied together within six hours. From start to finish, the entire process took about five months to complete, four months less than if the house had been built conventionally.

CUSTOM HYBRID: THREE MODULES STITCHED TOGETHER ON-SITE

CONTROL QUALITY

In typical modular construction, the entire house is framed and finished in a factory, then assembled on-site. Walls are painted, cabinets are installed, flooring is placed, and the roof is put on. Once the modules show up, most of the remaining work involves tying them together. Here, there was more site work to complete. A shed roof and two walls were built to tie the modules together and to create the large living area. Custom cabinets and the stairs to the second floor were installed as well.

HELP SUBCONTRACTORS

Plumbing and electrical work (from rough-in to finish) is done in the factory. Wiring and piping are left long to make connections in the field. Modules come equipped with access panels to allow plumbers and electricians to make these connections. HVAC systems are installed on-site after the modules are set. The process didn't change for this hybrid approach. Small problems can arise from the factory, but they aren't common. On this project, the plumber found a leak in the vent stack during inspection, but it was easily fixed.

SUSTAIN RESOURCES

Sustainability is one of the major strengths of modular construction. Because modules are built in an enclosed environment, framing never sees the weather, and there's no opportunity for mold. Some argue that because laborers aren't fighting the elements as they build, their work is better, as is the result. Workers aren't driving as far or as often to a site, so less fossil fuel is burned. There's also little waste because scraps from one project become blocking, cripples, and other pieces for the next project. That means less material goes in the landfill, and it also means high profit margins for the manufacturer.

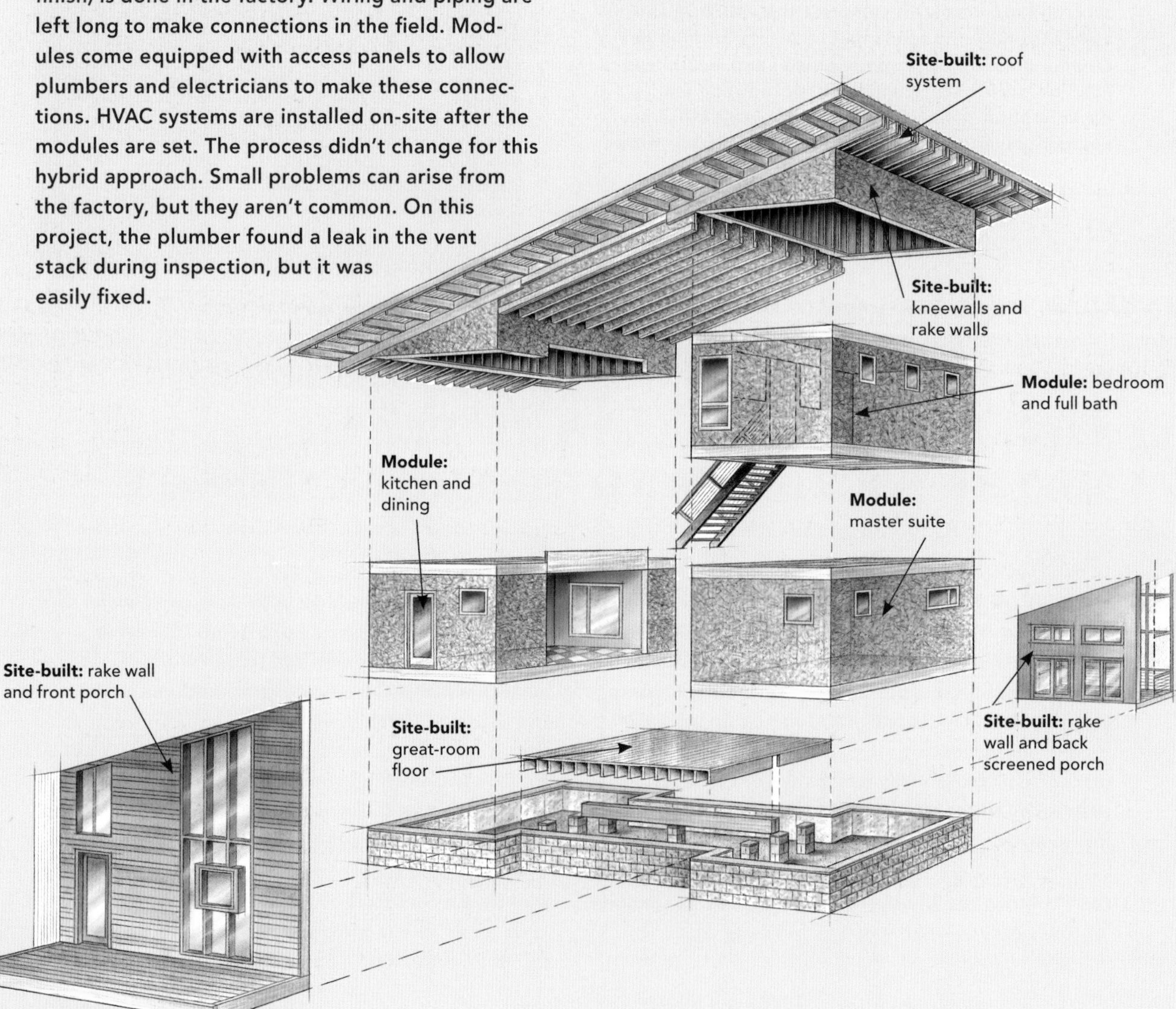

Designing for Privacy and Views

BY GREG WIEDEMANN

My firm's client Joan owned a small 70-year-old cottage in Bethesda, Md., that was slowly deteriorating. Although the suburban lot was narrow, toward the back it had great views to the northwest of the parkland that runs along the Potomac River. The view to the northeast, however, was not as pastoral. Joan's neighbor had built the tallest house in the area, and Joan felt overshadowed.

At first, our discussions centered on the idea of remodeling the existing house, but the more we talked, the clearer it became that it would be easier just to start over. The new house would take advantage of the parkland views and would use a two-story bedroom wing as a privacy screen for a secluded backyard (see the photo at right).

Joan's requirements for the house were modest: In addition to the requisite living spaces, she requested two bedrooms and a ground-floor office that could be converted to a bedroom in the future. The kitchen and the dining and living rooms could be combined in a single space. The only extravagances would be an in-ground pool, an outdoor shower, and a one-car garage. By Washington D.C., standards, the 2,100-sq.-ft. design was small.

FACING THE STREET WITH A POKER FACE. Fewer windows on the front (above, taken at A on floor plan) maintain the owner's privacy. In back, however, the house opens to a leafy yard with a pool and views beyond (see the photo on p. 138).

Selective views determine the shape of the house

The T-shaped plan combines a two-story bedroom wing with a one-story great room that contains the kitchen and living room. An entry hall stitches the two wings together and provides a connection from the entry to the rear terrace.

A T-SHAPED PLAN SHELTERS THE YARD

Built on a narrow lot with neighboring houses on both sides within a stone's throw, the house is oriented across the lot's width to create a secluded backyard. The floor plan is a T-configuration built of a main structure joined at right angles by the entry hall. The first-floor office can be easily converted into a bedroom suite. In the bedroom wing, the master bedroom and office suite occupy the rear of the house, where the views and privacy are best.

SPECS

- Bedrooms: 2, plus office
- Bathrooms: 3½
- Size: 2,100 sq. ft.
- Cost: $225 per sq. ft.
- Completed: 2006
- Location: Bethesda, Md.
- Architect: Wiedemann Architects; Greg Wiedemann, design principal; Felix L. Gonzalez, project architect
- Builder: GN Contracting, Arlington, Va.

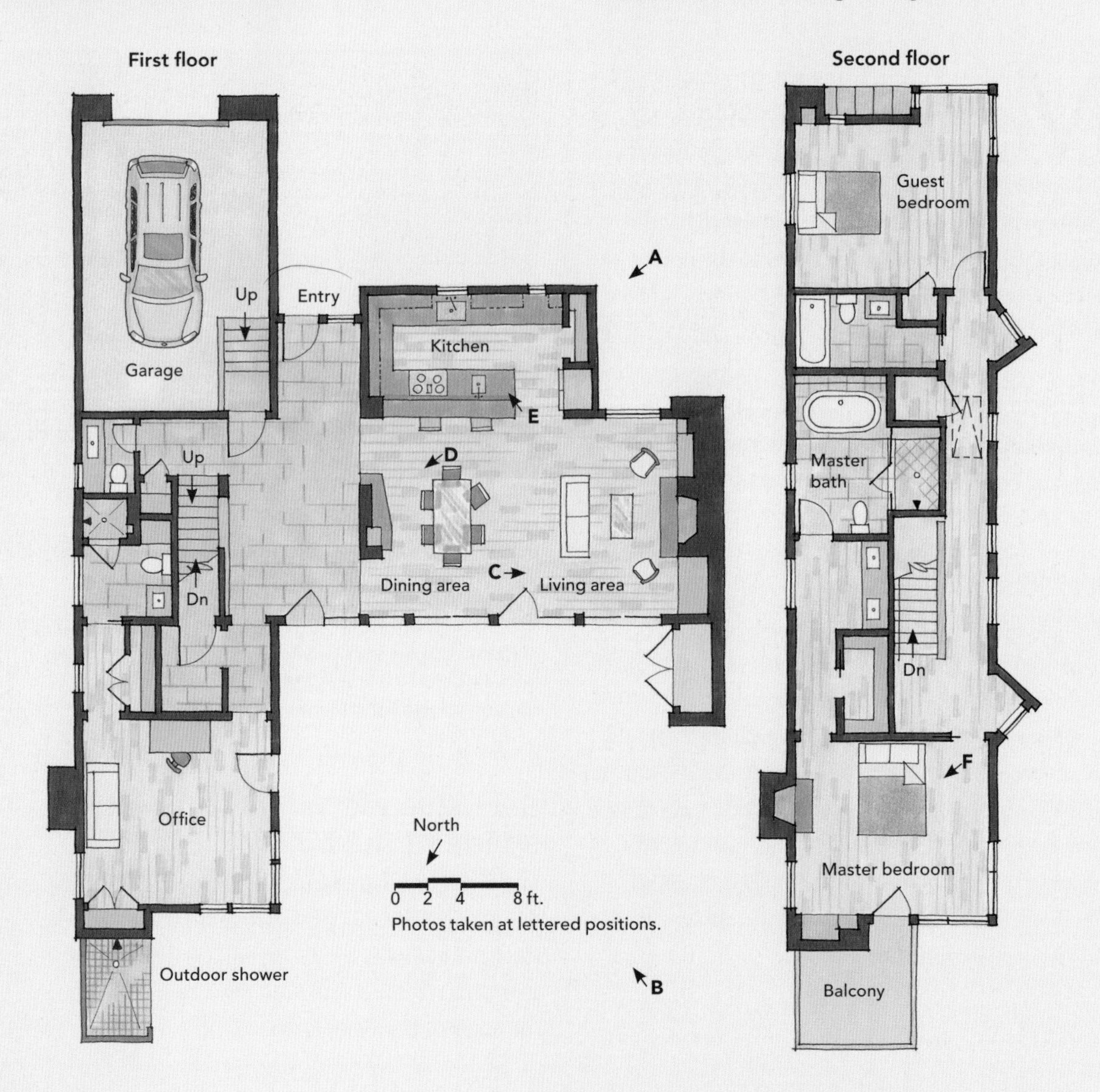

Photos taken at lettered positions.

OPEN TO THE INSIDE. Located on the street side of the house, the galley kitchen's windows are small for privacy's sake. A breakfast counter separates the kitchen from the dining area but maintains the sense of open space. Photo taken at E on floor plan.

RESPITE WITH A VIEW. The master bedroom takes advantage of its position at the rear of the house with a big window and an open balcony that overlook the pool. A gas fireplace adds to the comfort level. Photo taken at F on floor plan.

GEOMETRY AT WORK. In a house that's all about volume and space, the fireplace and bookcases showcase the designer's work in black granite and maple (above). Photo taken at C on floor plan. Dividing the entry hall and dining area, a freestanding unit maintains the open quality of the living area (facing page). Photos taken at C and D on floor plan.

BACKYARD SECLUSION. In a dense neighborhood, the house is oriented across the lot's width to embrace a secluded outdoor space. Photo taken at B on floor plan.

Screened by trees, shrubs, and the bedroom wing, the backyard and the pool terrace are private. The office and all the main living spaces open directly onto the terrace, providing a sense of seclusion and expansive views, despite the small lot size. The second-floor master bedroom and its balcony overlook the pool as well.

Strategic windows promote privacy

The living room's glass wall opens to views of the pool and backyard. On the opposite wall, the lack of large kitchen windows creates privacy from the street. Although shielded by the kitchen, the living/dining room is day-lit by the encircling band of clerestory windows. Awning windows placed on the east side admit natural light, but are high enough on the wall to block the views of the neighbor next door. Corner windows and projecting bays on the second floor are oriented toward the backyard and the more distant views downhill.

The plan combines home and office with a flexible future

Our goal was to design the home office to be converted into a bedroom when climbing stairs became a challenge for the homeowner. The office is at the end of the front entry hall and opens directly onto the rear bluestone terrace. The office bathroom and all of the doorways on the first floor are wheelchair-accessible.

The T-shaped plan can be expanded readily. A second floor could be added over the living area and have a direct connection to the existing second-floor corridor and main stair. It would be a relatively easy way to create an additional bedroom and bathroom while preserving the outdoor spaces and most of the clerestory windows.

Making the most of materials

We wanted to use materials in the house that made some connection to the site, at least in terms of color and texture. We mixed brick, clear-finished mahogany siding, and lead-coated copper on the exterior. Facing the street, the terraced stairs and the lower part of the exterior are covered with dark manganese brick, creating a base that is unified in color and texture.

The clear finish on the Canberra mahogany tongue-and-groove siding brings out its warm color, which fits nicely with the surrounding foliage. Lead-coated copper squares soldered together on the projecting bays and the rear second-floor terrace provide a different geometric scale to the house and an additional color and texture to the exterior.

On the interior, we picked bluestone for the entry-hall floor. It's the same stone we used for the front walk and back terrace and makes a continuous pathway from front to back. The remainder of the first floor is covered in stained white oak, while the second floor is clear maple.

Designed for the Coast

BY GORDON A. NICHOLSON

New Village is a small development in Mount Pleasant, S.C., just across the Cooper River from Charleston in what's known as the Lowcountry. Unlike most new developments in the area that use design guidelines based on architectural style, New Village is focused on building performance: energy efficiency, thoughtful siting, and sustainability.

Most locals cherish the Lowcountry for its scenic coastal landscapes and its majestic historic homes. However, the region poses technical and aesthetic challenges for architects and builders, who have to design and construct homes in an area prone to hurricanes, earthquakes, floods, corrosive ocean air, and intense sun. When developer Pat Ilderton approached me to design a house in New Village, I welcomed the challenges and took the opportunity to try some new things, but I drew my inspiration from a traditional house form, the Charleston single.

THIS BOLD TAKE on a traditional Southern style incorporates sustainability and storm resistance into a new neighborhood home. Photo taken at A on floor plan.

A narrow floor plan promotes natural lighting and ventilation

I've always had an affection for the simplicity of Charleston's single houses. These long, narrow one-room-wide homes have undeniably great proportions, and they make ideal use of their typically narrow building lots. In New Village, I was working with a lot that was less than 50 ft. wide. The floor plan of a single house seemed to be perfect for making the most of the abundant sunlight and the gentle onshore breezes.

INSPIRED BY THE CHARLESTON SINGLE

THE CHARLESTON SINGLE, a popular architectural style during the 1800s, made efficient use of narrow building lots. The design was economical at a time when taxes were assessed based on a home's street frontage. Pushed all the way to one side of the lot, a typical single makes room for two-story, side-loaded porches that encourage outdoor living. With few interior walls and lots of doors and windows, the Charleston single promotes natural lighting and cooling cross ventilation, important in a hot, humid climate. Photo below taken at B on floor plan.

SPECS

- Bedrooms: 3
- Bathrooms: 3
- Size: 2,186 sq. ft.
- Cost: $200 per sq. ft.
- Completed: 2005
- Location: Mount Pleasant, S.C.
- Architect: Gordon A. Nicholson Architect, LLC
- Builder: Ilderton Contractors

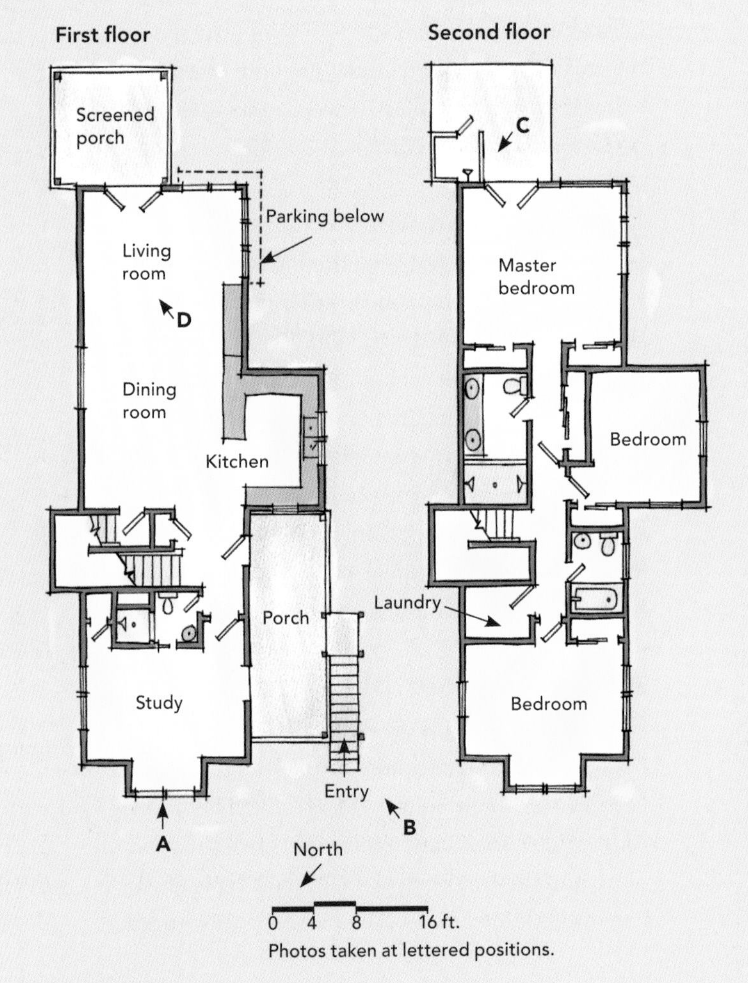

OUTDOOR REFRESHMENT AND INDOOR BREEZES. In the South, outdoor living spaces are a must. An alfresco shower (above right) is just steps away from the master bedroom. Inside, casement windows on the south- and west-facing walls catch the ocean breeze; a ceiling fan and awning windows on the east-facing walls keep cool air flowing (above left). Photos taken at C and D on floor plan.

Near the coast, the sunlight is bright and clear as it reflects off the water. To minimize dependence on artificial lighting, I designed the house to take advantage of natural daylighting. However, natural light can produce uncomfortable heat gain, so it was important to control where and how much light enters the house.

On the first floor, the entry-porch roof shades the foyer, the study, and the kitchen windows. Although these rooms don't get direct sun, they still are well lit on clear days without the help of artificial lighting. On the back of the house, a sunscreen hovers over the first-floor windows, marginalizing strong summer sun while permitting ample light deep into the open living and dining area. On the second floor, roof overhangs shield the bedroom windows from high summer sun but welcome lower rays during the winter.

Designing a one-room-wide house also allowed me to harness ocean breezes for natural cooling and ventilation. Each room has windows on at least two walls, so cross ventilation is easy to obtain. I selected casement windows for the south- and west-facing walls because they permit the homeowner to change the angle of individual window sashes and channel breezes into the house. Working with the ceiling fans, high awning windows on the east-facing walls keep the breeze flowing through the house.

Of course, the space that takes the best advantage of fresh ocean air is the two-story porch in the back. The lower porch is shaded and screened, while the upper porch is an open, sunny roof deck, complete with an outdoor shower just outside the master bedroom.

This single is 9 ft. off the ground

In the Lowcountry, strong storms and flooding are a serious threat, so builders and architects have to deal with strict codes that are meant to keep homes safe. The elevation of projected floodwaters in designated flood zones is used to determine the appropriate height of a home's first floor. Flood-zone requirements in coastal South Carolina usually place the first floor 5 ft. to 6 ft. above the ground. Building codes, however, allow 200 sq. ft. under the house to be used for purposes other than living space, so most homeowners opt to raise the floor to 8 ft. or 9 ft. and include parking and storage space below the house.

The most common foundations used to raise a house are driven wood piles or concrete-block piers built on concrete footings at least 18 in. below grade. Before construction begins, a soil engineer recommends the best choice based on a soil test. We used steel-reinforced concrete-block piers, which can be built quickly with little disturbance to the site or the neighborhood. Driven wood piles also can be installed quickly, but the pile driver is loud, and the finished piles are not always as accurate as block piers.

The design challenge of a raised foundation is making the solid portions of the house relate to the ground through the column structure. Painting the piers black and wrapping their perimeter in horizontal 1×6 lattice helped disguise the structural bays beneath the house. By matching the size of the lattice boards to the exposure of the siding and painting them the same color, the lattice has visual weight and substance.

To withstand hurricane-force winds, the entire house from the footings to the roof rafters is tied together with a series of straps and ties forming a continuous load path (see the drawings on the facing page). To create a strong shear wall, to prevent the plywood edges from buckling, and to deflect airborne debris that penetrates most easily at sheathing seams, solid blocking is installed behind all joints in the sheathing, which also requires strict nailing patterns. Corners are important for shear strength; for this reason, I avoid windows or other openings too close to the corners.

A commonsense approach to durability and energy efficiency

Sustainable homes get a reputation for being expensive or impractical when they focus solely on green products and the latest technology. For this house, I made simple, commonsense choices that boost energy efficiency and provide durability in a demanding climate.

The fiber-cement siding (James Hardie® Building Products; www.jameshardie.com) is accented with sections of corrugated-metal siding and a corrugated-metal frieze. Both are durable in a coastal climate and require less frequent maintenance than other options. Silver 5Y-crimped Galvalume® roofing (www.galvalume.com) helps keep the house cool by reflecting sunlight. Metal roofs are sustainable because of their largely recycled content and ultimate recyclability. Moreover, a metal roof has strong historical associations with architectural vernacular in the Lowcountry.

Beneath both the siding and the roofing is radiant-barrier sheathing: plywood with a thin layer of foil on one side. On the roof, the foil faces down and acts as a low-e coating, keeping heat out of the attic. On the walls, it faces out to reflect radiant heat. The ability to block radiant heat is important on the roof, which gets direct sunlight for most of the day. This low-cost assembly is effective at reducing heat gain.

Stability is a critical consideration for framing material. High humidity and the slow drying time on the coast can make movement in framing lumber a serious problem. The framers used engineered lumber and composite-decking materials that remain stable over the life span of the house.

Other high-performance aspects of this project include tankless water heaters, dual-flush toilets, compact fluorescent-light fixtures, high SEER-rated (seasonal energy efficiency ratio) HVAC equipment, low-e windows, and a pervious driveway. These simple choices can make a big difference in water and energy consumption. The dual-flush toilets, for example, save about 33% of toilet-water use.

With a traditional side porch and a central stairwell for a clear sense of entry, a strong gable and deep overhangs for shading and shelter, and a bold but judicious use of modern materials, this house is a translation of an old form into something new. To me, the most satisfying aspect of this project is that by measure of recent heating and cooling bills, the operating costs of the house are well below average. In this way, the house embraces the spirit of living in the Lowcountry, one that not only respects traditions but celebrates the landscape they are built on.

STRAPS AND TIES CONNECT THE HOUSE FROM ROOF RAFTERS TO FOOTINGS

High winds can damage a house easily due to uplift, shear pressure, and airborne debris. To prevent uplift and racking, stacked framing members form a continuous load path from roof to footings. All the framing (2×4s, 12 in. on center) is strengthened with straps, ties, and continuous sheathing. Solid blocking strengthens sheathing joints and deflects flying debris.

CONNECTORS STRENGTHEN FRAMING
Simpson Strong-Tie® makes galvanized-steel connectors that stand up to the elements and strengthen the house's framing connections. For a look at all of Simpson's products, visit www.strongtie.com.

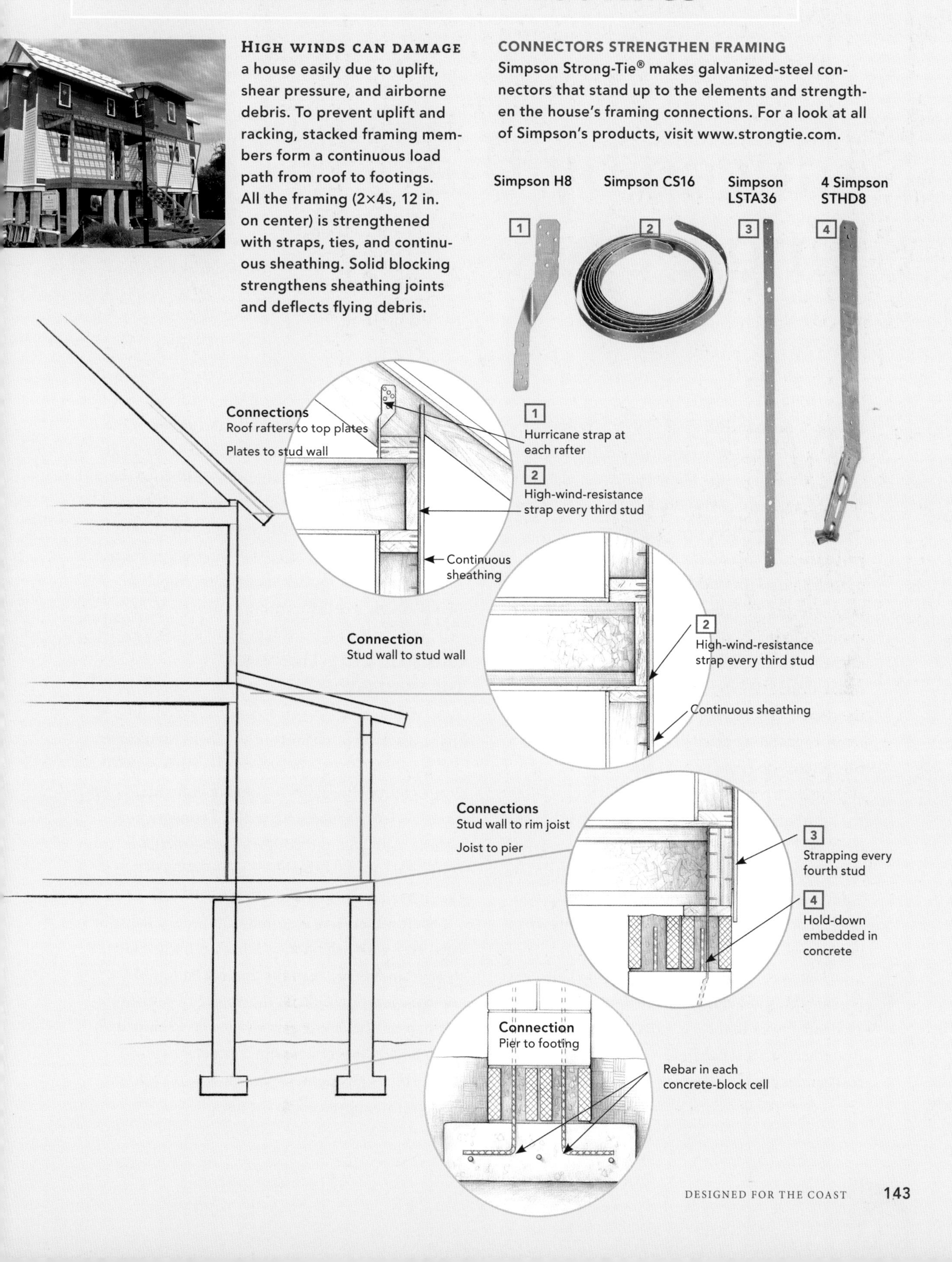

Seduced by the Shingle Style

BY ARLETA CHANG

When the Whalens bought lakefront property in Wisconsin, they didn't intend to build a new house but to remodel the small, simple cottage that occupied the site. Part of the planned remodel was nuts and bolts: fixing a moisture problem and strengthening some inadequate framing. The kitchen needed an overhaul, too, but the rest of the remodel would have been an effort to make the place cozier with trim details, paneling, and some built-ins here and there.

Before long, however, builder Rick Mueller uncovered a widespread mold problem that would require rebuilding much of the structure. At Rick's suggestion, the homeowners agreed that the old cottage wasn't worth saving, and we went back to the drawing board with a new shingle-style house in mind. The Whalens' choice of the shingle style fit the lakeside location perfectly. Born from Queen Anne Victorians, the shingle style is dramatic and bold on the outside, comfy and casual within. It's a designer's dream.

Of course, this project wasn't without challenges. For one thing, the shingle style originated in New England; I work in the Bay Area, a stone's throw from the Whalens' full-time residence; and this cottage was built in between—in Madison, Wis., on a narrow lot (see the photo on the facing page). The first question people always ask is "What was it like to design a house from so far away?" Although the cottage is filled with exacting details, the construction process was remarkably smooth (see "Communication is the Key . . ." on p. 149). In fact, this house might be the only project our firm has completed that is exactly like the working drawings.

Maintaining the view for everyone

Lake Mendota Drive is an established neighborhood tightly packed with a mix of permanent residences and vacation homes. The houses vary from early-20th-century bungalows to contemporary mansions along a street popular with walkers, runners, and cyclists. Although the shingle style captured the spirit of the neighborhood, we still needed to find the right size, scale, and location for the house.

Lakefront setbacks required that the new house be sited even with neighboring homes, pulling it farther away from the lake than the original house. Although a location right on the water can be exciting, pulling back the house gave us the opportunity to add a large stone terrace with a great lake view. The terrace offers an outdoor space close to the kitchen and is only a short walk to the dock.

THE NEW COTTAGE makes the most of a narrow lakeside loft with charming details outside (and comfy nooks within). Photo taken at A on floor plan.

Luckily, the homeowners didn't want a large house. The site is small and particularly narrow. Because it sits above the lake, we didn't need to use height to capture views. Instead, we used the full 36-ft. buildable width of the lot. This approach saved plenty of space for gardens and landscaping, and the house's low walls and roof massing allow passersby on the street to enjoy a lake view across the property.

Simple shapes with curvy accents

A descendant of Queen Anne Victorians, the shingle style also borrows details from a few early-American architectural styles. Shingle-style houses frequently share an asymmetrical exterior with a blend of strong, crisp geometric shapes contrasted against playfully exaggerated curved details. The

(Continued on p. 148)

DESIGNED FOR LAKESIDE LIVING. To keep a low profile from the street, the house consumes the full buildable width of the lot. A raised terrace offers a place to relax outside, and lots of windows reel in lake views. Photo taken at B on floor plan.

THERE'S MORE TO THE SHINGLE STYLE THAN JUST SHINGLES

In the late 1800s, formal, colorful Queen Anne Victorians were all the rage. While the shingle style might be the Queen Anne's casual cousin, don't be fooled by the modesty that cedar shingles create. This house has its own set of intricate, charming details.

ARCHED BUTTRESSES support a large second-story overhang. The rear entry beyond is bumped out from the wall and is cloaked with windows to gather light and lake views.

EYEBROW DORMERS are always charming, but their shape goes particularly well with a shingle-style house. Notice the contrast between the dormer's sweeping curve and the crisp eave lines.

ROLLING SHINGLED CORNERS at a recessed second-story window keep the shingles flowing with a soft transition from wall to window.

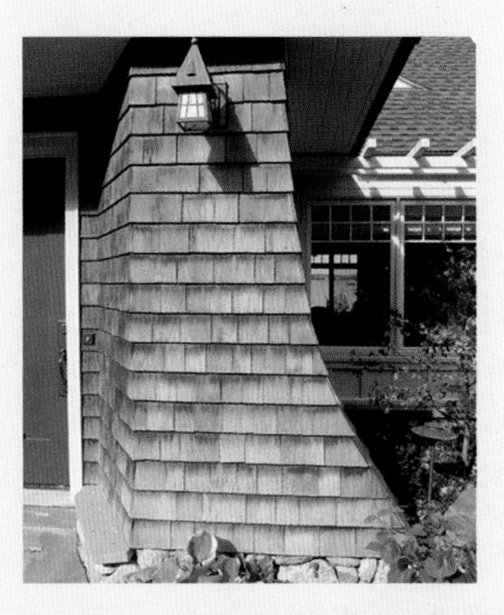

SWEEPING BUTTRESSES accentuate the corners of the first-floor sidewalls. Below, a fieldstone foundation grounds the house to the site.

Built-in gutters maintain a razor-sharp eave

The rain gutters are built into the roof, eliminating the need for a fascia and keeping the eave line sharp. To execute this detail, the builder terminated the rafters with a plumb cut in line with the sidewall and fashioned a rafter tail from four pieces of glued-up ¾-in. plywood. The outside pieces of plywood extend up the rafter and are glued and nailed for strength. A trough cut into the plywood rafter tail is sheathed with ACX plywood and covered with a peel-and-stick roofing membrane. A seamless copper sheet lines the gutter and extends to the eave edge.

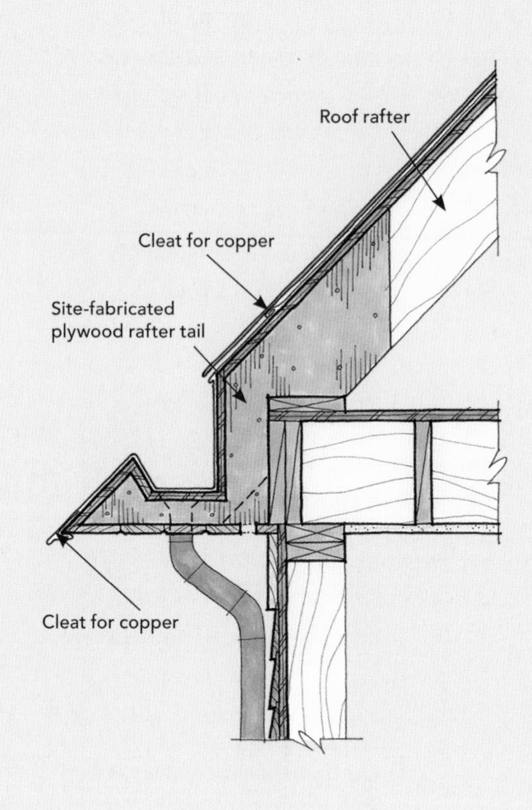

Lake Mendota cottage has all these elements on the street-front elevation, where a single, dominant gable springs from walls that curve outward as they meet the ground. The big arched window is echoed by an eyebrow dormer in the roof, and the sidewall shingles curve inward to meet the vertical jambs of the upstairs window. Built-in gutters maintain unobstructed triangular eaves (see the sidebar above).

Unlike the front entry, which is inset, the back entry projects outward and is wrapped with sidelites and transom windows, topped by a double-gable dormer that overlooks the lake. The texture of the cottage's weathered wood shingles has a quiet and natural effect, while the stone terrace, chimney, and foundation walls ground the house to its sloping site.

Multiple levels of cozy spaces

Varied ceiling heights often are used to create a sense of both intimacy and expansiveness in a house. On a sloped site like this one, varied floor levels are a natural alternative. Keeping the mudroom and the landing inside the front entrance at grade level with a low ceiling creates a dramatic effect as you step down into the living areas. Not only are the lake views brought to life with the appearance of the horizon, but suddenly, the small house also feels open and spacious.

To support a modern lifestyle, the kitchen and the dining and living rooms are open to one another (see the floor plans on p. 150). Instead of creating one open room, though, we defined each space with large cased openings. Box-beam ceilings in the living and dining rooms further distinguish these more formal spaces (see the top photo on p. 151).

Each room in the house has its own personality, defined with color, built-ins, and detailed trim. Different nooks and alcoves create layers of intimate spaces within each room. The living room, for instance, steps up to a sunny inglenook lined with built-in daybeds, which in turn steps up to a window bay. A built-in bench near the front door makes a window seat in the mudroom; recessed bookshelves create yet another alcove nearby.

Because the rafters spring from the first-floor walls, the second-story bedrooms and bathrooms are tucked under the roof. Dormers bring sunlight and views to the second floor and create charming nooks for desks, closets, and more built-ins.

Although a vacation home can offer some luxury in design, that wasn't a conscious part of this project. Charming details and cozy spaces are inherent to the shingle style, and I think a family would be happy to live full-time in this compact home.

COMMUNICATION IS THE KEY TO A HEALTHY LONG-DISTANCE RELATIONSHIP AMONG ARCHITECT, BUILDER, AND HOMEOWNER

Architects frequently work on long-distance projects, but such projects can present challenges. We traveled to this site only once before the project began, when we still intended to remodel an existing cottage.

Knowing that we wouldn't be on site to answer questions for the builder, Rick Mueller, we took extra care with the working drawings: We carefully dimensioned each plan and section drawing; we tried to predict questions and placed notes where they would be found easily on the plans; and we illustrated all the fussy areas with large-scale details. The roof was a big challenge because a deviation of 1 in. in plan meant a deviation of 1 in. in height; a small error could cause a second-story bathroom to miss code minimums. So we included written guidelines that described the framing sequence for each roof section.

To keep communication open and easy, Rick's son set up a Web site to host construction and material photos. Nothing could be clearer for architects, builders, and clients thousands of miles apart than immediate access to photos of the work in progress, followed by conference-call discussions.

You could say this was one of our most accessible job sites; the computer is next to the drawing board and never shuts down. I visited the site for the second time after construction was completed. The house is as close to how we drew it as any other project I've worked on.

FROM COMFY TO COZY TO INTIMATE

Open floor plans are great for keeping people connected, but when the time comes to curl up with a good book or retreat with your thoughts, there's nothing like a comfortable, private space. This house has it all, with a kitchen, a dining room, and a living room that are open to one another, and no shortage of more intimate areas. Upstairs, dormers gain headroom so that three bedrooms, two baths, and a large laundry closet all fit under the cottage's roof.

SPECS

- Bedrooms: 3
- Bathrooms: 3
- Size: 2,190 sq. ft.
- Cost: N/A
- Completed: 2004
- Location: Madison, Wis.
- Architect: Jarvis Architects
- Builder: Rick Mueller
- Structural design and architectural consultant: Arlan Kay
- Landscape design: Thomas B. Mohoney & Associates

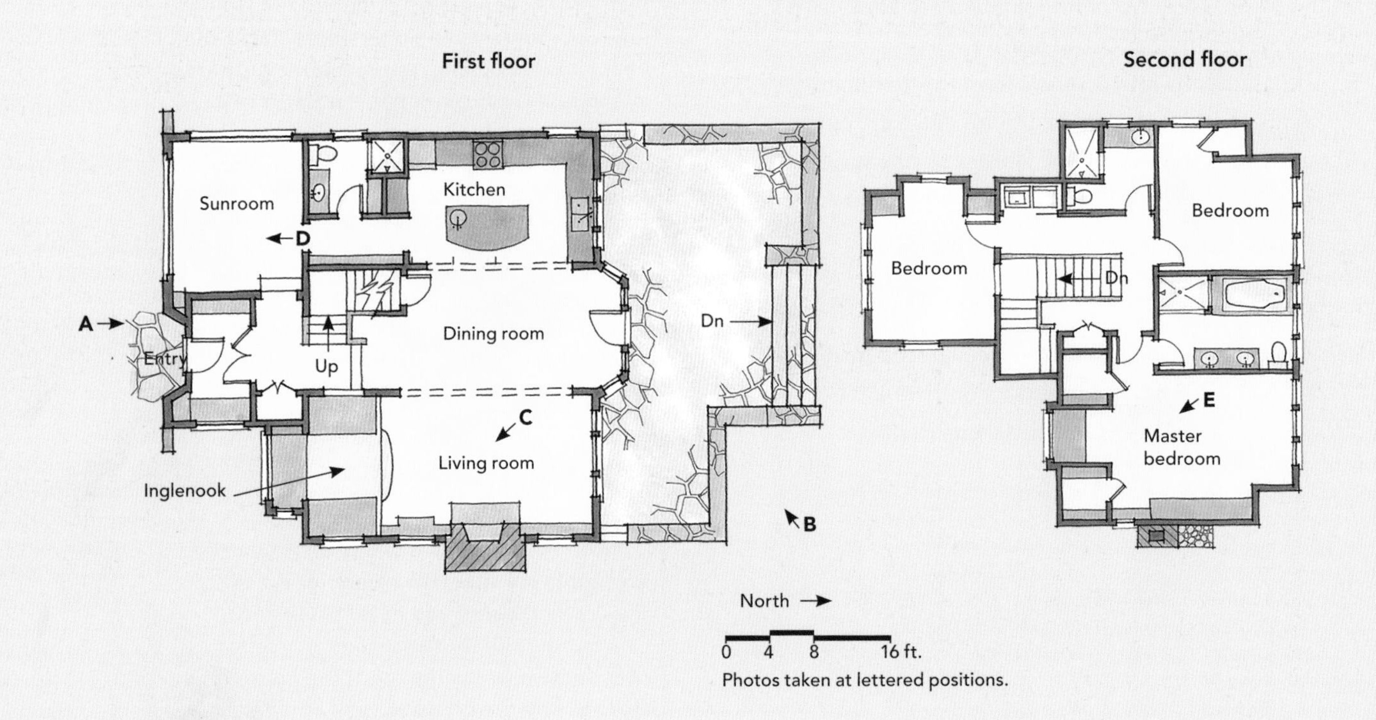

Photos taken at lettered positions.

ABOVE: AN INVITING INGLENOOK AWAITS. Curved brackets shape the opening to a raised alcove bordered with built-in daybeds and finished with a sunlit bay-window seat. Photo taken at C on floor plan.

LEFT: A STRIKING VIEW OF THE GARDENS. A large, arching window has a dramatic effect on the sunroom. The window captures southern exposure and frames a picturesque view of the gardens. Photo taken at D on floor plan.

BELOW LEFT: SUNNY SANCTUARY IN THE MASTER BEDROOM. A built-in dresser, tall wainscot, narrow closet doors, and distinctive windows add character to a small master suite tucked beneath the roof. Photo taken at E on floor plan.

Beauty on the Beach

BY JO LANDEFELD

When the opportunity arose to design a vacation house on the Oregon coast for my family, images of the simple beach cottages we had rented years ago on Fire Island, N.Y., immediately came to mind. Those unwinterized cottages often didn't have drywall covering the framing, and I found it comforting to see what was holding up the roof. I wanted to replicate the simplicity and the outdoor focus of those beach retreats for our vacation house. Although the coastal Oregon climate dictated quite a different approach to weatherizing our house, I always assumed the structure would be entirely exposed.

Steel instead of wood

The structural system I designed consists of heavy timber beams and trusses supporting a ceiling of exposed, rough-sawn fir planking. In a compact house like ours, the spacing of supports and windows has an important impact on the rhythm of the house. Windows fill the spaces between the exposed, rough-sawn posts in the living area and capture the views of the dunes and ocean.

Stronger in tension than wood, steel provides a sleek tension member at the bottom of the trusses in the main living area. Not only is this an interesting twist on basic wood-truss design, but it also allows the space to flow up to the peak without a heavy wood bottom chord on the truss. The steel pieces are a combination of standard eyebolts and turnbuckles welded to ½-in.-dia. and ¾-in.-dia. threaded steel rods and ¼-in.-thick steel plates.

Steel was used in a less obvious way to connect the wood members of the framing. In true timber-framing, intricate joints are made in the end of each beam, and the pieces then are slid together and pegged. Steel brackets and bolts were less time intensive, and although the brackets had to be designed and fabricated individually, the cost savings over timber joints was compelling. To design the brackets, the structural engineer determined the minimum bracket and bolt requirements; then

TIMBER FRAME WITH A MODERN TOUCH. The steel connectors are the defining design element of the large living space and cost less than wood joinery. The rough-sawn framing serves double-duty as window trim. The windows butt directly against the exposed 4×6 posts; a simple piece of 1×2 fir trim covers the joint. Photo above taken at A on floor plan; photo on facing page taken at B.

I adjusted the shape or increased the size to improve the aesthetics.

Spending money where it counts

We wanted a simple but wonderful cottage by the sea that we could share with family and friends. The exposed structure creates that special place but is more expensive than standard framing. To offset the cost, we chose durable, economical finishes. I believe the success of the house shows that the floor plan and the shape of the rooms were more important than expensive finishes.

We chose to have a large living space but made the bedrooms and bathrooms rather small. There are no giant Jacuzzi® tubs in the bathrooms; all the plumbing fixtures are modest and occupy minimal space. The house feels big because the windows incorporate the views to open up the space and the decks expand the living area.

We will own this house forever, so we tried to design for timelessness. Rather than choose trendy colors, we worked with a color palette selected from the hues of the site. The endless shades of green and blue outside the windows are repeated inside the house.

Most of the flooring in the house is wood-colored linoleum. We used more expensive slate in the entry for its weather-resistance and in a small strip along the hallway to reinforce the L-shaped floor plan.

The kitchen's stock cabinets and plastic-laminate countertops also are economical choices. The guest-friendly open shelving not only costs less but also makes it easy to find a plate or a glass.

In the end, the combination of my love of structure and a desire for simplicity, durability, and economy helped me create a unique house in an amazingly scenic spot where family and friends can enjoy the beauty of the natural environment.

A WEEKEND RETREAT SHOULDN'T BE HIGH-MAINTENANCE

We built this vacation house to relax in, not to create work for ourselves. That's why we chose to use durable, low-maintenance exterior materials.

Before moving to Oregon, I designed a house on Martha's Vineyard, where I saw 100-year-old homes with their original cedar shingles. Their longevity influenced my decision to use cedar shingles for the exterior siding of our cottage. Sometimes, though, aesthetic considerations outweighed the practical. The cedar trim at the windows and fascia is stained and will need to be maintained (photo taken at D on floor plan). But the house needed some color to contrast the natural shingles and the no-maintenance vinyl windows. These windows are inexpensive and come with a lifetime warranty.

For the roof, I chose a composite, polymer-modified fiber-cement shingle that looks like slate. On the decks, Trex® synthetic decking is combined with copper-tubing balusters for low maintenance.

To stand up to the corrosive salt air, all the exterior light fixtures are made of natural brass, and the exterior hardware is made of stainless steel. Photo taken at D on floor plan.

SITING AND SCALE CREATE THE PERFECT BEACH HOUSE

The low profile of this house lets it blend into the landscape, and because prime space is dedicated to public rooms with expanses of glass, the interior feels larger than it really is. To combat Oregon's harsh coastal environment, the house's L-shape creates a microclimate in the courtyard on the sunny south side that is protected from the prevailing winds.

SPECS

- Bedrooms: 2, plus media room and library as guest rooms
- Bathrooms: 3
- Size: 2,200 sq. ft.
- Cost: N/A
- Completed: 2001
- Location: Neskowin, Ore.
- Architect: Jo Landefeld
- Builder: Blue Mountain Contractors Inc.; John Manca, Randy Wilson
- Structural engineer: Stricker Engineering; Andy Stricker

LIGHTING FOR DAY, NIGHT, AND STORMY WEATHER. The soffit running through the kitchen, dining, and living areas has fluorescent strip lights on top that create general lighting on gray days and dramatic lighting at night when they set the wood ceiling aglow. The soffit's downlights combine with pendants in the kitchen to highlight task areas. Multiple interior-lighting sources also define activity spaces within the open living area. Photo taken at C on floor plan.

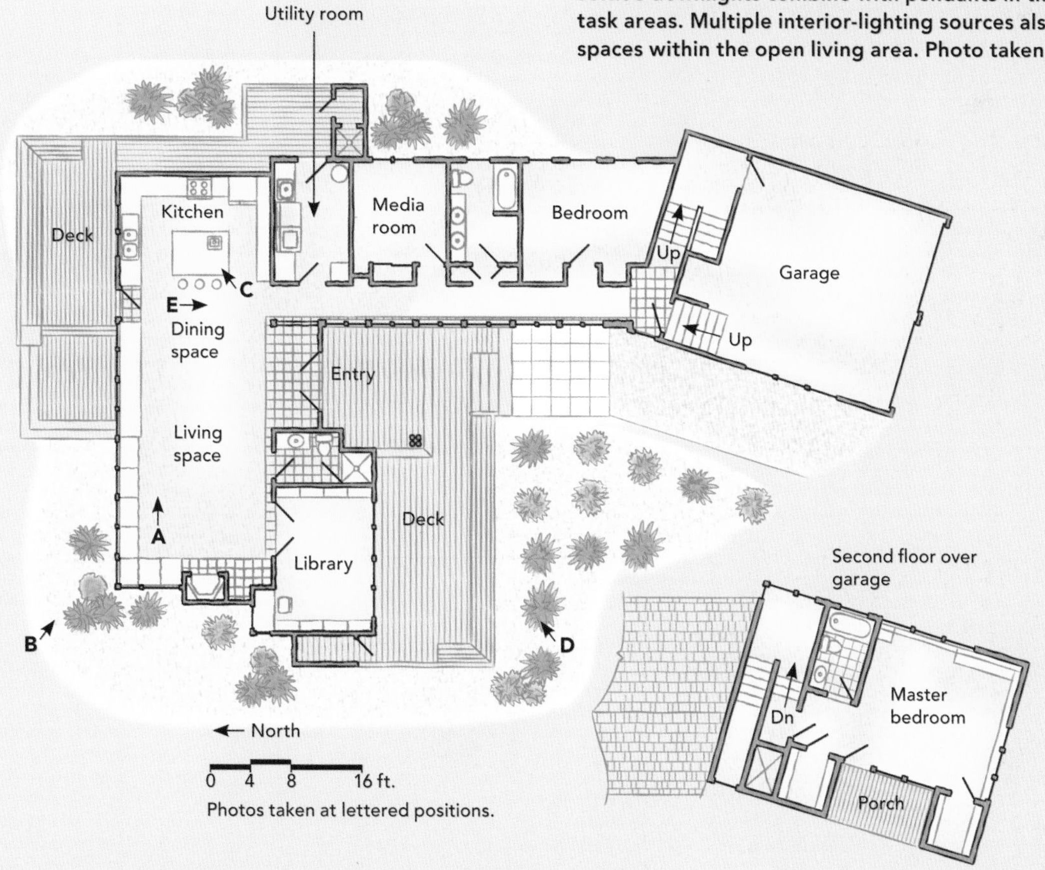

Photos taken at lettered positions.

STRUCTURAL NECESSITY BECOMES DESIGN OPPORTUNITY

The engineer required a shear wall in the entry, where the architect had hoped for a half-wall closet. The solution was steel cross-bracing of threaded rod and turnbuckles that echoes the truss's bottom chord. The steel design elements repeat through the main living areas and support the 24-in.-deep soffit and the 4×8 mantel. All the steel components are fabricated from stock parts. Photo at left taken at E on floor plan.

A Rustic Design for a Rugged Climate

BY MARTIN MCBIRNEY

In 1992, having had my fill of California, I moved to Sandpoint, a scenic town of 5,000 near the top of the Idaho panhandle. Using the proceeds from the sale of my California property, I immediately built a large contemporary home with dramatic views overlooking the Cabinet Mountains and Lake Pend Oreille. Unfortunately, while searching (like so many others) for a simpler, less hectic life, I unwittingly built a home that precisely reflected the sensibilities I had wanted to leave behind.

As luck would have it, I met and married a woman raised in the area, and over the first few years of our marriage, I gained a great appreciation for her tastes and scaled-down sense of proportion. In 1998, we accepted an offer on our house, which allowed us to design and build a home much more in keeping with the area and our simple lifestyle.

We worked with the same architect and builder responsible for our first house because the two were perfect for the job. The architect, who shared our vision of a compact and natural home, has a great feel for artistic, inviting spaces. The builder is a meticulous craftsman who works for the most part by himself and welcomes client participation. Together, we spent the better part of a year designing our new house.

Rugged and well insulated from top to bottom

Northern Idaho's climate is hard on houses, largely because the winters are not cold enough. Often, winter days hover at 32°F, creating annoying freeze/thaw cycles that can result in moisture problems. Having dealt with these issues in our previous house, I wanted our new house to be a building that would live up to the challenge. We chose to build the house's exterior walls using an insulating concrete form (ICF) system known as Rastra (see "Rastra Panels: Lightweight, High-Strength Building Blocks" on p. 159).

We liked the high insulation properties that Rastra offered and its impressive 4-hour fire rating (important for a rural home in the woods). The rough surface of the blocks allowed us to apply the interior and exterior plaster finish without any mesh. The blocks also have ecological value; they are made mostly of recycled polystyrene foam that otherwise would have ended up in a landfill.

Of the various available sizes, we chose 12-in.-thick Rastra blocks because of their increased insulation values and the resulting deep windowsills.

For the roof, we opted for the sturdy construction of structural insulated panels (SIPs), which are made by sandwiching foam insulation between two sheets

STRONG BONES. Energy-efficient Rastra walls, a type of insulating concrete form, provide a strong, fire-resistant framework for this mountain overlook. Photo taken at A on floor plan.

of oriented strand board (OSB). The 12-in.-thick SIPs were manufactured to our dimensions (thus reducing construction waste) by a local manufacturer, then shipped directly to our site. A crane lifted the panels into position so that crew members could screw them to the rafters.

Connected, multiuse spaces make up the floor plan

Taking cues from Sarah Susanka's first book, *The Not So Big House* (The Taunton Press, 1998), we designed a floor plan to match the way we live. This seemingly obvious concept actually represents a significant departure from most planning processes. Rather than start with a conceptual floor plan, our architect pushed us to think of the ways in which we truly would use each room of the house.

We focused most of our design attention on the activities we thought would occupy most of our time: preparing and eating meals, taking in great views, and relaxing by the fireplace.

The result was an open floor plan that makes it easy to move among kitchen, dining, entry/foyer, and living-room areas (see the floor plans on p. 160). The interior walls that normally separate these spaces are gone, but functional distinctions are still evident, thanks to more subtle devices. For example, the foyer and the living room are separated by the

RASTRA PANELS: LIGHTWEIGHT, HIGH-STRENGTH BUILDING BLOCKS

Rastra is an insulating concrete form (ICF) system that combines 85% post-consumer recycled polystyrene with 15% cement in lightweight building blocks. When stacked, reinforced with rebar, and glued together with foam sealant, Rastra forms provide a framework that then is filled with concrete to create load-bearing walls, shear walls, stemwalls, and other building components. The 5¼-in.-dia. circular channels running vertically and horizontally through each Rastra wall are designed to provide high strength with a relatively small amount of concrete.

Each 15-in.-high Rastra panel is available in 8½-in., 10-in., 12-in., and 14-in. wall thicknesses, with lengths of 7½ ft. and 10 ft. (custom panels are available as well), and can be set in place without the use of cranes. Forms can be cut and tooled with saws, routers, or rasps, then glued or clamped together until the concrete is poured.

Unlike traditional wood and concrete wall systems, Rastra does not hold or wick water, and does not promote mold or mildew growth. Its porous composition is effective at blocking heat and cold (R-values for 12-in.-thick panels range from 26.4 to 31.9) but also allows for a slow interchange of air.

For more information, visit www.rastra.com.

AN OPEN, CASUAL FLOOR PLAN

THIS PLAN MAXIMIZES VIEWS AND OUTDOOR ACCESS, especially in the public spaces, which are open to one another but still defined clearly with ceiling treatments, timber posts, and a freestanding fireplace. Having sacrificed an attached garage in favor of a porch, the owners instead built a small, separate garage (visible at far left in the photo below).

SPECS

- Bedrooms: 2 (plus one unfinished upstairs bedroom)
- Bathrooms: 2 (plus one unfinished upstairs bath)
- Size: 2,250 sq. ft. (1,800 sq. ft. downstairs plus 450 sq. ft. partially finished upstairs)
- Cost: $175 per sq. ft.
- Completed: 1999
- Location: Sandpoint, Idaho
- Architect: Bruce Millard, AIA
- Builder: Mike Murdock

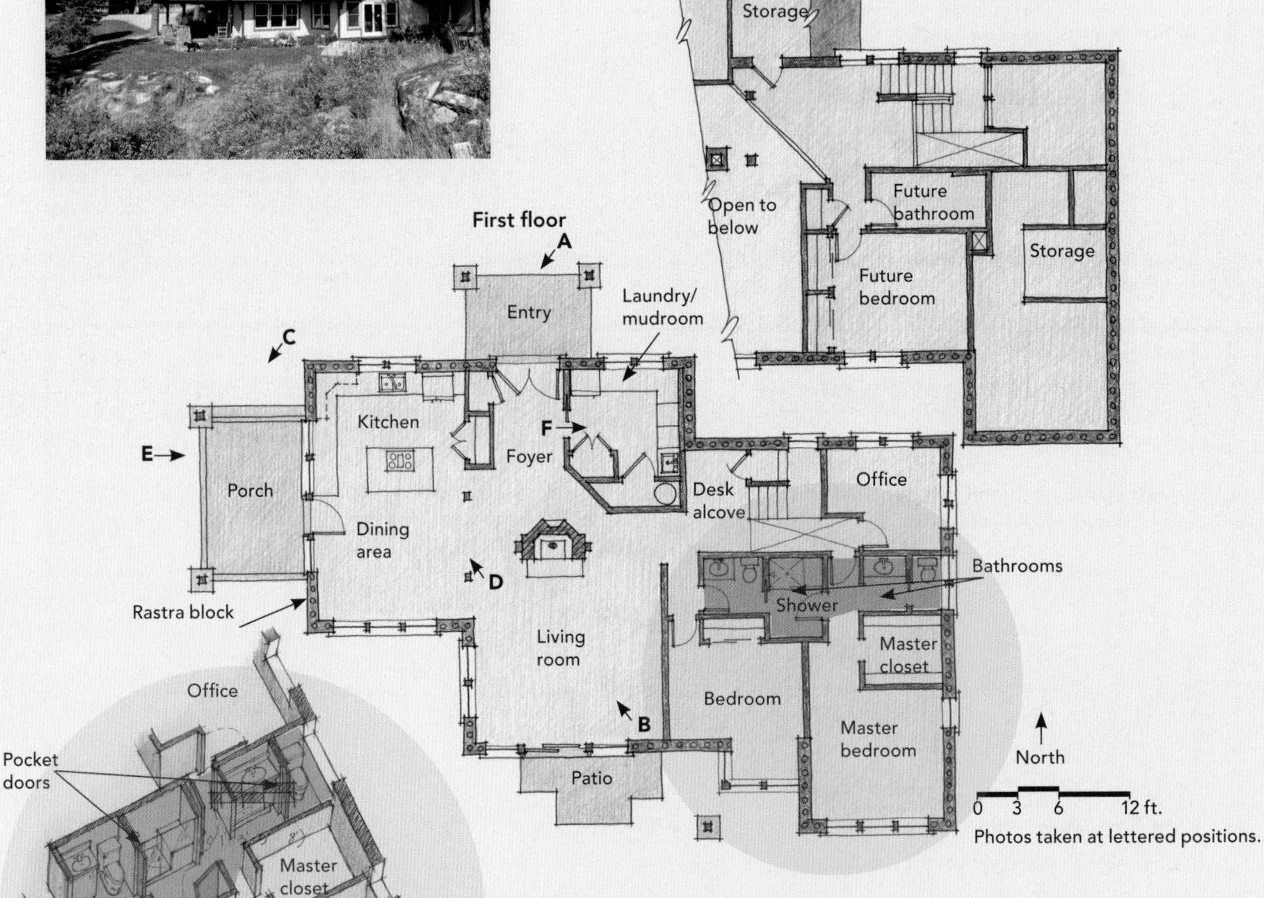

SHARING A SHOWER

Reducing the costs and space typically lavished on bathrooms, two half-baths share a common shower in this plan. One half-bath serves the master bedroom. The other doubles as the daughter's bath and a family powder room. Pocket doors retain privacy and help keep these spaces from feeling congested.

LONG VIEWS AND AN OPEN FLOOR PLAN ALLOW THE FAMILY TO STAY CONNECTED, whether they are reading in the living room, eating in the dining area, or cooking at the stove. Subtle details, like decorative nuts on the mantel, transform functional threaded rods into attractive focal points. Photo taken at B on floor plan.

fireplace and chimney. The kitchen is set apart by a change in ceiling height, as well as by the placement of a few timber posts.

The main floor's open plan does more than create an easy, informal atmosphere indoors. It also makes the most of outdoor views and outdoor connections. Big windows, a patio off the living room, and a porch off the kitchen and dining area (see the bottom left photo on p. 162) enhance our enjoyment of a beautiful site.

The west-facing porch and the amplitude of windows were made possible by our decision to rethink the role of the garage. Both my wife and I find the car a necessary evil and don't like its dominance in life and in much of residential architecture. The current formula, which usually includes a large attached three-car garage, leaves a house that is as much about cars as it is about people.

To counteract auto emphasis, we built a small, detached two-car garage about 150 ft. from the house. In the space where an attached garage would have been, we have large windows and a beautiful porch. Sure, carrying groceries in bad weather sometimes can be trying, but the inviting quality of each room more than makes up for it.

CHOOSING MATERIALS THAT GET BETTER WITH AGE. Soapstone countertops, oiled fir floors, and recycled timbers all contribute to a kitchen that doesn't shy away from the abuse of daily living (above). The adjoining open-air porch is an attractive and relaxing extension off the west side of the house, perfect for watching a sunset (below left and right). Photos taken at C, D, and E on floor plan.

Downplaying the bathroom makes other spaces better

Typical high-end homes have large, lavishly appointed bathrooms that consume valuable exterior-wall space and require no small amount of cleaning. Because most people spend less than 5% of the day in bathing and related activities, why devote so much of the budget and the floor space to bathrooms?

Answering this question led us to plan for a single-shower room between two single-sink bathrooms. This compact "suite" of bathrooms is adjacent to both main-floor bedrooms, so convenience and privacy aren't compromised. The consolidation of the bathrooms freed the floor plan so that most of the other rooms had at least two exterior walls to take advantage of natural lighting and the beautiful surrounding views (see the floor plans,on p. 160).

The decision to forgo a bathtub also had a personal element. Having used a bathtub roughly once a year since childhood, I saw no sense in including one on the main floor. Because my wife and daughter do like to take baths on occasion, we compromised and included one in the second-floor plan, part of a space we will finish sometime in the future.

THE ONE ROOM THAT GOT BIGGER. Upsized from the homeowners' previous house, the laundry/mudroom in this plan grew larger to provide floor space where the family needed it most. Photo taken at F on floor plan.

A house that wears in, not wears out

The reality of everyday living in a northern climate is that many surfaces are bound to take a beating. Cosmetically perfect floors and countertops that look pristine for years are tough to achieve out in the woods.

Our response was to choose soft, natural finishes whose defining characteristics are the lack of such perfection. We opted for oiled fir floors, natural-slate entryways, soapstone countertops, tinted gypsum-plaster walls, and recycled 100-year-old fir columns and beams. In each case, these surfaces become more interesting and beautiful with age, taking on a wonderful patina as they respond to the bumps and grinds of daily living. When a counter gets dinged, a dab of mineral oil restores the color, and it looks as though it has always been that way.

An unfinished second floor helps the house to adapt

Although we designed our house as a story and a half, our goal was single-floor living—at least at the outset. Knowing that there soon would be a time when our daughter would want to be separate from us (and vice versa), we included an upstairs bedroom and bath in the design. With time running out on the builder's schedule (we built at the rate of around 100 sq. ft. per month), we opted to finish the main floor completely and to leave the upstairs unfinished. How soon we choose to finish that room will depend on how fast our daughter grows up. If the pace to date is any indication, we'll probably be addressing the unfinished floor fairly soon.

PART 2

Adding On But Staying Small

Small Addition, Big Improvement

BY LYNN HOPKINS

When most people start thinking about additions to their houses, they think big, and rightfully so. Additions are the most direct route to an extra bedroom or a bigger kitchen. Sometimes, a few small changes can have an equally large impact on a house. In our case, adding only 50 sq. ft. radically changed the little Cape my husband and I bought a few years ago.

We loved the tree-lined, kid-filled neighborhood made up of small "starter" Capes built just after World War II. But our house's front entry was a problem. There was just a door in the wall (see the photo at right), nothing that acknowledged the importance of the front door as a symbol of hospitality. The lack of an overhang or roof meant that we got wet as we fumbled for our keys in rainy weather. Plus, the entry landing was so shallow that we had to back down the steps when we opened the front door.

Once through the door, visitors and family alike walked directly into the center of the living room, where there was no place to hang coats or leave muddy boots, backpacks, briefcases or any other bundles. Because of the constant traffic, the living room was not used much and became more like a hallway with a fireplace. My goal was to solve these problems without ruining the integrity of the house.

BEFORE

Relocating the door was key

I knew that we needed more space for a closet, larger stairs outside and some sort of shelter over the doorway. As I was thinking about these ideas, it occurred to me that the entry location of our house, opening directly into the living room, was something of an anomaly. Most houses have a front entry that opens into a foyer that's centered on the main stairs with the public rooms opening off to either side. This arrangement separates these rooms from the hubbub

EXTENDING A WARM WELCOME. Half hidden by shrubbery, the Cape's old, unsheltered front door had narrow stairs and was difficult to use (see the photo on p. 165). A new covered vestibule and stairs create an inviting, more hospitable entry.

of entrance traffic. My first change, then, was to move the front door approximately 7 ft. to the right, aligning it with the stairs and the passageway from the living room to the kitchen. Most of the foot traffic now circulates across the end of the living room instead of diagonally through it, making the living room a quieter place.

The new entry vestibule I designed measured just 5 ft. deep and 10 ft. wide (see the bottom photo on p. 168). I put a window next to the door that not only lets in light but also lets us see who is at the door. I chose bluestone for the floor because it can tolerate wet and muddy things that will be brought into the house; I used the same stone on the porch landing and steps. I also made sure that there was space for a hall tree with a bench, coat hooks and mirror. (Luckily for me, my father is an avid and willing furnituremaker; he made quite a few of the pieces in the house in addition to the hall tree.) Finally, I made enough space for a closet for coats, hats, and boots.

Relocating the front door made it possible for me to put in a pair of windows where the old door had been (see the top photo on p. 168). This greatly improved the natural light in the living room. The sofa could now be located under the windows, directly across from the fireplace. This in turn made a much better conversational grouping of the rest of the furniture.

The size of the vestibule also fit the scale of the existing house and the rest of the neighborhood. On the gable end, I added a truss that would emphasize the span of the roof. To support the projecting roof, I designed curving brackets that were simple but substantial (see the bottom right photo on p. 169); these brackets also introduce a design theme revisited inside the house.

Historic details lend stylish charm

Like most Capes, my house has double-hung windows with divided lites in a six-over-six configuration. These smaller panes give the house a lovely domestic scale that I could not ignore. Instead of one large window, I put a pair of double-hung windows in the living room, the same size and configuration as the existing windows. The window in the vestibule also has authentic divided lites and panes that are the same proportion as the double hungs.

The siding was also an important consideration. Much to our delight, our builder, Loren French, began the job by ripping off the aluminum siding, replacing it with white-cedar shingles at the appropriate time. White-cedar shingles are usually 16 in. long, 2 in. shorter than red-cedar shingles. Consequently, white cedar needs to be installed with a tighter exposure: 5½ in. compared with 7½ in. for red cedar. I find that this narrower exposure looks better on a small house. Because they are smaller and have not been squared and rebutted, white-cedar shingles are also significantly less expensive than red-cedar shingles and produce a shaggier, more rustic look, which is typical of many historic Capes.

Just because it was small doesn't mean it was cheap—I would love to say that this project was accomplished for peanuts and pass on miraculous money-saving techniques, but I would be lying. The

CHANGING THE FRONT DOOR'S LOCATION MADE THE LIVING ROOM A REST AREA INSTEAD OF A TRAFFIC CIRCLE

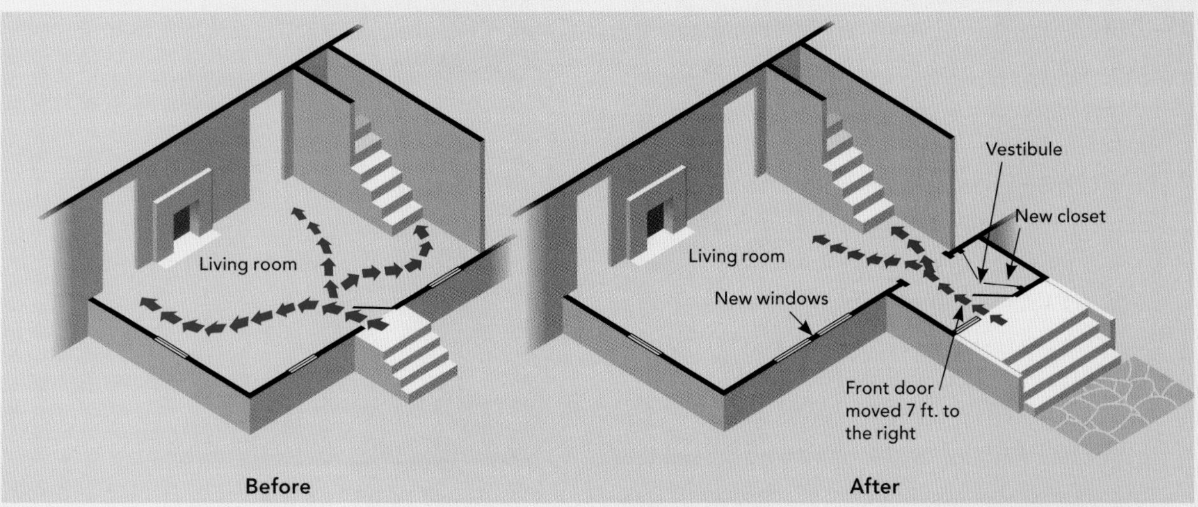

The front door opened directly into the living room, which became nothing more than a large hallway with a fireplace that led to the kitchen.

The new vestibule not only emphasized the location of the front door but also made a place for dropping off coats and wet boots. The living room became a place to gather, not just a transition between inside and outside.

TWO NEW WINDOWS provide natural light and a better place for sitting and chatting.

renovation, which also included a new roof, cedar siding for the rest of the house and a snowballing list of minor improvements, threatened to equal the square-footage cost for building a nuclear-power plant. Without any additional changes to the house, the addition would still have cost just over $370 per sq. ft. But the end result was well worth the expense and effort. These modest changes transformed our home, making the entire house more attractive, comfortable, and convenient.

By careful evaluation, I was able to make changes that were modest and still most effective. Each little decision was treated as a design opportunity. Less can be more.

THIS SMALL VESTIBULE has all the necessary ingredients for a functional entry. A hall-tree bench, a weatherproof bluestone floor and ample closet space provide room for coats, hats, wet boots, and umbrellas.

BRACKET THEME IS ECHOED AROUND THE FIREPLACE AND WINDOWS

ONCE THE SOFA WAS CENTERED ON THE FIREPLACE, I felt compelled to redesign the mantel (photo at bottom left). The new mantel is made of cherry to match the rest of the furniture in the house, all built by my father. The brackets that support the mantel shelf are reminiscent of those used outside (photo at bottom right). The bracket theme is repeated again at an even smaller scale as supports for the deeper-than-usual window stools (photo below). —L. H.

Home Remedies

BY KEYAN MIZANI AND ALEXIA ZERBINIS

Our first tour of the home of Jeanne and Joe Kaliszewski and their children was full of surprises, each eliciting a sharper gasp than the last. After interviewing several designers, the homeowners clearly had begun to anticipate the shock effect of showing one bungled space after another, and they enjoyed our growing expressions of disbelief. Built in 1928, the house had all the usual markers of a building's trip through time, such as multiple layers of peeling wallpaper and thick shag rugs in unfortunate colors. But there also were many odd and often unsettling things.

Almost all the original divided-lite wood windows had been replaced with inoperative single sheets of glass, some as long as 11 ft. Mirrored surfaces abounded on the interior, including orange-tinted reflective valances over windows and a wall-to-wall mirror in the dining room. The layout of rooms and hallways in this house of mirrors created a sense of labyrinthine, circuitous travel, with many dead ends. "But wait, there's more," said Jeanne, as she led us farther into the depths of the house.

To be sure, the house had many challenges but also some great opportunities. Jeanne and Joe took a leap of faith in buying it, recognizing its potential to become a long-term home for their family. First, though, changes were in order from the roof down. The homeowners wanted a master bedroom, a family room near the kitchen, and an office. The body of the house needed its arteries unclogged for circulation to make sense and for daylight and views to have pathways into the house. Every existing room needed new finishes.

We achieved these goals with one major change followed by many smaller ones. Like the squares of a Rubik's Cube, the changes were interrelated and had to work together to solve the puzzle. The solution included the early involvement of our general contractor, RMJ Construction, who provided pre-

LEAKY ROOFS OVER THE ORIGINAL UNSHELTERED ENTRY ARE A THING OF THE PAST. The new roof swoops down low from the ridge of the master-suite addition to cover a new porch that shelters the front door. Two new dormers add detail to the roofscape and daylight to the bedrooms. The casement windows open parallel to one another so that they catch prevailing breezes.

liminary cost estimates, allowing us to evaluate and prioritize the changes under consideration.

Rescue the upstairs with a bold stroke

When Jeanne and Joe first sat down with our design firm, two of their top priorities were to improve the house's front facade and to add a master suite to the second floor. We saw an opportunity to accomplish both with a second-story addition (see changes 1–5 in the sidebar on p. 172).

The house had some potentially prime real estate lurking under the low roof over the living room. The awkward relationship of this roof to a separate roof over the entry also was the main contributor to the clumsy appearance of the front of the house and to drainage problems caused by the valley between the roofs.

In their place, a new roof now matches up with the highest ridgeline of the house, extending over the living room to provide just enough space for a master suite without expanding the house's footprint. On the north side, the new roof sweeps down in a dramatic curve, sheltering a prominent covered entry porch.

PRESCRIBE A NEW ROOF TO ADDRESS MULTIPLE PROBLEMS

CHANGES 1–5

1. 400-sq.-ft. master-suite addition and covered entry porch
2. New 30-in. dormer
3. New laundry, plus open stairwell
4. Expanded bath for children
5. Interior windows for daylighting

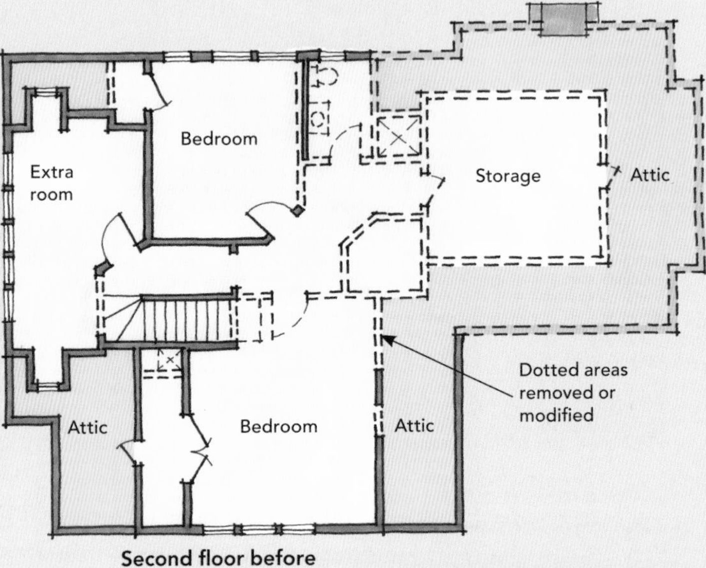

Second floor before

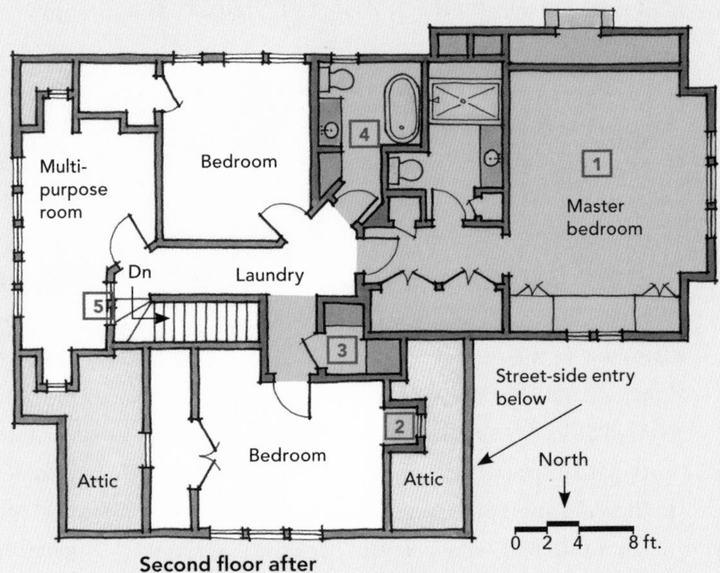

Second floor after

A master bedroom occupies the majority of the addition, with large windows facing the front and additional windows in a north-facing dormer. Closets are positioned on both sides of the hall, a way of getting double-duty out of its floor space.

The original upstairs bedrooms and bath were fairly workable, with some adjustments. We expanded the existing bath to include a claw-foot tub, a linen closet, and more wall area for towel racks. Then we annexed space from the overly deep north bedroom to carve out a modest laundry room and to open the hall to the stairway. The reorganized bedroom became more similar in size to the other bedrooms, and brighter due to its shortened depth and the addition of a dormer window. To bring daylight into the hallway, we added east-facing interior windows to the wall between the stair and the multipurpose room.

Cure circulation, and heal the floor plan downstairs

Inexplicably, the main route between the living and dining rooms crossed through the entry foyer, leaving it difficult to furnish and forcing travel down and then up two short stairways. Somewhat counterintuitively, we took out the stairs and filled in the wall between the foyer and the dining room. These changes created a more intimate foyer, protected the dining room from entry traffic, and offered a clearly defined route into the house (see changes 6–14, in the sidebar on p. 174).

This route leads into the central corridor, which previously was dark and underused. We widened it by 6 in., expanded its opening into the living room, and cut a 5-ft.-wide opening in the dining-room wall opposite the frosted French doors of the new office, bringing light into both spaces. The net result of these changes is a welcoming hallway that connects the house front to back and side to side.

To gain an extra measure of light, we removed the door to the stairway and replaced the adjacent wall with a railing. This change has created a focal point at the newel post and allows light to flow in from multiple sources, both upstairs and down. The hall's greater degree of openness also allows for outdoor views and cross ventilation.

What probably started as a bedroom turned into an improbably large laundry room somewhere along the line. Its location next to the living room made it a poor spot for a laundry but an excellent place for a home office. Large windows added to the south wall of the room, along with new frosted-glass French doors opening onto the hallway, admit light into the center of the house.

Adding an upstairs master suite allowed us to convert the downstairs bedroom to a family room. We removed a closet and created a passageway to the kitchen, making the family room's location ideal.

Next, we converted the downstairs bathroom into a new entry for the family that includes a half-bath and a mudroom with lots of open, kid-accessible storage and a coat closet. The new entry includes a 40-sq.-ft. bump-out, which is the only change to the house's original footprint. Joe and Jeanne hadn't asked for this space initially, but it appeared as a golden opportunity and now gets heavy, daily use between the heart of the house and the detached garage.

Rehabilitate the kitchen

The kitchen abounded with problems—poor circulation, wasted space, limited views of the yard, dreary cabinets—all of which produced a closed-in feeling. A pair of sliding-glass doors in the northeast corner neutralized an otherwise-desirable place for a table. In addition, an unused chimney, hanging cabinets that cut the space in half, and a pantry closet too deep to be used efficiently cluttered the room. We got rid of everything and started over (see changes 15–19, in the sidebar on p. 177).

We put two pullout pantries in the space formerly occupied by the chimney, which in turn freed the area previously clogged by the original oversize pantry. In this space, we relocated the back door, added more windows overlooking the yard, and

CURE CIRCULATION PROBLEMS DOWNSTAIRS, AND REASSIGN ROOMS

CHANGES 6–14

6 Laundry to home office
7 Bedroom to family room
8 Full bath to half-bath (creates space for mudroom)
9 Hallway expanded; new French doors to office
10 Dining room closed to foyer; steps removed
11 Mudroom enlarged with 40-sq.-ft. bump-out; new steps to garage
12 Walls and door removed at stairs
13 Family room and kitchen connected by passageway
14 Dining room opened to hall

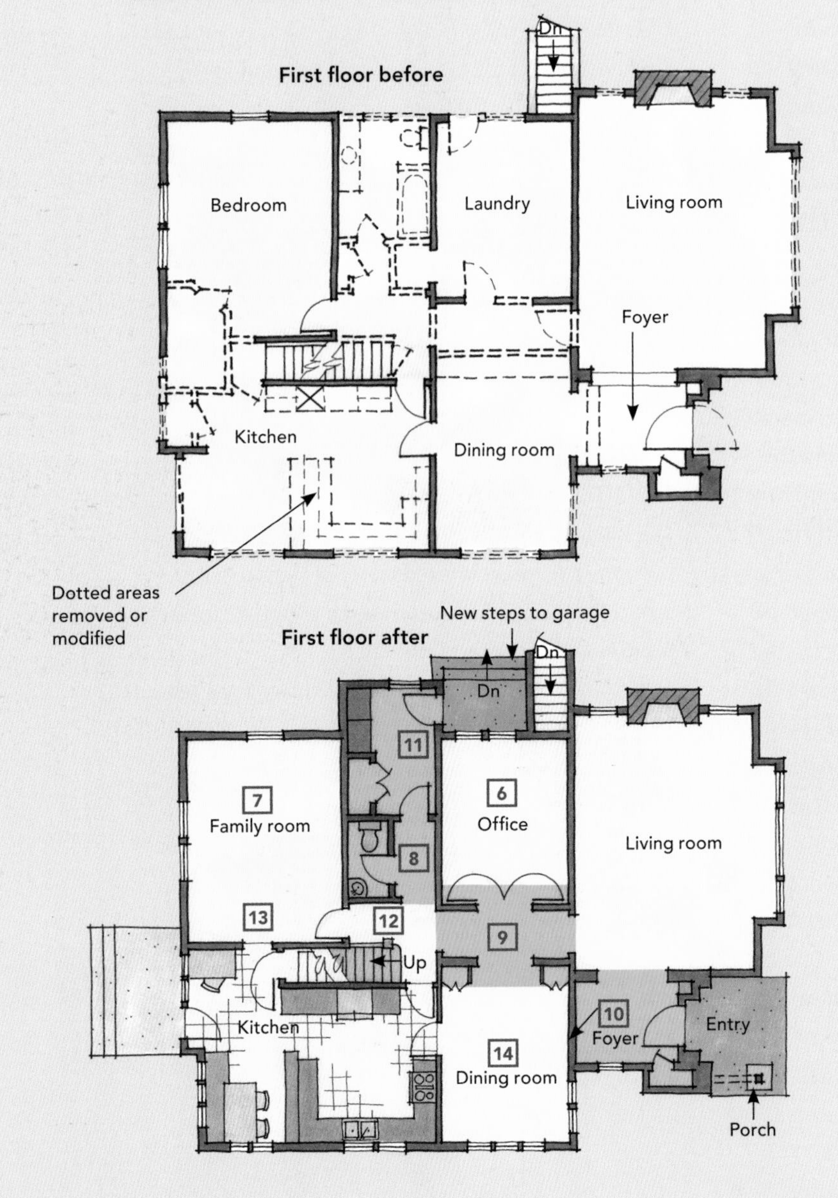

IN THE ORIGINAL HOUSE, both the living room and the dining room were open to the foyer. The new configuration leads visitors from the foyer to the living room and into the central hall. This passageway has been widened and opened to adjacent rooms and to the upstairs, improving daylighting and circulation.

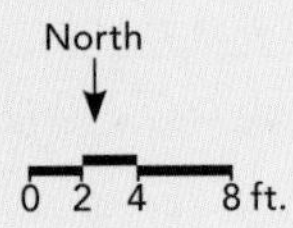

found enough room for a homework station. An adjacent breakfast nook, with a built-in bench and new windows in place of the sliding doors, has become a favorite place for daily gatherings.

The rest of the kitchen's layout remains largely the same, but we fine-tuned it to enhance the sense of space. We moved the stove to the wall formerly dominated by the refrigerator and replaced all the drab woodwork with stock frame-and-panel cabinets and trim painted white. Linoleum floors, laminate counters, and tile backsplashes were selected to evoke the original style of the house and to help the project stay within budget. These light-colored surfaces impart a bright, roomy feel to the kitchen. It is now the heart of the house, with places along the perimeter for enjoying a meal, reading the paper, doing homework, or just hanging out.

SIMPLY RELOCATING THE BACK DOOR ALLOWED FOR SIGNIFICANT IMPROVEMENTS TO THE BACK OF THE HOUSE. The northeast corner is now a breakfast nook with a cushion-covered bench for the kids. The parents, who typically need more mobility at the table, have chairs on their side. The new back-door location allows a view to the yard. And the dark, dreary plywood cabinets (photos above) have been replaced with new cabinets in keeping with the original Craftsman style of the house.

ATTEND TO THE KITCHEN AND MAKE PLACES TO HANG OUT

CHANGES 15–19

- [15] Back door relocated
- [16] New cabinets; fridge relocated; half-wall separates breakfast nook
- [17] New breakfast nook
- [18] Pantry replaced with homework station
- [19] Obsolete chimney replaced with pullout pantries

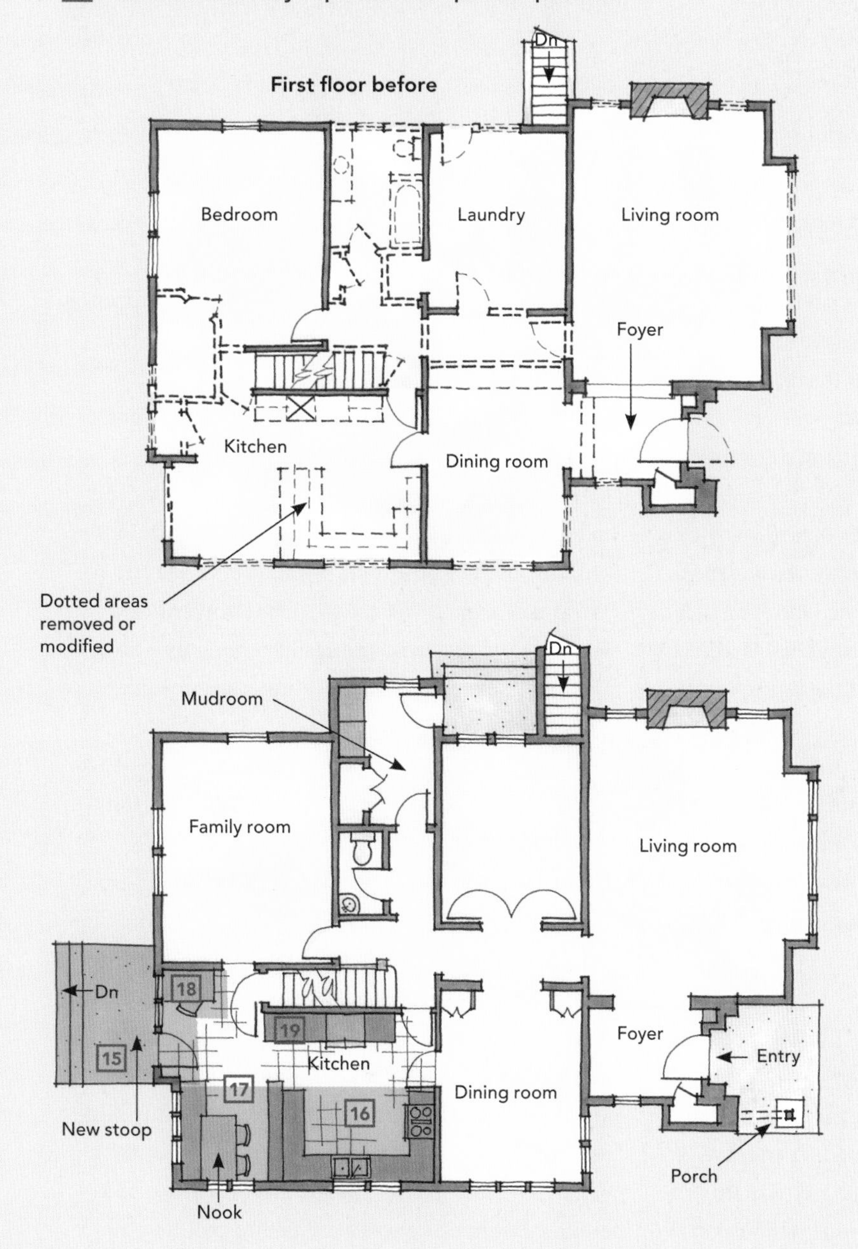

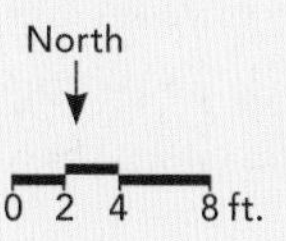

Living Lightly on the Whole Lot

BY GEOFFREY HOLTON

In 1993, my wife, Margaret, and I bought a house in Berkeley, Calif., that had been nearly gutted by its previous owner, an architect with imagination and a penchant for unfinished projects. Margaret and I are both hands-on people, so the clean slate was one of the house's best features.

We started with a modest budget and a commitment to as much reuse and recycling as we could muster. We took on commonsense conservation items first: insulation, upgraded windows, weatherstripping. We also spent a lot of time searching local salvage yards for cool stuff that looked like it would fit into our emerging sense of what the house might become. I collected chunks of old bowling alley and reclaimed Douglas-fir beams, while Margaret worked tirelessly, stripping the beautiful old beadboard we pulled out of the house's tumbledown back porch. All these materials and many others eventually found their way into the cabinets, finishes, and structure of the house.

Realizing the house's potential, inside and out

When we first acquired the house, the twin urgencies of rising energy costs and climate change were not so clearly upon us. As they emerged, our thinking about how we could minimize our reliance on the resources that we had always taken for granted began to evolve. As an architect who preaches the virtues of sustainable building, I think it's important for our house to walk the talk that my clients hear from me on a regular basis.

We decided to take advantage of the resources available to us, such as sunshine for electricity, gardens for food, and rainwater for irrigation, and to lessen our reliance on cars by making room for our day jobs at home. Our big project in the late 1990s was a small workshop for me and a studio where Margaret could pursue her career as a potter. Housed in a single small building, the two spaces share daylight through a translucent wall; a large barn door opens onto a patio workspace. The patio also has room for an outdoor grill just steps from an outdoor dining room (see the photo on the facing page).

Our son was born in 2000, which gave us the impetus to build a second-story master-suite addition in 2006. Its roof provided the real estate for a solar water-heating system and a 2.7-kilowatt photovoltaic (PV) array. The PV system supplies all our electricity, averaged out on an annual basis, including Margaret's electric-kiln firings (8 to 10 a year). The system cost about $16,000 after rebates and tax credits. Given our energy use before building the

MULTIPLE LEVELS ENRICH THE HOUSE. A backyard dining deck off the kitchen takes advantage of Berkeley's seasonable weather. The deck off the upstairs master bedroom doubles as a roof over the home office.

addition, and assuming a 5% annual increase in energy costs, we're looking at a 15- to 20-year payback period. Of course, if we get a hoped-for plug-in hybrid in the next few years, it will be akin to having free fuel for as long as we own the car. This will accelerate payback. We've slightly oversized the PV system to make that possible.

We use the solar-thermal system for domestic hot water (DHW) and for radiant-floor space heating. At about $26,000 installed, it was significantly more expensive than a straight solar-thermal DHW system (generally $7,000 to $12,000). But our price included all the radiant tubing, aluminum heat-distribution plates and insulation, a 100-gal. storage tank, and a boiler—basically, a whole new heating system.

LIVING AND WORKING WITH EVERY SQUARE FOOT

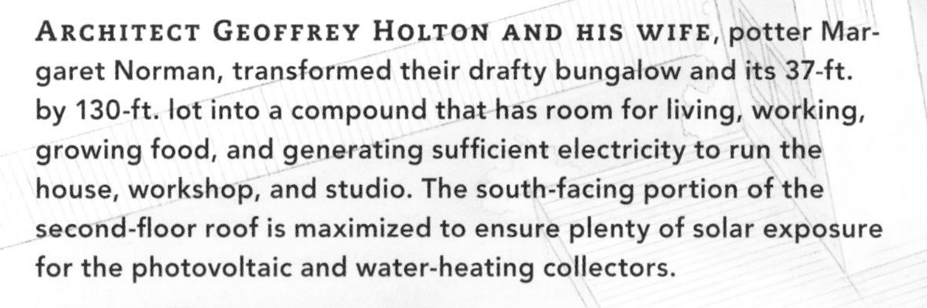

Architect Geoffrey Holton and his wife, potter Margaret Norman, transformed their drafty bungalow and its 37-ft. by 130-ft. lot into a compound that has room for living, working, growing food, and generating sufficient electricity to run the house, workshop, and studio. The south-facing portion of the second-floor roof is maximized to ensure plenty of solar exposure for the photovoltaic and water-heating collectors.

A woodshop and a pottery studio share space in the northwest corner of the lot and make for a very short walk to work. A sliding barn door extends the shop workspace into the backyard.

A lower-level deck bridges the gap between the kitchen and the patio grill, creating the perfect space for outdoor dining.

The backyard is home to a small vegetable garden, an herb garden, a raspberry patch, and a couple of small fruit trees, making for fewer trips to the farmer's market.

The homeowners' love of cycling is reflected in a steel-wheel motif on the deck and on stair railings throughout the house. A small garage at the back of the lot provides ample bike storage when they're not pedaling around town.

Gray water from the house flows to the backyard, where it's collected in a tank made from a defunct hot tub and is used to water the garden.

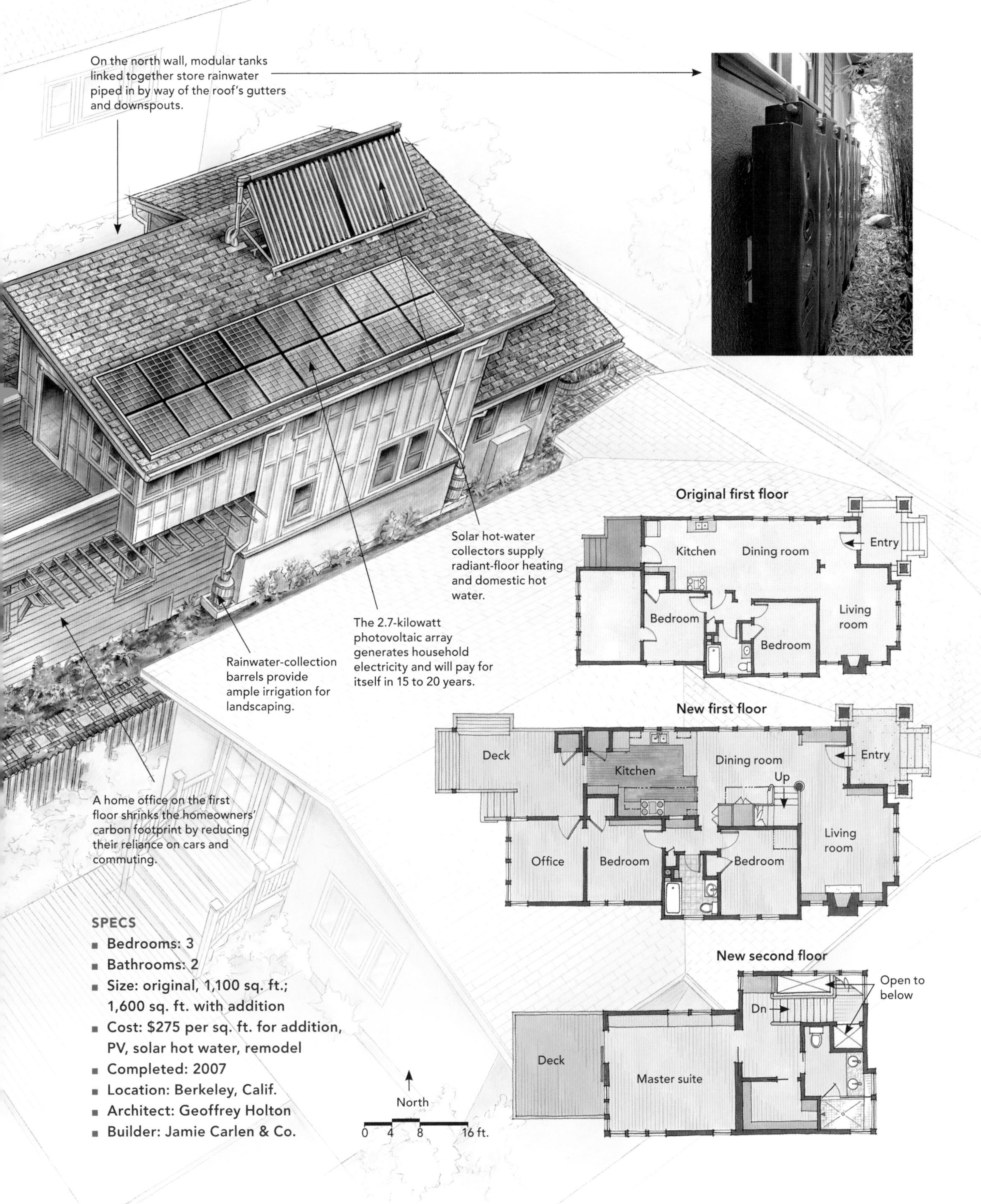

On the north wall, modular tanks linked together store rainwater piped in by way of the roof's gutters and downspouts.

Solar hot-water collectors supply radiant-floor heating and domestic hot water.

The 2.7-kilowatt photovoltaic array generates household electricity and will pay for itself in 15 to 20 years.

Rainwater-collection barrels provide ample irrigation for landscaping.

A home office on the first floor shrinks the homeowners' carbon footprint by reducing their reliance on cars and commuting.

SPECS

- **Bedrooms: 3**
- **Bathrooms: 2**
- **Size: original, 1,100 sq. ft.; 1,600 sq. ft. with addition**
- **Cost: $275 per sq. ft. for addition, PV, solar hot water, remodel**
- **Completed: 2007**
- **Location: Berkeley, Calif.**
- **Architect: Geoffrey Holton**
- **Builder: Jamie Carlen & Co.**

GRAY-WATER DOS AND DON'TS

Living with a gray-water system requires you to be aware of what's OK, and what's not OK, to put down the drain.

Conventional gray-water wisdom is that all soaps and shampoos are OK because they will be highly diluted. The rule is "Keep an eye on the plants, and if they don't seem to like it, make some changes." We use old-fashioned soaps like Kirk's Castile soap for hand and body washing. For clothes washing, we use biodegradable detergents such as Ecover®, Bio Pac, or Oasis. If you can't find these products, check the ingredients list on other brands, and be careful not to use soaps that contain salts of any kind. In general, liquid soaps and detergents contain fewer salts than powdered varieties. Also steer clear of chlorine bleach, boron, borax, or bicarbonate of soda.

Avoid drain cleaners as well. Our system has a valve that can divert the gray-water flow back to the city's sewer line. If we need to use a drain cleaner or bleach, we engage the diverter and keep it there for a while to rinse out residue.

Don't grow root vegetables, such as beets or carrots, with a gray-water system. Instead, stick with aboveground fare such as tomatoes, beans, and berries.

For more on gray-water systems, study the book *The New Create an Oasis with Greywater* by Art Ludwig (available at www.oasisdesign.net).

Stretch the water supply

In California, water use and groundwater replenishment take on more importance every day. We've approached that problem in two ways. First, we installed a row of modular rainwater-holding tanks along the north wall of the house (www.rainwater-hog.com; see the photo on p. 181) and a couple of old-fashioned rain barrels on the south side. Gutter downspouts run through a leaf catcher/filter and feed into the tanks and barrels. At current capacity, we can bank about 500 gal. of rainwater for irrigation.

The water-saving feature that we're most excited about, though, is our gray-water garden (see p. 180). This very simple technology takes advantage of the ability of plant-root systems and naturally occurring soil bacteria to filter and clean water. Here's how it works:

The clothes washer is connected to a drain line that leads to a gravel-filled collection tank in the backyard. (The toilets, the kitchen sink, and the dishwasher drain to the city sewer line.) Water-loving plants grow in the gravel, largely cleansing the gray water. The outlet from this "constructed wetland" leads to a perforated pipe buried in mulch, 8 in. below ground, beneath a native-plant garden and two fruit trees. Two similar perforated pipes run from bathroom sinks and showers to a lush raspberry patch and to a second native-plant garden in the front yard. Both pipes are also buried at least 8 in. below ground, where public-health officials like them to be.

Seeing the garden thrive on water that would otherwise have gone down the drain and into San Francisco Bay is a delight. And keeping the water here is a small step toward making our city and the natural systems that support it healthier and more drought resilient.

RESCUED MATERIALS ADD STYLE, UTILITY, AND A TOUCH OF WHIMSY

STAIR TREADS MADE FROM OLD GYMNASIUM BLEACHERS lead to the master suite (right). Above them, a railing composed of bike wheels rolls on up the stairs. The metal risers are industrial scrap.

The master bath has a concrete-vanity counter with aggregate made from obsolete porcelain toilets, which are notoriously hard to recycle (below right).

In the kitchen, recycled beadboard from the back porch finds new life as cabinets (below). The wall opening below the skylight lets daylight into the center hall.

Urban Farmstead

BY ERIC ODOR

In 1990, my wife, our two cats, and I relocated from Santa Monica, Calif., to Minneapolis and started house hunting. Cory and I never much liked Dutch colonials, but we found one with maple floors and 10-ft. ceilings, and we made an offer on the spot. When we realized that we could remove virtually every wall on the first floor, we gutted all 1,200 sq. ft. in less than a month's time.

After an initial flurry in 1992, we settled into a long, slow process of tackling little projects inside and out as money allowed. When interest rates finally took a dive, we decided to roll the remainder of the work into a refinancing. We hired a local contractor, Mike Knutson, to add an orchid room, a potting shed, a new garage, and a 10-ft. by 33-ft. screened porch.

We owned a small house on a large lot that had been a prime candidate for a teardown, but we had other interests here. As there were only four of us (don't forget the cats), we weren't interested in maximum volume; rather, we were interested in a symphony of spaces, inside and out. We wanted an expansive summer home that would engage the entire site, a cozy winter retreat from which to observe our domain, and a country cabin without the commute. We opted for a village of simple forms.

Stay small, but add lots of variety

It took us a while to see the Dutch colonial for what it really was, but once there, the village idea quietly morphed into an urban farmstead. The barnlike house was built in 1905 and was moved to its present location in 1925. Roughly 20 ft. by 30 ft., it hugged the north setback, approximately 30 ft. west of the sidewalk. Over the years, the small garage had sunk about 4 in. at a glacial but persistent rate. We needed a new garage and a screened porch.

The porch was a social necessity. We spent as much time as possible each summer on the uncovered front porch until the mosquitoes drove us inside. We needed screens, and we needed them front and back.

Cabin without the commute

When the existing garage was stripped from the house, the purity of the barn shape and its clapboard siding made the next move obvious. We needed another form, complete in itself, to define the property's southern boundary. To this end, we built a corrugated-metal granary to house a car and some storage, its simple shed roof reflecting the upper slope of the barn's gambrel roof. These two structures defined a 10-ft. chasm that the screened porch spans from front

(Continued on p. 190)

HEAD FLASHING WITH AN ATTITUDE. To get inexpensive weather protection for a side door that leads to the basement, the author designed a galvanized aluminum cowling to echo the gutters and corrugated garage siding. Photos taken at A and B on floor plan.

KEEP THE SHAPE, JETTISON THE REST

THE ORIGINAL 600-SQ.-FT. HOUSE had circuitous circulation at best. The kitchen was tucked behind the stairs, accessible only by passing through the living and dining rooms. The initial renovation cleared the first-floor partition walls and made kitchen access a clean walk from the front door. Upstairs, the homeowners rearranged the bathroom layout and cleaned up the closet space. During the second stage of renovation, the orchid room, the screened porch, and the new garage were added.

SPECS

- Bedrooms: 2
- Bathrooms: 1
- Size: 1,320 sq. ft., plus 330-sq.-ft. porch
- Cost: approximately $200,000
- Completed: 2009
- Location: Minneapolis
- Architect: Eric Odor, SALA Architects; Jerry Palms of Archistructures, structural engineer
- Builder: Knutson Custom Remodelers

BEFORE

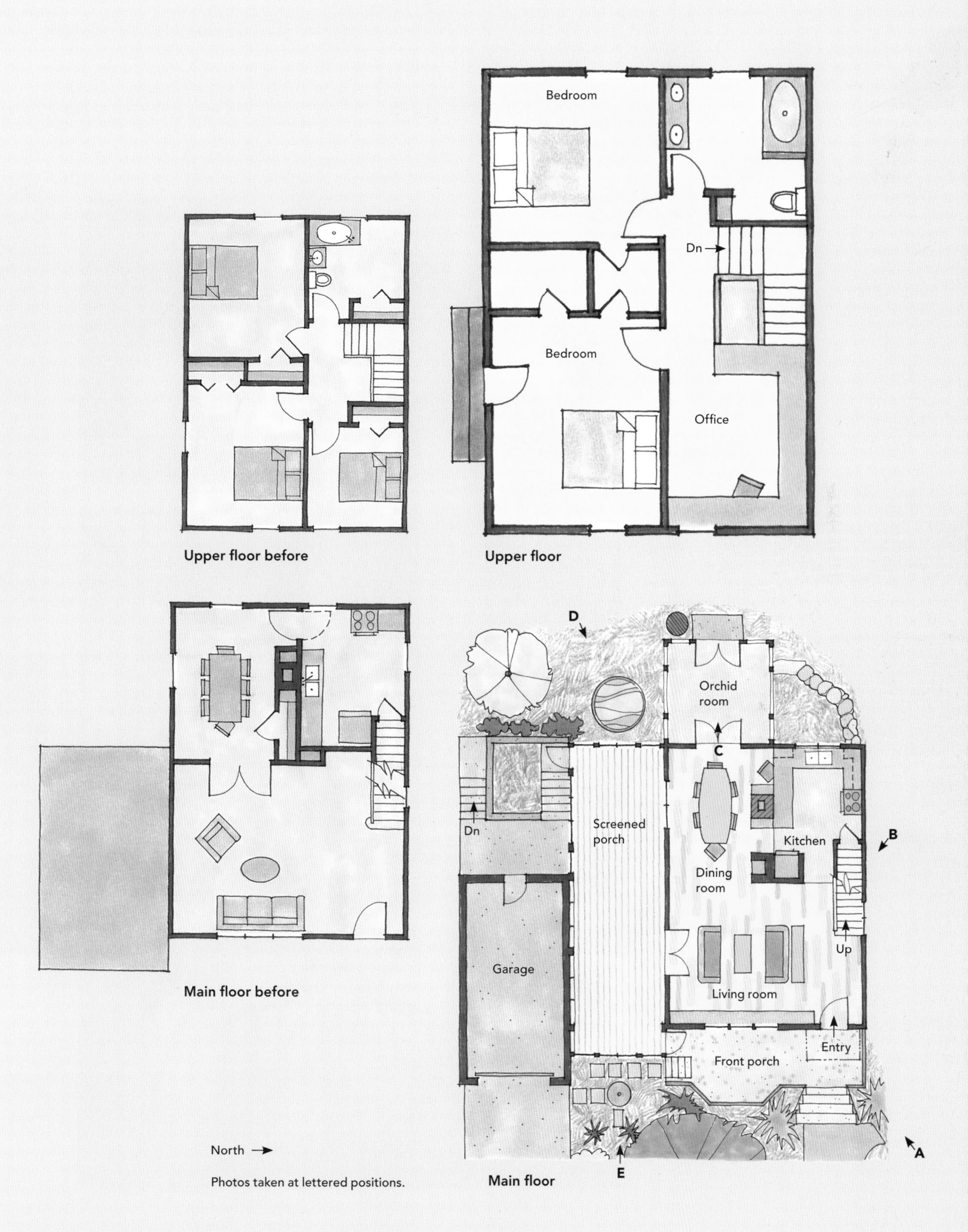
Bedroom
Dn
Bedroom
Office
Upper floor before
Upper floor
D
Orchid room
C
Screened porch
Dn
Kitchen
B
Dining room
Garage
Up
Living room
Entry
Front porch
Main floor before
North
A
E
Photos taken at lettered positions.
Main floor

SMALL ADDITIONS BRING LARGE VALUE

After the interior was remodeled, a new garage and two key elements were added. The enclosed orchid room and screened porch increased the floor plan by only 450 sq. ft., but they created a cozy winter sunroom and a breezy summer hangout, respectively. Both overlook the backyard's gardens.

BEFORE

WINTER'S RETREAT. A surplus of orchids and the need for a sunroom drove the addition of the orchid room. Its foundation serves as a potting shed accessible from the backyard. Photo taken at C on floor plan.

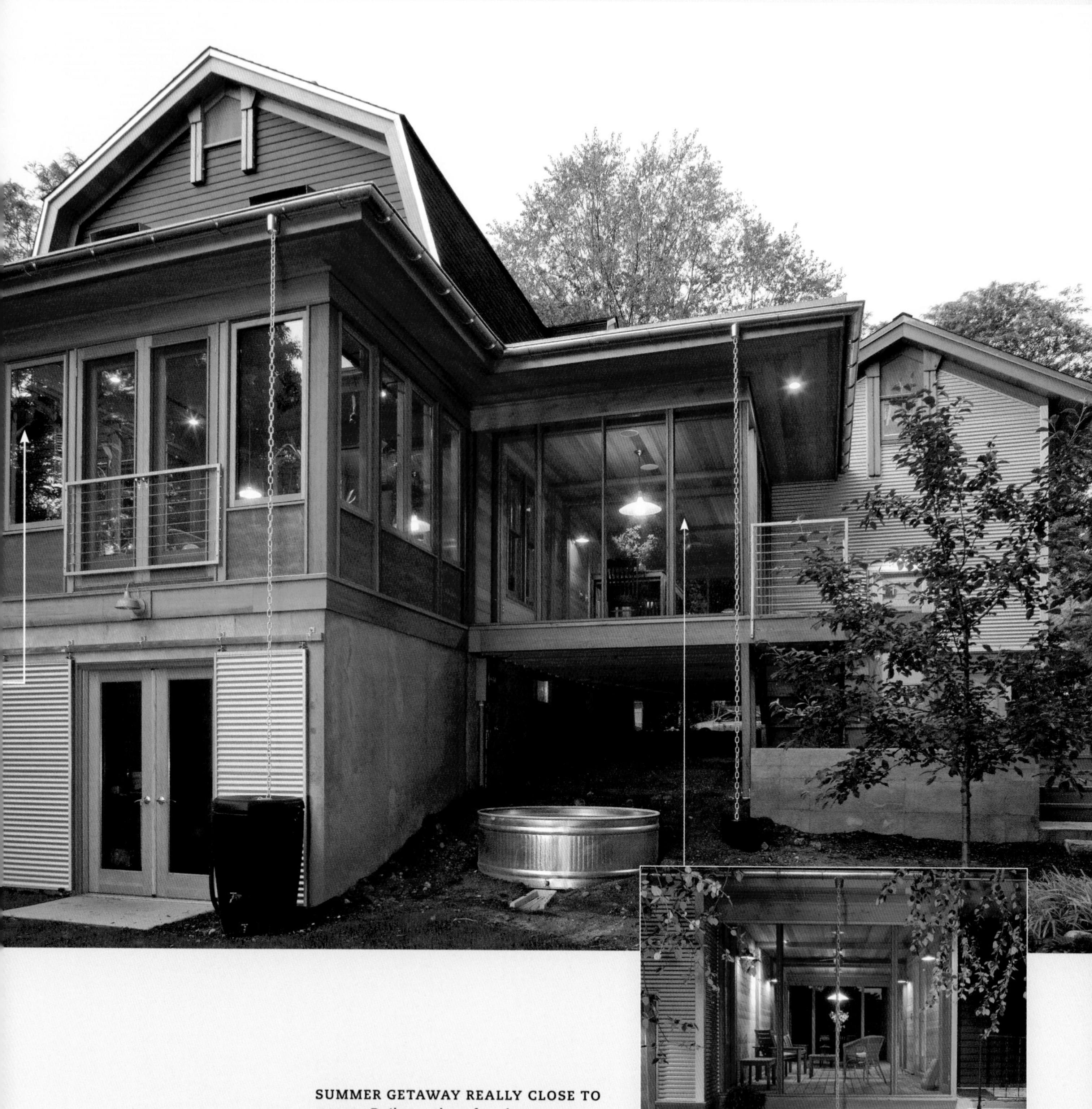

SUMMER GETAWAY REALLY CLOSE TO HOME. Built as a bug-free breezeway, the porch hangs suspended between the house and the garage. Photos taken at D and E on floor plan.

PROJECT COSTS

Although the entire project stretched out over 15 years, most of the cost came when we added the garage, orchid room, and screened porch. Because my wife and I renovated the main house ourselves, the estimated cost is a little harder to separate into labor and materials.

OUR WORK INSIDE THE EXISTING HOUSE:

- Approximately $50,000

CONTRACTOR'S WORK:

- Re-side existing house with fiber-cement clapboards and 5/4 clear-cedar trim: $17,000
- New concrete-block chimney and three-tab asphalt roofing on existing house: $10,000
- New 11-ft. by 12-ft. orchid-room and potting-shed foundation: $40,000
- New 12-ft. by 22-ft. garage and 10-ft. by 33-ft. screened porch: $103,000

- Total: $170,000

to back, forming a bridge and breezeway that hovers over the ground. This interstitial perch also became the cabin without the commute.

Gaining space in the plant world

The orchid room was a late addition to the project. After an initial orchid rescue some 10 years ago, our plant population seemed to take off and now needed a home of its own. As fate would have it, the foundation of that home became the basement walkout that we always needed as well as the potting shed of Cory's dreams.

Staying close to the agricultural roots of the project, we borrowed frugal, sustainable methods and materials common to farm life, using recycled and recyclable elements such as high-fly-ash concrete, corrugated steel and fiber-cement siding, and harvested rainwater. With water being a precious resource soon to be scarce, we spent a great deal of time and effort figuring out how to manage it. We ended up using a variety of tools, including rain chains, rain barrels, rain gardens, and a 6-ft.-dia. livestock tank as our reservoir.

Seamless in Missoula

BY CHARLES MILLER

Angie Lipski is a stickler for authenticity. When she and her husband, Dean Johnson, decided to enlarge their one-story bungalow in anticipation of starting a family, Angie saw a twofold opportunity to improve their house. As an architect adept at working in historic styles, she's well aware that a proper bungalow presents its primary gable to the street. As a consequence, job number 1 was to fill in the missing gable and make it look as though it had always been there. Job number 2: Take advantage of the 600 sq. ft. of unused attic space by adding what amounts to a major doghouse dormer to both the front and back of the house (see the photo on p. 192).

The original house had two upstairs bedrooms flanking a full bath. The new configuration spreads living spaces to all four corners of the bungalow's footprint, bringing the upstairs total to three bedrooms, a study/sewing room for Angie, a new master bath, and a multipurpose space adjacent to the hallway (see the floor plans on p. 195). This room, a remnant of one of the old bedrooms, is the most engaging of all the new spaces (see the top photo on p. 193). Open to the hall and the stairwell, it shares its views and light with the rest of the upstairs. It's a display space, library, and potential TV room, and it no doubt will serve as nursery and study hall.

BEFORE

A year after the big blue tarp came down and the expanded second story started to settle into the fabric of the neighborhood, Angie had a chance encounter with the lady who lives across the street. Standing on the sidewalk, she pointed at the new gable and asked Angie, "Have those two windows always been in that wall?" Now that's seamless.

PROBLEM: A NEW STUDY IN THE HALLWAY NEEDED TO BALANCE PRIVACY WITH OPENNESS.

Solution: The entry to the hallway study is framed by a box beam supported by pilasters at each end. They aren't structurally necessary, but they give the space a sense of sturdiness and separation from the rest of the house. Photo at right taken at A on floor plan.

PROBLEM: THE CHIMNEY FLUE INTRUDES INTO THE UPSTAIRS HALLWAY.

Solution: Replace the old heater in the basement with a high-efficiency heater that vents out the side of the house. Fortuitous consequences: The new heater lowered energy costs by 20%, even though the size of the house increased by 33%. The chase for the old flue provided space for laundry drain lines and a new heating duct.

A SECOND-STORY ADDITION to a classic bungalow (facing page) looks as though it has been there forever.

PROBLEM: THE OLD BATHROOM LOST DAYLIGHT ACCESS.

Solution: A transom window over the shower in the original bath grabs light from the new bath. Photo at left taken at B on floor plan.

PROBLEM: THERE'S NO PLACE FOR CRAFT ACTIVITIES.

Solution: Build a sewing room off the master bedroom. Photo taken at C on floor plan.

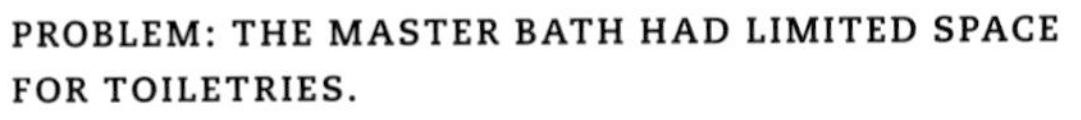

PROBLEM: THE MASTER BATH HAD LIMITED SPACE FOR TOILETRIES.

Solution: Install his and hers deep drawers next to the closet. Top photo taken at D on floor plan.

PROBLEM: THE MASTER BEDROOM CLOSET LOST SPACE.

Solution: Tuck a closet into the low-ceilinged wedge-shaped space in the bathroom.

SHARE THE VIEWS, SHARE THE LIGHT

WHEN ANGIE LIPSKI first started sketching potential upstairs floor plans, her plumber was fixing the downstairs shower valve. He made an offhand comment about upstairs bathroom placement: "If you put the baths next to each other, you won't screw up the downstairs ceiling, and you'll save on the cost of plumbing." That idea drove the design.

SPECS (UPSTAIRS ONLY)

- Bedrooms: 3
- Bathrooms: 2 (one new)
- Size: 600 sq. ft.
- Cost: $230 per sq. ft.
- Completed: 2009
- Location: Missoula, Mont.
- Architect: Angie Lipski
- Builder: Scariano Construction

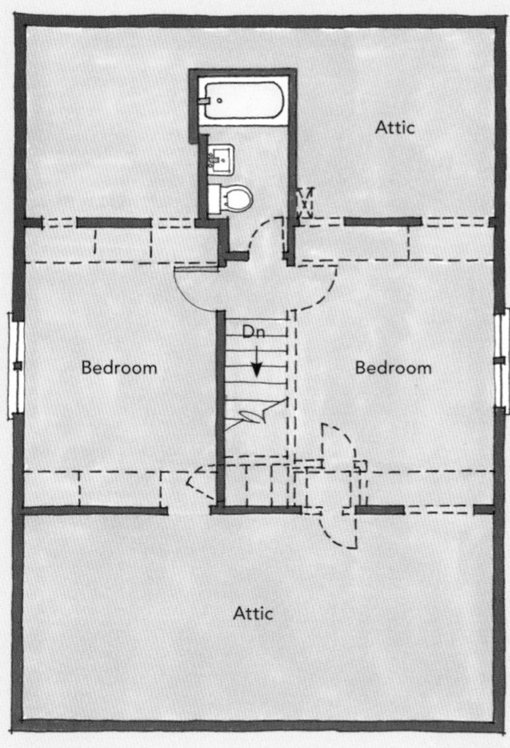

Before

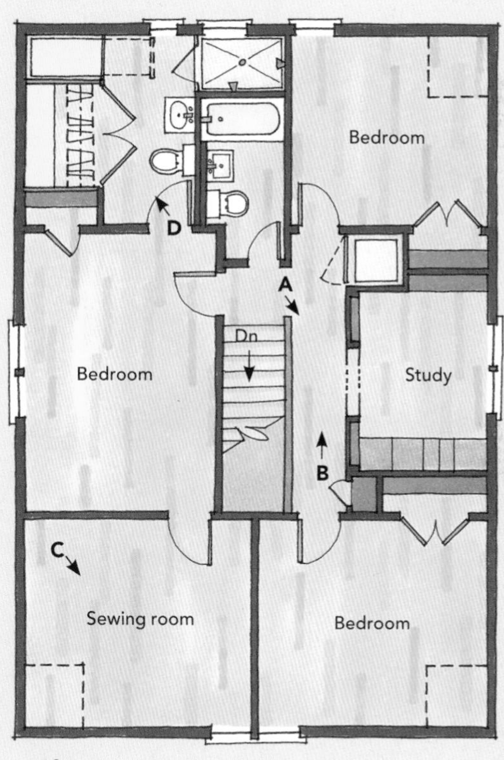

After

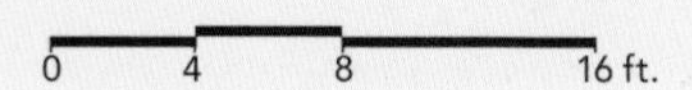

Photos taken at lettered positions.

HOW TO EASE THE PAIN OF AN UPSTAIRS ADDITION

Muddy boots, roofing nails, falling debris, rain squalls, and the carting of bulky materials through finished spaces are just a few of the potential hazards that can damage a house when building a second-story addition. There's also the loss of privacy. Here are three ways that Angie and Dean's builders minimized the pitfalls.

1 Scaffolding in the front and back served as bearing points for a beam that held aloft a tarp large enough to tent the entire house. Worries about water damage to existing finishes evaporated. Cost: about $3,000

2 A temporary exterior staircase led straight to the job through an upstairs window, meaning no endless tromping through the downstairs.
Cost: $900

3 Oriented strand board (OSB) shields at strategic ground-level locations protected exterior finishes and landscaping. Cost: Lost in the round-over

From Small to Big Enough

BY BILL MASTIN

This modest California bungalow served its present owners, a photographer and a general contractor, quite well for more than 10 years. They added a small darkroom and a home office at the basement level, and replaced the home's aging board-and-batten siding with cedar shingles, turning it into a little cousin to the famous "Berkeley brown shingles" across town.

As their two daughters grew up, however, Bill Jetton and Janet Delaney's cozy two-bedroom house began to feel cramped. The teenagers could no longer share a bedroom, Janet needed proper studio space for her growing photography career, and everyone wanted a second bathroom. Their search for a bigger house began during the Bay Area's merciless dot-com bubble.

Janet and Bill spent a frustrating two years looking for a reasonably located and big-enough place; charm became optional. Potential buyers crowded Sunday open houses, reeling at inflated prices. The search was draining, and the numbers never really added up in favor of moving. The houses for sale, though larger than the bungalow, all seemed to have flaws in their layout, and many needed extensive structural or finish work.

While the work Bill and Janet had done on their house—new foundation, shingles, and basement space—would be attractive to buyers, they likely wouldn't recoup what they had put in. And the kitchen still had its original plan, which was not up to current standards. What to do? It was time to assess the potential for enlarging their little bungalow.

Because we were old friends, I was familiar with Bill and Janet's house. Having attended many birthdays and holiday celebrations, I knew the kitchen's flaws firsthand. I had worked with Bill on residential projects over the years, so I also knew the many building skills he and his team could put into action. Here was a rare opportunity to help good friends make the place they loved grow to serve their evolving needs.

At the end of an otherwise functional list, Janet added: "Don't forget to have fun."

The floor plan was perfect—for 1910

When we pondered the house's next chapter, we all agreed the bungalow had a homey, sheltering quality and a simplicity in its basic layout that were worth keeping. It was built in 1910, just a few years after Berkeley booster and poet Charles Keeler wrote *The Simple Home*. He advocated a home where "all is quiet in effect, restrained in tone, yet natural and joyous in its frank use of unadorned material." Good

advice. We considered what natural touches we might bring to the design.

Bill and Janet had heard their house described as a "worker's bungalow." It was affordable partly because of what was omitted. The house had a welcoming little front porch but no foyer. A table at the back kitchen window had a view of the garden, but there was no dining room. Passage to the front and rear bedrooms was directly through the small living room and kitchen because there was no central hallway. Between the bedrooms, the lone bathroom had a door into each but no link to the other living areas. These three features—foyer, dining room, and

(Continued on p. 202)

KEEP THE PROFILE LOW ON THE STREET SIDE. With a charming porch setting the tone, the new second story repeats its gable shape with a dormer that contains the master bedroom. Photo taken at A on floor plan.

ABOVE: FIVE FEET THAT MADE A BIG DIFFERENCE. Bumping out the back wall 5 ft. made room for the dining table. Photo taken at D on floor plan.

RIGHT: A SCULPTURAL STAIR OVERLOOKS THE ACTION. Crafted of maple and cherry, some of the stair's balusters are tapered slightly and of random width, suggesting their forest silhouettes. The kitchen island is on wheels, allowing it to be rolled out of the way for big dinner parties. Photo taken at C on floor plan.

HOUSE GROWS TOWARD THE BACK

Simple in plan and modest in amenities, the original house was virtually intact. The only changes (by previous owners) had been the addition of another bedroom in the back and a deck off the kitchen. Now, the newly remodeled house includes a second-floor bedroom, bath, and studio, along with an expanded kitchen and a carefully revised deck. Moving the ridge toward the backyard and placing a high, shed-style dormer for the studio behind it kept the bulk of the upstairs addition largely hidden from view. Photos taken at B on floor plan.

SPECS

- Bedrooms: 3
- Baths: 2 + a bedroom lavatory
- Size before: 1,077 sq. ft.
- Size after: 1,967 sq. ft.
- Builder: Jetton Construction
- Cost: $198 per sq. ft. (includes both new and remodeled space)
- Completed: 2001
- Location: Berkeley, Calif.
- Architect: Bill Mastin

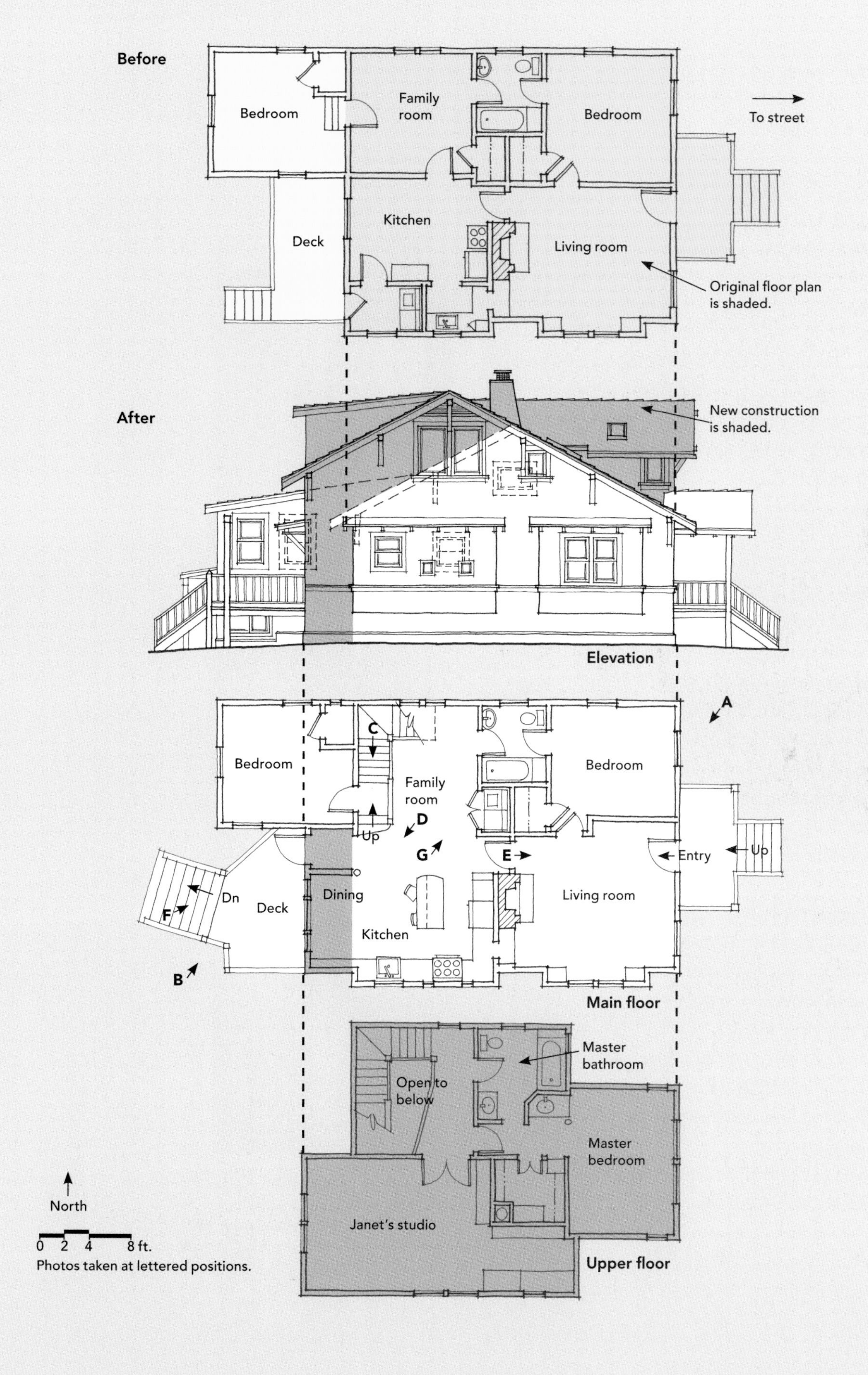

Photos taken at lettered positions.

central hallway—are typical in the many Craftsman-inspired bungalows around the Berkeley area. As we started to enlarge the house, we felt their absence.

"To improve circulation, take a bite out of the bedroom."

First, improve circulation

The original kitchen plan was a chopped-up jumble of three small rooms: one for the sink; one for the laundry and the back entry; and one for the stove, refrigerator, and table, with almost no usable counter space. But the plan's main flaw was poor circulation. The diagonal route disrupted cooking and dining, and it made laundry and outdoor access difficult. Entertaining could be a bruising affair. Thus getting a straighter route established from the front door through the house to the backyard became a key organizational idea (see the floor plans on p. 201).

The first move was to get the piano out of the way of the front door (photos at right). A slice of space taken from the front bedroom resulted in an alcove for the piano and for coats. While not a foyer, it helped with traffic flow and added charm to the living room.

The old house did have a usable attic, with storage space and a roof steep enough for moving around easily. By pushing back the ridge, we exploited this volume for a new second floor, without adding much height or apparent bulk. The new upstairs became the parents' realm.

Our first instinct had the master bedroom facing the quieter back garden, and Janet's studio on the street. These locations switched early, though, because we decided it was essential to maintain the house's 1½-story appearance from the street. A cozy master bedroom could be shaped with a gable dormer and take its detailing cues from the original house. In the back, the studio's larger shed dormer could lift up for its needed volume, without the low-slope, torch-down roof becoming a dominant element from the street. Because of its door arrangement, the new upstairs bath serves as a master bath that also can be used by the rest of the household. A small vanity sink in the master bedroom takes the pressure off the bathroom at rush hour.

Carving out a slice of the adjacent bedroom made an alcove for the piano, a place to hang coats, and a much clearer path to the front door. In the bedroom, the alcove's ceiling is a storage shelf. Photos taken at E on floor plan.

CORNER TABLE, SUNSHINE IF POSSIBLE. A little deck, elevated above grade enough to make the most of the sunlight, is framed by a built-in bench and a beefy red-cedar mast that anchors one end of a clothesline. Photo at right taken at F on floor plan; photo below taken from studio window.

LAUNDRY IN A BOX

A WASHER AND DRYER, elevated for easier accessibility, reside in a former closet. Shelves hang on the inside of the flush hollow-core plywood doors, which are stiff enough to take the extra weight. Faux frames applied to the outside of the doors give them the frame-and-panel look of the original doors. Photos taken at G on floor plan.

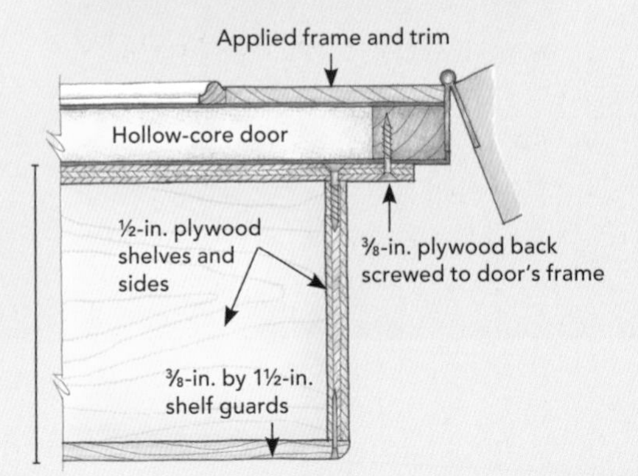

By selectively removing walls on the main floor, we opened space for a stairway that overlooks the new center of the house. A former closet became the laundry, with storage above and shelves attached to the doors.

This island can float out of the way

The old kitchen was just too small, so we expanded it by pushing the west wall 5 ft. toward the backyard. Now there's space for pull-out pantry cabinets and a dining table with a garden view. This move also made room for an island and a couple of stools. The island is on wheels (with brakes!), so on special occasions, the kitchen can be transformed into a festive mead hall with sit-down dinner space for 20 people.

Secrets of a great outdoor room on a small lot

Elevated to catch the sun, the new deck takes its shape from the views it either protects or enhances. The deck is oriented so that it deflects stair traffic away from the bedroom window adjacent to the back door while also giving some breathing room to the ground-floor window below. The nearly 7-ft.-wide steps provide a sitting perch with a view that's angled away from a nearby storage shed and toward the flowerbeds in the far corner of the garden.

The new deck is about the same size as the old, but this one has a built-in bench. A timber-frame trellis with beefy 6×6 masts defines the corner of this outdoor room and anchors one end of the clothesline. The windows next to the breakfast table turn into pass-throughs when the grill is fired up.

Screening with greenery can make a small urban lot feel more private. Here, it also provides shade and helps define garden pathways. Cables bring climbing vines up the south wall, where they provide filtered light for Janet's studio. A spectacular climbing rose survived construction and is now a flowery cape that wraps around the path leading to Bill's basement office.

Ranch Makeover, Bungalow Style

BY DANIEL S. MORRISON

Before and after images of David and Kathy Griffin's Arlington, Va., house have a lot in common—except for appearance. Both the original 1950s brick-and-block rambler (commonly known as a ranch house in other parts of the United States) and the early-20th-century bungalow design the Griffins copied filled the affordable-housing needs of a growing population. Both styles evolved with little input from architects and were built en masse for the middle class.

Ramblers make a great start

Utility and affordability are common traits of both house styles, but the bungalow design, with its outgoing porch and sheltering roof, has become desirable while the introverted rambler hasn't. Brick-and-block ramblers may not offer much to look at, but they present an excellent starting point for renovation.

Practically bombproof, the foundation and the first-floor walls are typically strong enough to support a second floor without additional reinforcement, and because they're plentiful, ramblers are relatively affordable. They are residential blank slates, allowing you to go in almost any direction: Cape, colonial, contemporary, or in this case, bungalow.

Some parts, however, are more worth saving than others (see "Obstacle or Opportunity" on p. 209). The Griffins collected photographs and illustrations of details, fixtures, and materials that they wanted to incorporate into their renovated house. David and Kathy compiled their preferences in a three-ring binder and presented this idea book to their design team, principal architect Charles Moore and project architect Sarah Farrell.

Double the living space without doubling the footprint

A few years before the transformation, the Griffins hired Moore's firm to update the house with new energy-efficient windows and to add a new kitchen wing and porch to the back of the house. The planned bungalow transformation, while an extreme makeover, had a strict budget: The Griffins required that the kitchen stay nearly intact and that the windows be salvaged.

The opened-up kitchen wing was closed partially to create a more formal dining room, but with a peek-through over the stove (see the photo on p. 208). The replacement windows were reused in the front wall, which was moved toward the street about 1½ ft., the maximum that setback requirements allowed (see the floor plans on p. 207). Moving the

(Continued on p. 208)

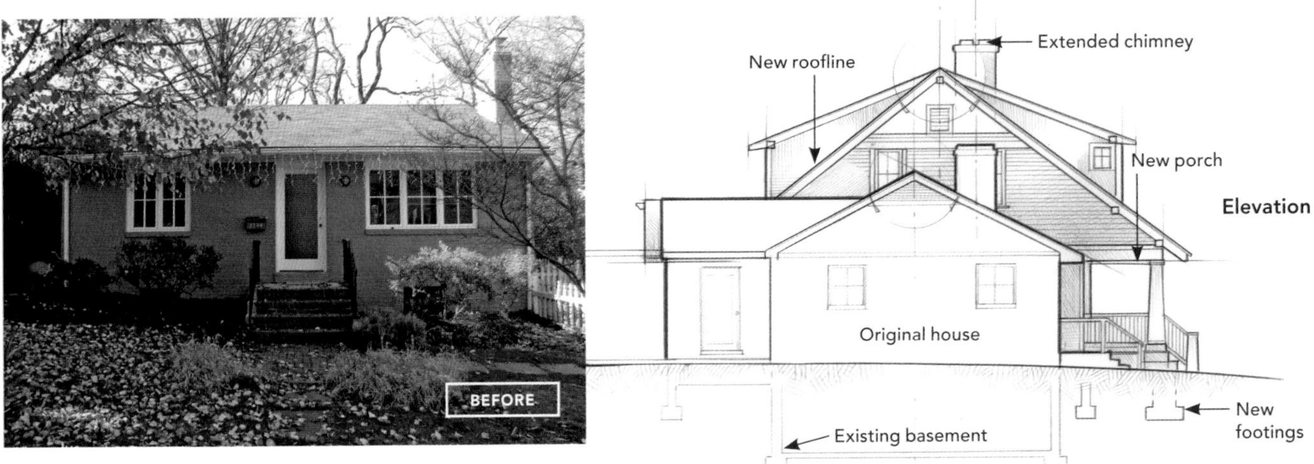

GO UP AND OUT

A strong foundation and wall framing, along with existing power, water, and sewer service, can make even an extreme makeover much faster than building new. Postwar ramblers and ranch houses provide an excellent starting point in an established neighborhood at an affordable price. Another asset is a mature landscape that's already in place. Photo above taken at A on floor plan.

DEFINED YET OPEN, SPACIOUS YET COZY

This makeover doubled the living space without enlarging the footprint very much. By adding as much to the front of the house as setbacks allowed and by tucking a second floor under a big roof, the plan succeeded in making the house look as if it were still one story. It feels cozy because you can see from one end of the house to the other. Public and private spaces are defined by half-walls with tapered columns, pass-throughs, and ceiling beams.

SPECS

- Bedrooms: 3
- Bathrooms: 2
- Size: 925 sq. ft. (before), 1,857 sq. ft. (after)
- Cost: $250,000
- Completed: 2003
- Location: Arlington, Va.
- Architect: Moore Architects; Sarah Farrell, project architect
- Builder: Gabe Nassar, GN Contracting Inc.

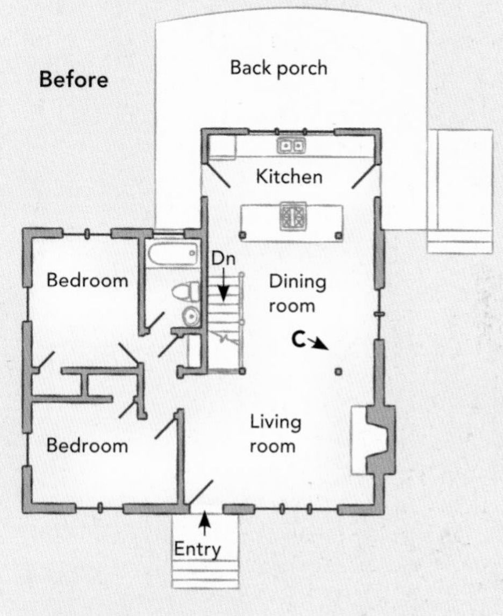

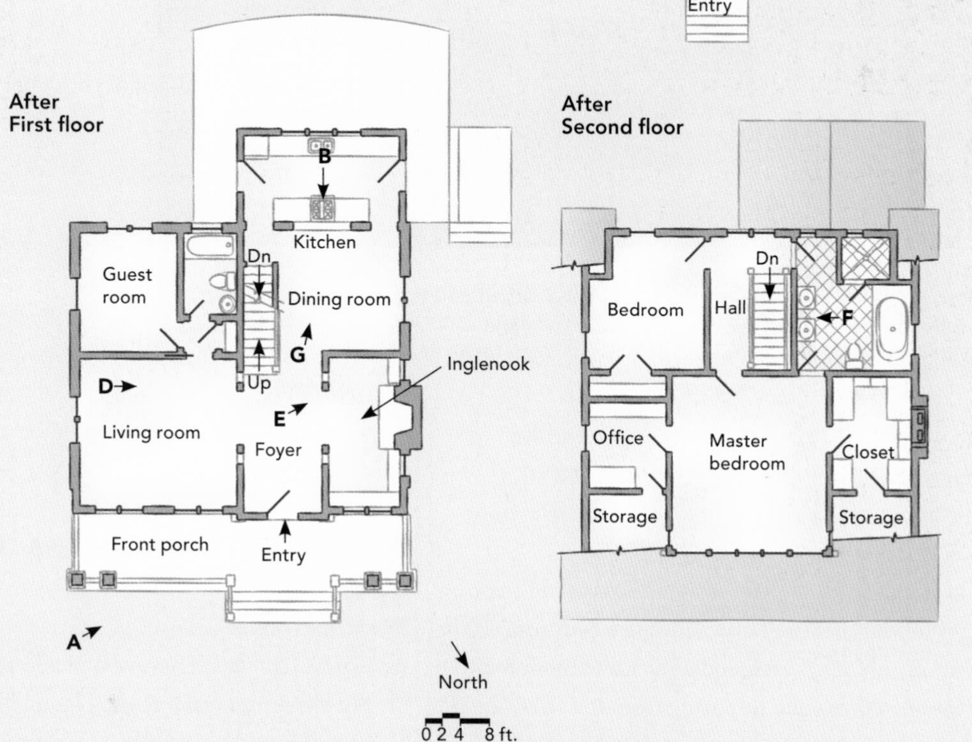

Photos taken at lettered positions.

A WALL OPENING EXTENDS THE VIEW. **This kitchen addition took place before the full renovation. The wall opening above the stove links interior spaces and provides a view straight through the house. Photo taken at B on floor plan.**

front wall of the house this small amount added enough to the front rooms to boost their utility while leaving plenty of space for a comfortable front porch and yard.

The architects doubled the living space (and the height) of the Griffins' house, adding a bedroom, a bathroom, an office, and storage space without making the structure seem imposing from the street and without making it look like a two-story house. In fact, moving the house closer to the street makes it more inviting with its deep, neighborhood-friendly porch and its sheltering roof.

Subliminal boundaries in an open plan

Inside, the comfortable-yet-practical feeling continues. Bungalow trim elements are typically simple in profile but elegant in proportion. Flat moldings combine to form wide casings, and cornices support the classical proportions of earlier architectural styles while rejecting the level of ornamentation. Extravagant details, if used at all, are saved for formal areas. To keep this project affordable, the architects chose paint-grade trim rather than the dark-stained wood common to bungalows. Their decision allowed for a higher level of refinement (tall wainscot paneling and coffered ceilings) without a significantly higher level of cost.

Because they'd lived in this house for a few years, the Griffins knew the existing floor plan's strengths and shortcomings. The circulation patterns devised for the updated floor plan are from models of actual living patterns, and visual cues make these patterns subconsciously apparent. Partial walls with massive tapered columns define individual spaces without chopping up the floor plan. In the Griffins' home, you can see from one end of the house to the other in both directions, yet semiprivate spaces, such as the inglenook (see the photos on p. 210), are defined clearly.

The architects also used color to distinguish different spaces. The main color, gray, is used in the central portion of the house (foyer and dining room). Other colors (yellow in the inglenook and kitchen; green in the living room and bathroom) have the same value as the central gray. For these earth-tone colors to separate the spaces effectively, they're placed adjacent to the central gray. Yellow rooms don't touch each other, nor do they touch green rooms. Both yellow and green touch only gray. In this way, the colored rooms are clearly secondary destinations from the central travel lane.

Ornate light fixtures are a trademark of bungalow design because bungalows were among the first houses built with electrical wiring. The fixtures celebrated this technological advancement with decorative-glass shades and brass bodies (www.rejuvenation.com).

OBSTACLE OR OPPORTUNITY?

Photo taken at C on floor plan.

HOW TO PRIORITIZE A LARGE-SCALE HOME RENOVATION

It can be tempting to err on both sides of the salvage equation. If you demolish everything, you'll undoubtedly rebuild much of it. But saving too much can waste time, effort, and money. Here are five tips from the architects for figuring it out.

- **Work around the fireplace.** It will suggest at least part of the layout. Because it's expensive to move, the fireplace dictates a cozy zone. It can be a living-room centerpiece, part of a den, or, as in this house, an inglenook.
- **Work around the stairs location because it defines the circulation path.** Stairs are not expendable. Rather than reframe the floor to accommodate a new staircase placement, let the stairs show you the circulation paths and landing locations.
- **Move plumbing and electrical if necessary.** Electrical cable and plumbing pipe are cheap, and electricians and plumbers are good at rerouting them. The current location of the kitchen or bathroom might not be right for the updated floor plan.
- **Save the floor, not the ceiling.** The existing ceiling framing most likely will be undersize for a second floor, so don't worry about saving it. On the other hand, an already installed hardwood floor is protected easily during construction and is worth saving.
- **Be committed to a great final product.** Know what you want and be willing to pay for it. Actively defining your wants by collecting photos and studying use patterns goes a long way toward speeding up a job while experiencing fewer surprises and keeping closer to budget.

EIGHT SIGNATURE ELEMENTS OF A BUNGALOW

Bungalows differ regionally, incorporating elements of various styles. They all have a few things in common, though: Bungalows are simple, earthy, and practical. Although bungalow style has no formal definition, these eight common elements will help you get into the bungalow ballpark.

INTERIOR ELEMENTS

1 Half-walls with tapered columns define rooms without closing the floor plan. The columns accentuate the strong symmetry crucial to bungalow designs. Photo taken at D on floor plan.

2 An inglenook provides a cozy fireside retreat. Besides a fireplace, the recessed area typically includes built-in seating, built-in bookcases, or both. Natural lighting is important. Photo taken at E on floor plan.

3 Elegant trim details are based on simple profiles. High wall paneling, coffered ceilings, picture-rail bands that wrap around windows, and door head casings are common trim elements in bungalows. The joinery and detailing are exquisite. Photo taken at F on floor plan.

4 Period light fixtures reflect the fact that bungalows were among the first houses to be wired for electricity. Lighting fixtures were chosen with the same care as art might have been. Light shades were made with mica, amber glass, or stained glass, and the fixtures often were brass. Photo taken at G on floor plan.

EXTERIOR ELEMENTS

5 A large dormer is an efficient way to create space but keep the house profile small. Either a shed or gable dormer set into a deeply overhanging roof makes the bungalow look like a one-story house when, in fact, it is two stories.

6 Stout columns anchor the roof. A deep, sheltering roof is the dominant exterior feature. Eaves and gable-end overhangs give the roof a protective and massive presence.

7 Abundant windows offer natural light, fresh air, and an outdoor connection. One of the original concepts of bungalows was healthfulness. Lots of fresh air and natural light promise clean living as well as a clear head.

8 A sheltered porch invites neighborly interaction and provides an intermediate layer of protection between indoors and out. The porch also is a transition from private to public space—from the house to the neighborhood.

5
7
6
8
3
4

A Cool Texas Remodel

BY ALAN BARLEY

For the past 25 years, I've been working with my business partner, Peter Pfeiffer, designing sustainable homes in Austin, Tex., and around the country. We've found that the most practical way for a house to work in our hot climate is to build it as if it were sitting under a big, shady umbrella. When you're out in the sun, you wear a broad-brimmed hat and light-colored clothes. The same ideas apply to designing houses.

A hundred years ago in Texas, houses didn't have furnaces and air-conditioners. Folks had to lay out their homes in logical, practical ways to deal with the harsh climate. Deep overhangs, porches, and thermal convection were basic passive-cooling tools that made living in this area more comfortable in the summer. They are the same passive strategies we use today.

Because of our approach to sustainable building, we were sought out by a young professional couple who had purchased a one-story home built in the early 1940s that had good bones and perfect orientation. Their new house was approximately 1,300 sq. ft., and they gave us three main goals for the remodel:

- Keep within a tight budget.
- Enlarge the living space to approximately 2,000 sq. ft.
- Rearrange the house's existing footprint for better function.

Sustainable passive design

What works in central Texas doesn't necessarily work in Montana or New Jersey. Each of these climates requires a unique response. Designing site-specific means that the layout of a house takes its cues from the features of the particular site that it's built on. Factors such as solar orientation, prevailing breezes, topography, septic, access, views, water, trees, and neighbors show you how a house wants to be laid out.

Here in Texas, century-old passive-cooling techniques combined with modern-day radiant barriers and insulation allow houses to stay cool during much of the year without having to resort to air-conditioning. Because the house is now cooler and more comfortable, the air conditioner can be smaller and used less frequently, and in turn, it costs less to purchase and to operate. Seen in a larger context, the house also uses less energy from the grid.

In the end, the more passive strategies a house uses, the less expensive it is for the homeowner. The fewer moving parts, the less chance for things to break down.

A REMODELED RANCH stays in the same footprint but gains a master suite and a passive cooling strategy.

An upper floor makes sense on many levels

With these ideas to guide the big picture, we suggested a few specific items to make this house habitable for today's lifestyles. We wanted to add a new master suite and another bathroom. If we removed the fireplace, the living room could be opened up more to the street. The owners wanted to be able to walk directly from an expanded kitchen out to a rear deck. All the mechanical systems, electrical, and plumbing, as well as the entire exterior, would have to be reworked, too.

Our clients had a few thoughts on how the spaces should be organized. They suggested adding the new master suite at the rear of the house, extending into the backyard. Because they wanted to maintain a connection with the street, the living room could

BETTER LIVING THROUGH DEMOLITION. The original kitchen was segmented by partition walls. After the walls were removed, the unified space became brighter and, with new cabinets, more functional. Photo taken at C on floor plan.

remain facing front. The original two bedrooms and the bathroom required only face-lifts.

We pushed back a bit on their desire to add the master suite on the first floor. We were hesitant to put an addition anywhere on the south that would stop breezes from moving through the house. The possibility of children in the future also meant we wanted to leave as much yard space as possible for play.

With these issues in mind, we proposed the idea of going up, building over versus expanding the existing footprint. We then could just bolster the existing framing and foundation. By keeping existing yard space intact and by reusing as much of the house's structure as possible, we saved costs, materials, and shade trees.

Building up also had the benefit of reducing energy costs. In the new two-story scheme, one air

GO UP, NOT OUT

The bones of the original house were left intact or recycled, and the remodel didn't expand the footprint of the house. The garage, carport, and existing floor plan were left in place. Rather than use the space in the backyard, the architects added a second floor with a master suite and an additional bath and bedroom. The stairs fit easily between the dining and living rooms. A new front porch creates a better sense of street integration, and a new deck connects the kitchen to the backyard.

SPECS

- Bedrooms: 4
- Bathrooms: 3
- Size: 2,240 sq. ft. of conditioned space (increased from 1,319 sq. ft.)
- Cost of remodel: $125 per sq. ft.
- Completed: 2005
- Location: Austin, Tex.
- Architect: Barley & Pfeiffer Architects; Donna Tieman, project manager
- Builder: Ken Kahanek

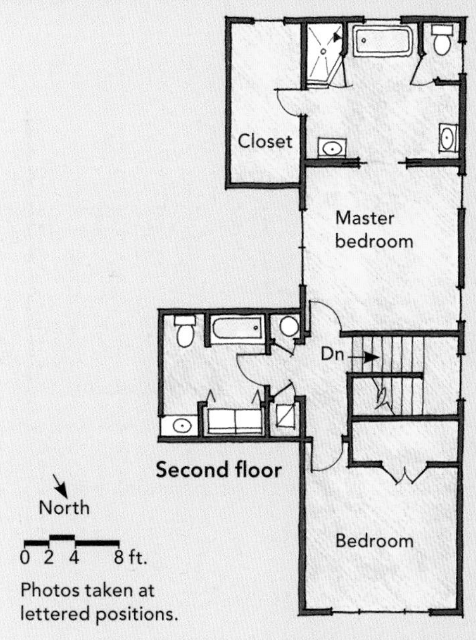

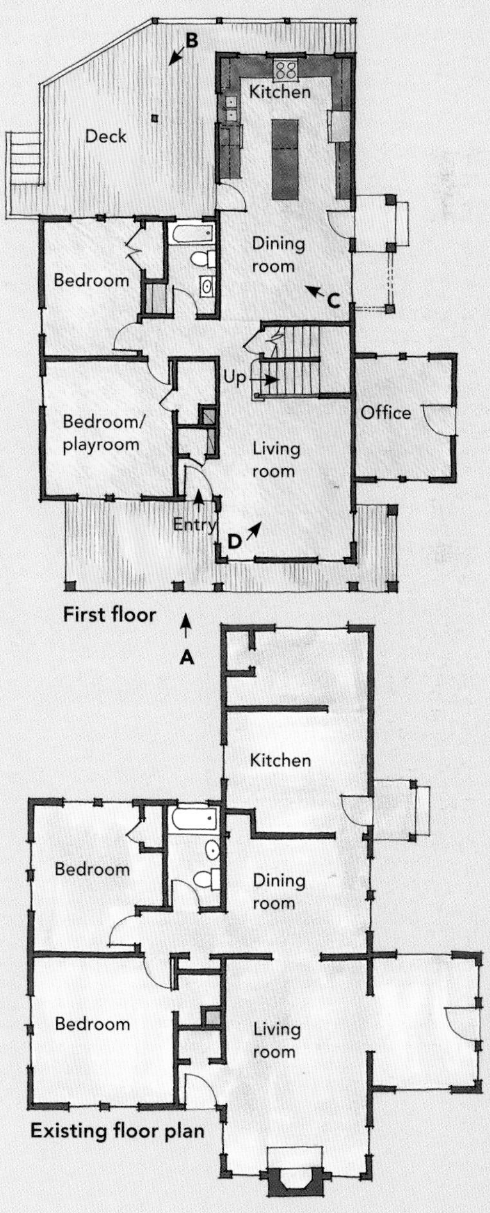

WORTH THE SPACE. The only additions to the house were a front porch and a kitchen-accessible deck. Sheltered by deep overhangs and two sidewalls, it's the ideal outdoor room for Austin's hot summers. Photo taken at B on floor plan.

ELEMENTS OF COOL IN A HOT PLACE

1 **SHADE** Deep overhangs above short second-story windows keep the upstairs rooms in the shadow of the eaves for the better part of the day. The mature trees next to the house also help shade the roof.

ZONED CONDITIONING
Instead of one large air-conditioner, there are two smaller units, one upstairs and one down, controlled by a programmable thermostat.

2 **INSULATION** To keep the budget lean, the house is insulated with fiberglass batts: R-13 in the walls, R-36 in vaulted ceilings, and R-22 in flat ceiling joists. Baffles promote airflow between the soffit and ridge vents and help cool the roof. A ½-in. layer of rigid polystyrene between the second-floor ceiling drywall and the ceiling joists thermally isolates the attic.

3 **STACK EFFECT**
The stairwell helps cool the house, except during the hottest months. When the breeze-side and stairwell windows are opened slightly, the resulting airflow pushes the rising hot air out of the upper stairwell, which in turn pulls in cooler air from windows downstairs.

4 **THE PREVAILING BREEZE**
The long axis of the house runs southwest to northeast and exposes one side to the prevailing southerly wind, which is allowed to enter through appropriately placed windows.

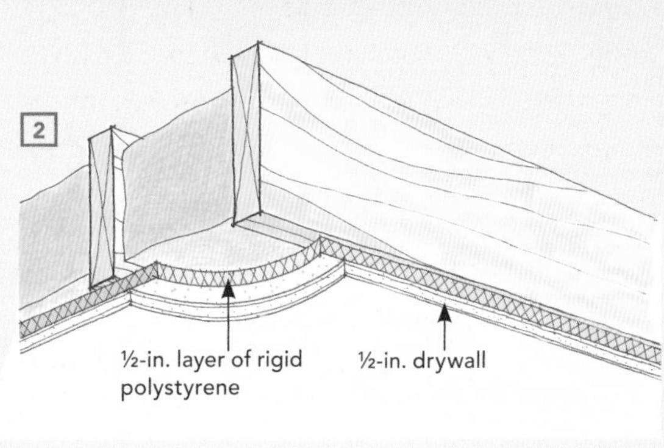

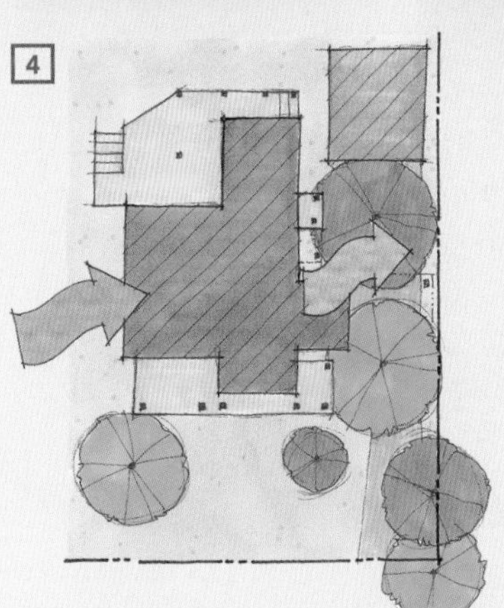

conditioner would serve the first floor and another unit would serve the second floor. With the main bedrooms all on the new second floor, the first-floor unit could be shut down at night, leaving the second-floor unit to keep the occupants cool.

Stairwell brings passive cooling

Adding a second level gave us the opportunity to use the stairwell to encourage the stack effect. We placed the stairwell between the living and the dining rooms and stole some floor space from each room. The new kitchen almost doubled in size, giving us space to add more southeast-facing windows for the breeze.

Positioning a group of four operable windows high on the stairwell under an extended overhang sets the stage for a convection current. Heat rises in the house and vents out the stairwell windows, in turn pulling in cool air from the lower level. The extended overhang protects the stairwell windows from the hot western sun. In the spring and fall, the outside air temperature is typically cooler than inside. Before leaving for the day, the homeowners can open the stairwell and southeast windows partially and shut off the air-conditioning.

Combined with a radiant barrier in the attic and properly sized roof overhangs, this practice lets the house vent itself naturally during the day and reduces heat buildup. When the owners arrive home in the late afternoon and the temperature is hotter, they shut windows and turn on the air-conditioning, which works less to cool the house and, in turn, reduces energy costs.

By locating the master suite upstairs, we made the house bigger without increasing its footprint. The more a house can be stacked, the more efficient it is to build, so we added an extra bedroom. We also fit a bathroom upstairs with a washer and dryer closet.

STAIRWELL WITH BENEFITS. Placed between the living and dining rooms, the new staircase and its high windows add natural light to the living room and contribute to air circulation. Photo taken at D on floor plan.

We still had to make the house respond to the street and to provide a deck off the new kitchen. A new front porch created additional outdoor living space and made the street side of the house more inviting. The new porch roof also eased the integration of the second-floor additions. In the back, we designed a partially covered deck off the kitchen that allows outdoor seating and provides a great view of the yard.

Bungalow Comb-Over

BY LEO ARTALEJO

When our first child arrived, my wife and I quickly realized that our family was outgrowing our little house. The idea of remodeling popped up one night while we were having dinner with our neighbors. They had recently added a second story to their house, and survived. We loved our neighborhood, but we couldn't say the same for our 1942 war box.

We knew we needed more space in the long term, but we weren't sure how to get it. We talked with our neighbors in depth about the pains and pleasures of remodeling, and they sent us home that night with a stack of *Fine Homebuilding* magazines. We found an article in the summer *Houses* issue titled "Ranch Makeover, Bungalow Style" (p. 205), which excited us because the house had been wrapped in what we referred to as a bungalow-roof "comb-over." The article featured a fairly nondescript house that had been transformed into a bungalow with great curb appeal. Maybe it was possible to stay in our neighborhood, keep the good parts of our existing house, and add some missing elements.

Our design process started with an empty photo album and a stack of shelter magazines. My wife and I would open a bottle of wine and start pasting in clippings of rooms and details that we liked. We also kept notes on things that we didn't like. This process equipped us with a visual language that allowed us to engage architects and builders in initial conversations.

After interviewing three different architects who had been recommended by friends and whose Web sites appealed to us, we settled on a small boutique outfit in Seattle called CAST architecture. We were impressed with their ability to balance contemporary uses of space, light, and materials in traditional houses. Our conversations were quickly distilled into four guiding principles that would inform the design of our home:

- Reconfigure and expand while staying in scale with the rest of the neighborhood.
- Orient the house toward the landscape to connect the living spaces with the yard.
- Maximize natural light to help offset the gray days of a Seattle winter.
- Focus on energy conservation, efficient use of space, and natural materials.

What to keep? What to toss?

We liked some parts of the original house and, for both financial and environmental reasons, wanted to keep them. We were pleasantly surprised to learn that the foundation was sturdy enough to carry a second story. We were happy with the size of the

FROM BOX TO BUNGALOW. The low-slung bungalow-style roof keeps the front of the remodeled house in scale with the rest of the neighborhood. Stucco piers and fiber-cement lap siding are topped with cedar posts and shingle accents. A welcoming porch leads to a front door that now opens into a vestibule. Photo taken at A on floor plan.

bedrooms, the hardwood floors, the layout of the bathroom, and the fireplace in the living room. But we wanted the new spaces to emphasize big changes, such as combining the new kitchen with the dining and living area for long diagonal views.

The reconfigured plan retains the southern half of the original house and radically rearranges the northern half (see the floor plan on p. 220). What used to be the back of the extra-deep garage became space for a new kitchen. We made up for the annexed garage territory by pushing it 8 ft. toward the street to the setback line. The front door, which used to open unceremoniously into the living room, now leads from the side of a small porch into an entry that includes an art niche, a closet, and a small bench.

At the center of the house, a two-story-tall window wall takes advantage of one of our favorite

(Continued on p. 223)

FIXING THE BOTTLENECK

THE FRONT DOOR TO THE ORIGINAL HOUSE entered into the living room/dining room at the intersection of the doorway to the kitchen. A new entry into a small vestibule eliminates the old arrangement. On the second floor, a family room with a couch, a computer station, and a shelf full of toys overlooks the dining area and rock garden. Two-ft. cantilevers beyond the downstairs wall provide enough extra room for a bathtub in the kids' bathroom and a little more space in the master bedroom.

SPECS

- Bedrooms: 4
- Bathrooms: 3
- Size: 2,294 sq. ft.
- Cost: $224 per sq. ft. (doesn't include owner's labor)
- Completed: 2008
- Location: Seattle
- Architect: CAST architecture; Tim Hammer, project architect
- Builder: Zoltan Farkas

NEW MEETS OLD AT THE POST PASSAGEWAY. Spruced up with fir trim, the old living room is separated from the new entry by a bench in the foyer, a display cabinet, and a low soffit. Long diagonal views, such as the glimpse of the kitchen from the living room, occur from several vantage points. Photo taken at B on floor plan.

NO TURNING BACK. The southern half of the original house (above) contained the living room, a bedroom, and a small bath that were worth keeping. But the northern half had to go to make room for an open kitchen and dining area. The revitalized living room (left) overlooks the new spaces. Photo taken at C on floor plan.

SPLURGING WHERE IT COUNTS

ALTHOUGH WE WERE WORKING within the original footprint of the house and keeping room sizes fairly modest, there were several places where we were willing to break the bank a bit to make the house memorable and inspiring to live in.

A TWO-STORY SPACE

Two of our guiding principles were to foster connections between the public parts of the house and to maximize natural light. When the architect suggested having a double-height ceiling above the dining room, we were hesitant to give up what was essentially an upstairs bedroom. Going with this design, however, proved to be a defining feature of our new home. The double-height space with its transom windows allows for ample light and views, which can be appreciated from both floors. It also allows for easy communication in the public spaces of the house.

ROCK GARDEN

Because we were reorienting the house toward the backyard, we decided to take advantage of the slope and create a rock garden. boulders aren't cheap, and they require impressive machinery to deliver and move into position. So one of the first things we did once the north half of the house had been carted away was to use the wide-open access to the yard to bring in the boulders. Cost of boulders and the labor to install them: $14,000

FOLDAWAY DOORS

To take full advantage of this rock garden, we wanted to be able to open the house to the outdoors and to let the patio mingle with the kitchen and dining area. To that end, we sprung for a 10-ft.-wide, four-door unit from NanaWall®. On warm, sunny days, it's a joy to fold open these doors and live in our own little campsite, with the kids doing a tricycle slalom around the patio. Cost of folding doors plus installation: $13,000

RADIANT FLOORS

We'd heard good things about radiant-floor heat. Because we were replacing a significant part of the existing subfloor and would be building an entirely new second story, we were pleased to discover an efficient radiant subflooring called Warmboard®. It's an aluminum-sheathed, pregrooved plywood panel that serves as both subfloor and heat radiator. The grooves are fitted with PEX tubing to route the hot water through the floors. For the part of the house that we were keeping, we chose to do a staple-up installation of PEX tubing under the existing subfloor. While not as efficient as Warmboard, this hybrid solution allowed us to use one boiler to heat the whole house. Cost of Warmboard, PEX, and boiler: roughly $16 per sq. ft.

A HIGH CEILING AND A ROCKY WALL Granite boulders and a row of mature poplars lend a rare sense of countryside to a house in a dense neighborhood. NanaWall folding doors accordion to the side to mingle the patio with the dining area. Photo taken at D on floor plan.

COOL DETAILS

In a corner of the kitchen, a handy desk for a laptop floats above a window with a view of the black bamboo outside. The window above the desk is frosted to let in light but maintain privacy from the house a few feet away. The bamboo peekaboo continues through the clear transom at the top. At the base of the stairs, a tokonoma-style alcove provides a place for an artistic display area adjacent to the busy crossroads of the house. Photos taken at E and F on floor plan.

things: our secluded backyard. This orientation brings in light and highlights a connection with nature that can be seen from multiple vantage points.

Rooms to let the good times roll

One of the things I love about our neighborhood is the wine-making club. Every fall, we buy a load of grapes from Washington State vineyards, divvy up the juice, and bottle the resulting wines. As soon as I had space in the new garage, I put up a batch of Remodel Red (see the photo on p. 220). Like the house, the wine was a big hit at the party we had for the builders and architects.

A House in Hiding

BY BRIDGET CAHILL

Things are not always what they seem. And in the case of this small house on Cape Cod, that's a good thing. The house's barnlike facade faces a street that buzzes with beach traffic from April to October. Beyond the big doors, you'd never guess there's a quiet, cozy retirement cottage designed for accessibility, privacy, and beautiful views of a nearby salt marsh.

This story begins a couple of years ago when my sister, Colleen, bought a home on Cape Cod. The property included an outbuilding that had served as a carriage house in the 1800s.

Whenever I visited, I found myself wandering in and out of the carriage house, taken by its charm and by lovely vantage points from upstairs windows. When my father's health started to decline, he and my mom began to think about finding a smaller place closer to their kids. I suggested that they move into an updated version of the carriage house. They'd end up with a great retirement home, and I'd have the chance to transform this charming old outbuilding.

Preserving the facade and the footprint

The building we had to work with was a 1½-story structure with a lean-to addition on one side.

Given the proximity to a busy street and the need to preserve some ground-floor space as a storage/workshop area, we decided that the barnlike facade could provide effective camouflage for the home behind it.

We also had to contend with the numerous state and local building regulations. Because the carriage house sat within 100 ft. of wetlands, adding on was not an option. Furthermore, the planning and permitting process included hosting a tea with a woman who had summered in the carriage house as a young girl in the 1940s. The tea and the affidavit she signed afterward were vital for us to have the carriage house grandfathered under local zoning laws as a residence.

Tearing down before building up

Long before the renovation became a realistic option, I had a revised floor plan laid out in my

STREET SMART. To the beach traffic on this busy street, the new carriage house looks the same as the old (above). The original doors on the lean-to section of the building became part of the siding (facing page). Photos taken at A and B on floor plan.

mind (see the floor plan on p. 229). First, the existing plan for the second floor—with its living space in front and sleeping area in back—had to be reversed.

In addition, part of the unfinished first floor, home only to paint cans, kayaks, and some out-of-work lobster pots, had to be included in the new plan if we were to have enough space for a full-time residence. The house's total living space would be only about 1,200 sq. ft., but by maximizing the use of space, it would be roomy enough for a comfortable home.

Sticking to the size and configuration of the original building helped us retain its charm. We kept most of the first-floor workshop area, located behind the barn doors, in its original condition. To keep the view from the street the same, we left the front gable end of the original structure. The lean-to part of the building was demolished, except for the barn doors, which we rehung to give the new siding an old look (see the photo above).

To support the new lean-to section of the carriage house, we poured a 3-ft.-deep concrete foundation with a French-drain system to channel away groundwater. The new foundation raised the entire first floor slightly. To make everything fit, we raised the shed-dormer roof slightly, which had minimal impact on the view from the street. I reconfigured the interior stairway with a landing to increase second-floor living space. I also widened the stairs to accommodate a chairlift, should that option ever be needed for my dad.

A new light on old-house charm

Although we gutted the original structure, I wanted both to recapture its essence and to add to its charisma. We brought in 200-year-old hand-hewn chestnut beams to span the ceilings on both floors. These nonstructural beams were the largest cosmetic expense of the entire project, but they were well worth it. On the first floor, the beams combine with a gas fireplace that has a stone-veneer backing to create a strong feeling of warmth.

OUTDOOR CONNECTIONS. The best views in the house can be found in the kitchen, through ample gable-end windows and a French door that opens on a small balcony. Inside, odd pieces of furniture combine to make the kitchen look as if it has evolved over time. Photo above taken at D on floor plan.

DECKS COMPLETE THE PLAN. The only additions to the existing footprint that were allowed are a second-floor balcony and a first-floor deck. Photo taken at E on floor plan.

To maximize the incredible views from the second floor, I incorporated as many windows as possible into the back wall (see the bottom photo on p. 226). The ample windows, cathedral ceilings, and skylights brighten and enliven the space, making it feel much larger than it is. To contrast and balance the high ceilings and openness, I combined various pieces of used furniture, including an oak dresser, a pine sideboard, antique desk drawers, and a glass-fronted curio cabinet. The result is a cozy country kitchen that seems born of necessity rather than of modern-day style and efficiency (see the top photo on p. 226). Custom cabinets that house the microwave and refrigerator help tie these elements together.

Modern convenience in minimal space

Because of my dad's deteriorating mobility, it was necessary to provide for handicap-accessibility and function in the first-floor bathroom. We tiled the entire bathroom floor with a drain in the center of the room to achieve this goal in a limited space.

"A small south-facing balcony extends from the kitchen, offering views of both sunrise and sunset."

We moved the second-floor master bedroom to the front of the house, giving the kitchen the best views of the marsh. To share the views with the bedroom, I separated the spaces with interior French doors. The doors not only increase the natural light and the feeling of spaciousness in the room, but they also let in refreshing sea breezes.

To maximize the use of space in the bedroom, I designed built-in closet/bureau pieces along with a headboard to surround the bed. To minimize the size of the master bath, we placed an oversize bathtub in the corner of the bedroom.

Decks move the outbuilding outdoors

The lean-to part of the carriage house is a bit smaller than the main building, making the whole footprint just shy of a full rectangle. Local zoning allowed us to complete the rectangle with outdoor spaces (see the photo on p. 227).

On the second floor, a small south-facing balcony extends from the kitchen, offering views of both sunrise and sunset. French doors swing open to help catch the cool breezes. On the first floor, a large, comfortable deck opens from the living room to provide an area for relaxing, barbecuing, and entertaining outdoors.

COMFORTABLE NEW SHOES IN AN OLD FOOTPRINT

Local regulations demanded that the rebuilt carriage house occupy the same footprint as the original building. The first floor houses a living room, an accessible bath, and a small bedroom. The stairs to the second floor are wide enough for a future chairlift. The second floor is wide open to take advantage of the views. French doors open the back bedroom to salt-marsh vistas.

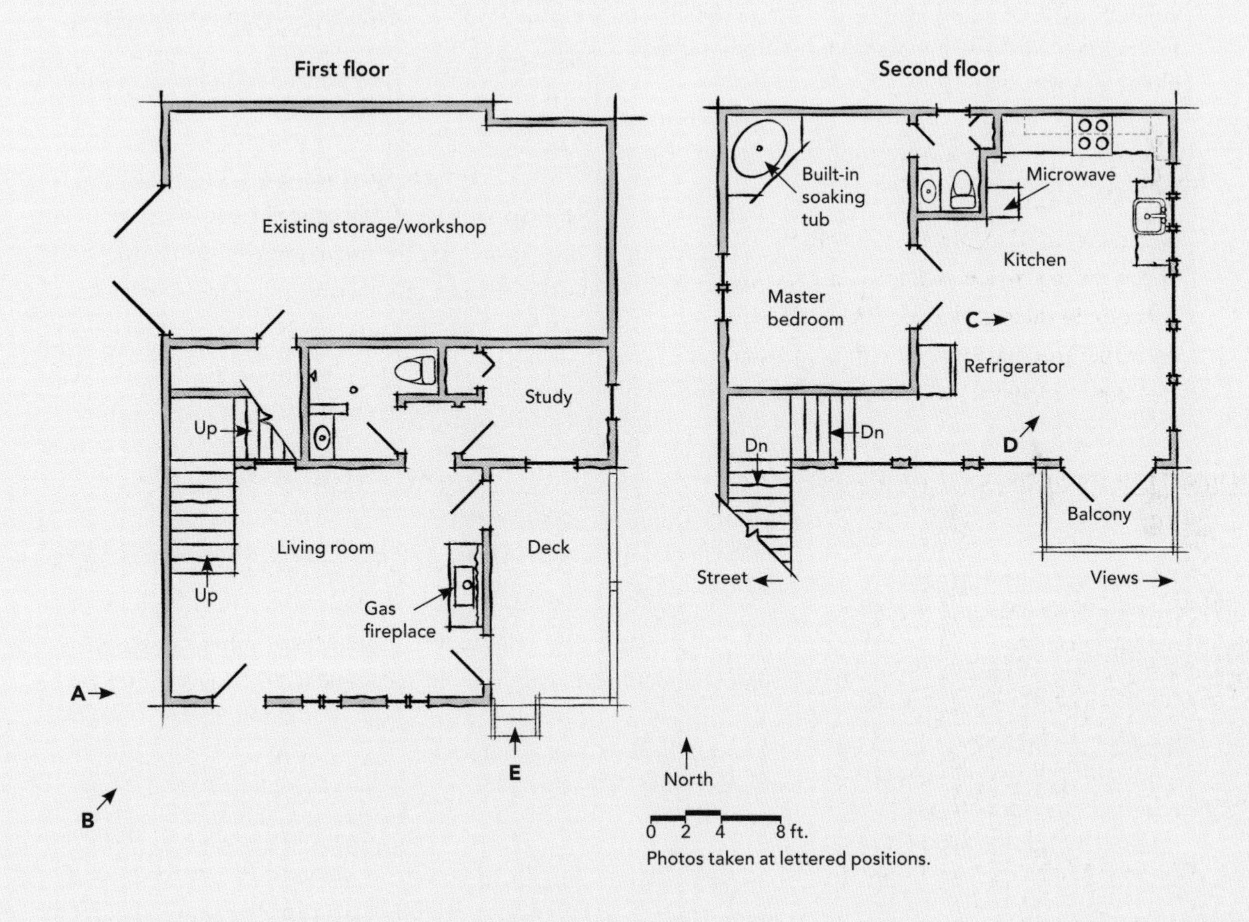

Photos taken at lettered positions.

CONTRIBUTORS

Leo Artalejo is a communications consultant, a remodel junkie, and an amateur winemaker, talking about all these topics and more at twitter:@leoartalejo.

David Baird is a designer, illustrator, and painter living in Berlin, Vermont.

Alan Barley AIA, is a principal in the nationally recognized architecture firm Barley & Pfeiffer Architects in Austin, Texas (www.barleypfeiffer.com) and specializes in high performance sustainable residential architecture.

Jill and John Bouratoglou (www.barchpc.com) teach and practice architecture in Brooklyn, N.Y.

Bridget Cahill (www.seasidedesign/build.com), a contractor based in Brewster, Mass, specializes in the redesign and improvement of homes on Cape Cod.

Arleta Chang is an architect at Jarvis Architects (www.jarvisarchitects.com) in Oakland, Calif.

Gene DeSmidt (www.desmidt-designbuild.com) is a contractor based in Oakland, Calif.

Chris Ermides is a former *Fine Homebuilding* associate editor.

Tina Govan (www.tinagovan.com) is principal of Tina Govan Architect, Inc. in Raleigh, NC.

David Hall is the architect/owner of STUDIOEDISON (www.studioedison.com) located in Edison, Wash.

Russell Hamlet is a principal at Studio Hamlet Architects (www.studiohamlet.com), an innovative and environmentally focused architecture firm based on Bainbridge Island, Wash.

Bryan J. Higgins is an architect who works at SRG Partnership in Portland, Ore.

Geoffrey Holton (www.ghadesign.net) is an architect based in Oakland, CA. His small firm specializes in green architecture, sustainable community and water smart design.

John Hopkins, architect, is the owner of Hopkins Studio (www.hopkinstudio.com) a green residential design firm located in Berkeley, CA.

Lynn Hopkins (www.lhopkinsarch.com) is an architect working and living in Lexington, Massachusetts.

Jo Landefeld is a practicing architect in Portland, Ore., and spends as many weekends as possible with her family and friends at their house in Neskowin.

Bill Mastin is an architect based in Oakland, Calif.

Martin McBirney moved to Sandpoint, Idaho in 1992 where he built his rugged, mountain home.

Michael McDonough (www.mcdonougharchitect.com) is an architect in Asheville, N.C.

Duncan McPherson is an architect and Principal with Samsel Architects (www.samselarchitects.com) in Asheville, N.C.

Charles Miller is editor at large at *Fine Homebuilding*.

Keyan Mizani is a principal at eM/Zed Design LLC (www.em-zed.com) in Portland, Ore.

Daniel S. Morrison is *Fine Homebuilding's* executive editor.

Gordon A. Nicholson (www.gnstudio.net) is an architect in Charleston, S.C.

Eric Odor (www.salaarc.com/profiles/eric-odor) is a managing partner with the firm SALA Architects in Minneapolis.

Dunbar Oehmig is one of the owners of Red House (www.redhousebuilding.com), a worker-owned cooperative based in Burlington, VT.

Kurt Ofer co-owns Altonview Architects (www.altonview.com) with his wife, Teresa Drerup, in Cooperstown, N. Y

Jim and Mark Picton are principals of Picton Brothers, LLC, in Washington Depot, Conn.

Al Platt (www.plattarchitecture.com) is an architect in Brevard, N.C.

Daryl S. Rantis is an architect who works in Asheville and Portland, Ore, and all points in between.

Christopher Stafford is an architect in Port Townsend, Wash.

Chris Stebbins designs, builds and helps to sustain low impact lifestyles in Eugene, Ore.

Greg Wiedemann's architecture firm, Wiedemann Architects LLC (www.wiedemannarchitects.com), is located in Bethesda, Md.

Alexia Zerbinis is a principal at eM/Zed Design LLC (www.em-zed.com) in Portland, Ore.

CREDITS

All photos are courtesy of Fine Homebuilding magazine (FHB) © The Taunton Press, Inc., except as noted below:

Front cover: main photo by Chris Ermides (FHB), top photos from left to right: Charles Bickford (FHB), Charles Miller (FHB), Charles Miller (FHB), Charles Miller (FHB), and Anice Hochlander (FHB). Back cover: top photo by Charles Bickford (FHB), bottom photos from left to right: Skot Weidemann (FHB), Charles Bickford (FHB), and Charles Bickford (FHB).

The articles in this book appeared in the following issues of Fine Homebuilding:

pp: 7-16: Big Ideas for Small Houses by Russell Hamlet, issue 187. Photos 1-5: Grey Crawford (FHB), Daniel S. Morrison (FHB), David Hall (FHB), Erik Kvalsvik, Charles Miller (FHB). Photos 6-10: Charles Miller (FHB), Grey Crawford (FHB), Art Grice (FHB), David Duncan Livingston (FHB), Brian Pontolilo (FHB). Photo p. 9 by Ken Gutmaker (FHB), photo p. 10 by David Duncan Livingston (FHB), photo p. 11 by Charles Miller (FHB), photo p. 12 by Brian Vanden Brink (FHB), top photo p. 13 by Charles Bickford (FHB), bottom photo p. 13 by Charles Miller (FHB), left photo p. 14 by Charles Miller (FHB), right photo p. 14 by David Duncan Livingston (FHB), left photo p. 15 by Erik Kvalsvik, right photo p. 14 by David Duncan Livingston (FHB), top photo p. 16 by Brian Pontolilo (FHB) and bottom photo p. 16 by Charles Miller (FHB). Drawings by Russell Hamlet except for floor plan drawing p. 12 by Paul Perreault (FHB) and drawing p. 15 by Vince Babak (FHB).

pp: 17-21: The Big Little Backyard House by John Hopkins, issue 187. Photos by Charles Miller (FHB. Drawings by Martha Garstang Hill (FHB).

pp. 22-26: A House That's Half Porch by Al Platt, issue 158. Photos by Daniel S. Morrison (FHB). Floor plan drawing by Mark Hannon (FHB). Drawing by Charles Lockhart (FHB).

pp. 27-33: A Simple Plan for Lakeside Living by Gene DeSmidt, issue 163. Photos by Charles Miller (FHB) except photo p. 31 by Gene DeSmidt (FHB). Floor-plan drawings by Paul Perreault (FHB). Drawings by Bob LaPointe (FHB) except for drawing p. 32 by Martha Garstang Hill (FHB).

pp. 34-40: Living with Only What You Need by Brian J. Higgins, issue 163. Photos by Charles Miller (FHB). Drawings by Paul Perreault (FHB).

pp. 41-44: The Small House Done Well by Kurt Ofer, issue 158. Photos by Charles Bickford (FHB). Drawings by Steven N. Patricia (FHB).

pp. 45-50: Form Follows Function by Daryl S. Rantis, issue 222. Photos by J. Weiland (FHB) except for photos p. 48 and p. 50 by Patrick McCombe (FHB). Drawings by Robert LaPointe (FHB).

pp. 51-56: Live Tall on a Small Footprint by Michael McDonough, issue 214. Photos by Chris Ermides (FHB). Drawings by Martha Garstang Hill (FHB).

pp. 57-59: Payback Time by Dunbar Oehmig, issue 219. Photos by Patrick McCombe (FHB) except right photo p. 58 by Chris Wojcik, courtesy of Red House Inc. Drawings by Martha Garstang Hill (FHB).

pp. 60-64: The Ever-Evolving House by Duncan McPherson, issue 212. Photos by Chris Ermides (FHB). Drawings by Martha Garstang Hill (FHB).

pp. 65-69: Downsizing for Comfort by Christopher Stafford, issue 187. Photos by Charles Bickford (FHB). Drawings by Martha Garstang Hill (FHB).

pp. 70-75: Building Better Affordable Homes by Kenyan Mizani, issue 224. Photos by David Papazani (FHB). Drawings by Vince Babak (FHB).

pp. 76-83: Year Round Cottage in the Woods by David Baird, issue 155. Photos by Charles Miller (FHB). Drawings by Steven N. Patricia (FHB). Floor plans by Paul Perreault (FHB).

pp. 84-90: A Low-Budget, High-Impact House by Chris Stebbins, issue 179. Photos by Charles Miller (FHB). Drawings by Martha Garstang Hill (FHB).

pp. 91-97: From Luxury to Leed by Jim and Mark Picton, issue 206. Photos by Rob Yagid (FHB).

pp. 98-104: At Home on a Hilltop by Charles Miller, issue 187. Photos by Charles Miller (FHB). Drawings by Martha Garstang Hill (FHB).

pp. 105-111: Pointed at the Sun by Charles Miller, issue 195. Photos by Charles Miller (FHB) except for right photo p. 107 courtesy of Arkin Tilt Architects. Drawings by Martha Garstang Hill (FHB).

pp. 112-116: Living Lightly on the Mountain by Tina Govan, issue 219. Photos by Rob Yagid (FHB) except for photos p. 112 and bottom p. 115 by Tina Govan (FHB). Drawings by Martha Garstang Hill (FHB).

pp. 117-124: A Duplex Grows in Brooklyn by Jill and John Bouratoglou, issue 179. Photos by Randy O'Rouke (FHB). Drawings by Jill Bouratoglou (FHB).

pp. 125-129: Privacy and Light on a Small Lot by David Hall, issue 195. Photos by David Hall (FHB). Drawings by Martha Garstang Hill (FHB).

pp. 130-134: Why Modular? by Chris Ermides, issue 209. Photos courtesy of Randy Lanou. Drawings by Don Mannes (FHB).

pp. 135- 138: Designing for Privacy and Views by Greg Wiedemann, issue 217. Photos by Charles Bickford (FHB) except photos p. 135 and p. 138 by Anice Hochlander (FHB). Drawings by Martha Garstang Hill (FHB).

pp. 139-143: Designed for the Coast by Gordon A. Nicholson, issue 187. Photos by Brian Pontolilo (FHB) except photo p. 139 by Sara Cook, house photo p. 143 by Gordon A. Nicholson (FHB) and product photos p. 143 by Krysta S. Doerfler (FHB). Drawings by Robert LaPointe (FHB).

pp. 144-151: Seduced by the Shingle Style by Arleta Chang, issue 187. Photos by Brian Pontolilo (FHB) except photo p. 145 by Skot Weidemann (FHB) and photo p. 146 by Arleta Chang (FHB). Drawings by Martha Garstang Hill (FHB).

pp. 152-156: Beauty on the Beach by Jo Landefeld, issue 173. Photos by Brian Pontolilo (FHB) except left photo p. 156 by Sally Painter (FHB). Drawing by Paul Perreault (FHB).

pp. 157-163: A Rustic Design for a Rugged Climate by Martin McBirney, issue 176. Photos by Justin Fink (FHB) except right photo p. 159 and photo p. 160 by Martin McBirney (FHB) and bottom photos p. 159 courtesy of Rastra. Drawings by Martha Garstang Hill (FHB).

pp. 165-169: Small Addition, Big Improvement by Lynn Hopkins, issue 119. Photos by Charles Bickford (FHB) except photo p. 165 by Ted Szostkowski (FHB). Drawings by Mark Hannon (FHB).

pp. 170-177: Home Remedies by Keyan Mizani and Alexia Zerbinis, issue 187. Photos of finished details by Charles Miller (FHB). Before photos by Keyan Mizani (FHB) and Alexia Zerbinis (FHB). Drawings by Martha Garstang Hill (FHB).

pp. 178-183: Living Lightly on the Whole Lot by Geoffrey Holton, issue 203. Photos by Charles Miller (FHB). Floor plan drawings by Martha Garstang Hill (FHB). Drawing by Don Mannes (FHB).

pp. 184-190: Urban Farmstead by Eric Odor, issue 219. Photos by Troy Theis (FHB) except bottom photo p. 185 and bottom photo p. 188 by Charles Bickford (FHB) and photo p. 186 by Eric Odor (FHB). Drawings by Martha Garstang Hill (FHB).

pp. 191-196: Seamless in Missoula by Charles Miller, issue 219. Finished photos by Charles Miller (FHB) other photos courtesy of Angie Lipski. Drawings by Martha Garstang Hill (FHB).

pp. 197-204: From Small to Big Enough by Bill Mastin, issue 179. Photos by Charles Miller (FHB) except before photos by Bill Mastin (FHB) and bottom photo p. 204 by Janet Delaney (FHB). Drawings by Martha Garstang Hill (FHB).

pp. 205-211: Ranch Makeover, Bungalow Style by Daniel S. Morrison, issue 171. Photos by Daniel S. Morrison (FHB) except bottom photo p. 206 by Charles Warren (FHB) and photo p. 209 by David Griffin (FHB). Floor plan drawings by Paul Perreault (FHB). Drawings by Bruce Morser (FHB).

pp. 212-217: A Cool Texas Remodel by Alan Barley, issue 213. Photos by Charles Bickford (FHB) except before photos by Alan Barley (FHB). Drawings by Martha Garstang Hill (FHB).

pp. 218-223: Bungalow Comb-over by Leo Artalejo, issue 211. Photos by Charles Miller (FHB) except before photos by Tim Hammer, courtesy of CAST architects. Drawings by Martha Garstang Hill (FHB).

pp. 224-229: A House in Hiding by Bridget Cahill, issue 169. Photos by Roe A. Osborn (FHB). Drawings by Paul Perreault (FHB).

INDEX